View of Fredericksburg, 1856, reproduced from colored hand-drawn map. With exception of railroads, steamboats, bridges, and dam, the picture gives a bird's-eye view of Colonial Fredericksburg.

Colonial Fredericksburg
and Neighborhood in Perspective

# Colonial Fredericksburg and Neighborhood in Perspective

by

## Oscar H. Darter

*Professor of History, Mary Washington College*

TWAYNE PUBLISHERS
New York

# FOREWORD

Historic Fredericksburg, Inc., has been established recently "to preserve the sites and monuments of historic, aesthetic and architectural value in Fredericksburg and vicinity . . . and to stress the significance of this city and vicinity as a factor in the development of our state and national life." The society has requested the present writer to prepare a brief historical sketch of Fredericksburg and neighborhood as an introduction to a perpetual Educational Campaign to inform the people of this community, state, and nation of the rich historical heritage of this section of Virginia.

This is the land of the Washingtons—George, his father and mother, sister and brothers; of the Lees—Richard Henry and Francis Lightfoot, signers of the Declaration of Independence, "Lighthorse" Harry and Robert E.; of George Mason, "father of the Virginia Bill of Rights;" of James Madison and James Monroe; of Edmund Pendleton and John Taylor; of John Paul Jones; of John Marshall; of Dr. Hugh Mercer; of John Mercer and his three sons, George, James, and John Francis; of Fielding Lewis and James Hunter, leading patriots and industrialists of the Revolution; of Matthew Fontaine Maury, "Pathfinder of the Seas."

It is the land of George Rogers Clark, "Conqueror of the Northwest;" of Dr. Thomas Walker, first explorer of the Kentucky wilderness to leave a written record of his journey. Walker preceded Daniel Boone by twenty years into that country.

It is the land of Giles Brent, "Leader of the Staffordian Frontiersmen in the Bacon Rebellion;" of Margaret Brent, "America's First Feminist," and the first white person to own the site of Fredericksburg and recognize it as suitable for a town.

It is the land of Alexander Spotswood and his Knights of the Golden Horseshoe; the cradle of the American steel industry; the seat of the first postoffice in the American colonies.

It was the leading medical center of colonial Virginia. Dr. Hugh Mercer, Dr. Thomas Walker, Dr. Lawrence Brooke, Dr.

Adam Stephen, Dr. John Tennent, Dr. Charles Mortimer, Dr. Robert Wellford, Dr. John Julian, and twenty-five others lived and practiced here.

Fredericksburg was the gateway to the West; the birthplace of the first "Public Manufactory of Arms;" the arsenal of the Revolution; the primary source of that Revolution; and the birthplace of many of the nation's leaders.

During the colonial period, Fredericksburg was a great metropolitan commercial center where more than 3,000 ships entered and left her wharves annually, from forty-three Atlantic and 125 West Indian and foreign ports.

Surely America should know these facts about one of her most historical regions; and it is hoped that this pamphlet may stimulate further interest in its history.

# PREFACE

The typical colonial town of eighteenth century America is usually thought of as being an isolated, largely self-sufficient, provincial center. The leading American historians almost invariably present this point of view. Some have ignored the existence of colonial towns altogether, especially towns of the southern colonies, with the exception of Charleston. A few authors state that with the single exception of Charleston no towns existed in the southern colonies. They describe colonial society under titles like "Provincial America" or "Provincial Society" without distinguishing urban from rural communities, and have, therefore, left the impression in the mind of the student or reader that the whole of American eighteenth century life was provincial. This, however, was not the case.

The primary concern of this study is to suggest that the commercial towns, even the smaller ones, and their contiguous neighborhoods were predominantly cosmopolitan, and that their economic, social, and intellectual interests were of a world-wide character.

In presenting this view the first step has been to make a study of a number of leading college textbooks on American history, currently in use in American colleges and universities throughout the nation, in order to determine the point of view which their authors hold regarding the question. To the list of general histories have been added a number of the best texts on the colonial period, and a third group of general works on American history.

The present study takes issue with the point of view held by most authorities that unmodified provincialism best describes American colonial communities. Falmouth and Fredericksburg have been chosen as typical colonial towns and have been treated as typical of many others of the period to demonstrate the opposite view. Instead of being provincial, the principal seaport towns and their vicinities have been found to be predominantly cosmopolitan.

The present dissertation attempts to support this statement by presenting the results of a study of the several different aspects of Colonial Fredericksburg and vicinity: the origin, size, composition (racial and national); the population; the influence of the geographic factor in determining the course of events; the activities, interests, and outlook of the neighborhood; the religious groups of the community; the economic life and contacts of the leading citizens; their social and cultural background; and numerous other aspects which affected or were responsible for a cosmopolitan outlook in the vicinity.

## ACKNOWLEDGMENTS

The author of this work wishes to express his gratitude to Mr. George H. S. King, genealogist of Fredericksburg, for his generous help on many points of this manuscript; to Mrs. Mary (Terretta) Burrell for her valuable assistance; to Professor Reginald Wilbur Whidden of the English Department of Mary Washington College for reading and editing the manuscript; to Professors Almont Lindsey, R. L. Hilldrup, and Carrol H. Quenzel of the History Department of Mary Washington College for reading the manuscript and offering valuable suggestions.

Also to the Graduate Council of the George Washington University, particularly Professor W. C. French, deceased, who served as Director of the study and Professor Wood Gray of the American History Department, the Assistant Director, and to the Graduate Committee of Examiners for their helpful comments and suggestions when this manuscript was prepared and presented as a dissertation for the doctorate degree.

The author wishes to express also his appreciation for the many courtesies and assistance given him by members of the library staffs of the several universities and the officers of other institutions, such as the Library of Congress, the Friends Library of Baltimore, the State Library of Virginia at Richmond, the Library of the University of Virginia, the Library of the College of William and Mary, the Library of the Restoration of Williamsburg, the Virginia Historical Society, the Public Library of New York City, the Clements Library of the University of Michigan, the Huntington Library of the University of California, and the Public Records Office, London, England.

Also to the clerks of the various counties in the Rappahannock Valley: Mr. A. H. Crismond of Spotsylvania, Mr. James Ashby of Stafford, Mr. E. G. Coghill of Caroline, Mr. L. B. Mason of King George, Mr. Albert Stuart of Westmoreland, Mr. R. I. Barnes of Richmond, Mr. O. B. Chilton of Lancaster, Mr. B. B. Roane of

Gloucester, Mr. A. D. Latané of Essex, Mr. C. W. Eastman of Middlesex, Mr. T. E. Barnestein of Fauquier, and others.

Gratitude is also expressed to Rev. Mr. Boogher, Rector of St. George's Episcopal Church of Fredericksburg for granting permission to use the Minutes of that church; to the Masonic Lodge of Fredericksburg for granting access to the Minutes of the Lodge; to Mr. J. W. Adams, Clerk of the Court, Fredericksburg, for his kind and valuable assistance; and to Mr. L. J. Houston, Jr., City Manager, for granting permission to use the Minutes of the Council of Fredericksburg.

It is impossible to mention by name all the many friends in and around Fredericksburg who permitted the author to use many private papers and other materials in their possession. Only a few can be named here: Miss Eliza Roy, Mrs. Fred H. Robinson, Miss Greenhow Scott, Miss Sallie Lacy, Mr. Harry Lightner of Falmouth, and many others.

Last but not least, special gratitude is expressed to my wife, Lela Mae Deere Darter, for her assistance, understanding, sympathy, and forbearance during the many years devoted to this study.

Finally, the author wishes to state that he is responsible for whatever errors this book may contain.

OSCAR H. DARTER,
Head of the History Department,
Mary Washington College

## TABLE OF CONTENTS

# List of Illustrations

# Introduction

The method of dealing with the present subject comprehensively was suggested by Lamprecht's teachings that the geographic, racial, religious, economic, and cultural life and social ways of a people must be taught if we are to understand their political history.

The problem itself was suggested by a project which the present writer directed—the preparation of a world map of modern Fredericksburg by the local International Relations Club of Mary Washington College.

The history of Fredericksburg, Virginia, and its vicinity and hinterland is conceived in terms of all the activities of its people: economic, social, literary and spiritual, as well as political. The history of any community is intimately related to its physical environment and is interwoven with neighboring people's history. The life and activities of such a community are not confined to its corporate limits or immediate environs. It is influenced by and wields an influence upon other areas which can be seen as extending in ever-widening concentric circles.

Town and country are inevitably interwoven, and urban and rural neighborhoods overlap with increasing interchange of goods, services, ideas, and people. The two are so interrelated and interdependent that no clear line of demarcation can be drawn to distinguish them. They are united in kinship ties, economic interests, political and social bonds, and religious and intellectual affiliations.

Likewise nations and peoples in all parts of the world in modern history impinge upon each other. Nations are interdependent; civilization is interracial; interacting forces and influences determine the course of history. Recognition of these cardinal underlying principles form the background and basis of "Fredericksburg in Perspective."

17

ও *1* ৯ও

## Provincialism vs Cosmopolitanism
## as Reflected by Standard Texts and
## General Works on American History

It is the purpose of this chapter to substantiate the charge that authors of college textbooks and general reference works on American history have failed to stress sufficiently the cosmopolitan character of colonial towns and their contiguous neighborhoods; that they have left the impression that these population groups were predominantly provincial; that this conception distorts the true picture when it portrays colonial American life in general as provincial and neglects to recognize the cosmopolitan character of the urban communities of the Atlantic seaboard and slights the importance of southern towns other than Charleston.

These authors have not failed to take into consideration the wide trade contacts of colonial towns, but they have treated them in such a manner that no clear distinction has been made between that very important element of urban population which developed and enlarged its world outlook, and that portion of the population which did live in more or less isolated settlements and was consequently narrow, self-contained, and provincial in their outlook. While portraying the world-wide economic activities carried on by the merchants and other classes within the colonial towns, the authors have failed to indicate the implications and impact of such relations upon the outlook of the urban population and their bearing upon colonial thought.

The present thesis does not take issue with the conception that much of colonial society was provincial; the point under considera-

19

tion is that there was a very considerable element in colonial make-up which was not provincial, but on the contrary, possessed a significant world-outlook and a cosmopolitan mind. It is further maintained that this portion of the population was responsible for much of colonial leadership, contributed largely to colonial culture, and shared to an important extent with the rural and frontier people in creating and developing those fundamental and distinct traits and ideals which characterize American culture and philosophy today.

The members of this predominantly urban group were the missionaries of political, social, and economic thought of the world of that day, particularly of American thought. It was they who did most to crystalize such concepts into movements and forces which became irrepressible. They formed the vanguard in championing commercial rights of free trade, which became the primary cause of the Revolution. It was they who resisted the Navigation Acts most ardently. They were also active members of the Committees of Correspondence.

There were still other ideas and doctrines with which they were closely associated, and, insofar as America is concerned, were perhaps the source of origin, although this fact is difficult to determine. Among such concepts may be listed expansion, manifest destiny, industrial development, the scientific spirit, arts and letters, and the international mindedness and goodwill which have been so significant in American history from William Penn's treatise on *"A European Diet or Parliament"* to Woodrow Wilson's League of Nations.

Before attempting to analyze in detail the point of view revealed in the best recognized works on the colonial period and in other reputable works on American history, a few general facts should be stated and should be kept in mind.

First, the element of urban population with which we are here concerned in many respects had a broader world outlook and was more conscious of world relationships, world interactions, world implications, and world bearings upon their interests than are urban people of America today. The leaders of these colonial centers were vitally and primarily concerned in developing markets in Europe, the West Indies, Central and South America, Africa, and Asia, and were secondarily interested in intercolonial or domestic markets.

Secondly, it should be remembered that the population of the United States has always been heterogeneous, and that from the time of the first settlers, this country has constantly received immigrants from the different countries of Europe and from other parts of the world. In addition, the seaports were great centers of trade and were, therefore, continually filled with sailors, merchants, travelers, immigrants, and other people from many places on the earth. The principal interest of these towns was commerce on a world scale.

This world perspective, from at least the economic point of view, remained the predominant outlook of the commercial and industrial classes of these port-towns throughout the colonial period.

With independence and the critical problems of readjustment which ensued, many of the great colonial commercial enterprises which had flourished under English protection went to the wall. This situation forced the new nation to turn to the development of domestic resources, the result was greater emphasis on national ideals, which came to be expressed in such doctrines as self-sufficiency and national economic independence.

Naturally this attitude on the part of new commercial and industrial concerns, which arose on the ashes of the once prosperous colonial enterprises, had a rich field to which it could turn—the provincial, self-sufficing, small and largely isolated, frontier settlements of rural America which has so predominantly characterized the agricultural population throughout colonial history.

Finally, attention should be called to the fact that the principal sources and centers of culture—science, drama, art, music, literature —of colonial America were in the towns and the planters' homes. The towns were the residence of practically all the prominent leaders of the professions—the clergy, lawyers, merchants, bankers and financiers, educators, journalists, scientists, political leaders, in fact all the chief patrons of culture of that day except the planters, who themselves maintained extensive urban contacts.

The following pages of this chapter are devoted to the analysis of leading textbooks on American history, texts on the colonial period, and general works on American history to determine their point of view regarding the provincial or cosmopolitan character of colonial towns. The aim has been to let the authors present the picture through direct quotations from their text, with only introductory and explanatory remarks added.

Strange as it may seem, the more recent textbooks in United States history give less attention to colonial towns than the earlier texts do. Such widely used books as Chitwood's *History of Colonial America,* Hicks's *The Federal Union,* Morrison and Commager's *The Growth of the American Republic,* Nichols and Nichols' *The Republic of the United States* give very little about colonial towns and neglect seriously the true character of a very vital part of colonial society.

Chitwood, for instance, fails to give very much about colonial towns or urban society. Even in his chapter headed "Social Life in the Colonies," he gives no indications of the impact of these factors on the character of life of that day in respect to urbanity or cosmopolitanism. He says that "At the end of the colonial period there were in the English colonies only four cities (Boston, New York, Philadelphia, and Charleston) which deserved the name."[1] He confines his attention to these.

Hicks in his *Federal Union* does better than Chitwood. Under the chapter headed "Colonial America," he says that "commerce was the chief concern of all colonial cities."[2] He states that "Annapolis, Williamsburg, and Wilmington . . . . were hardly more than villages . . . . Norfolk and Baltimore attained some importance as ports, and Charleston became a thriving little city."[3]

Morrison and Commager fail to treat colonial towns specifically as integral parts of colonial society, or as vital factors in shaping the outlook of colonial life. They mention Charleston and Williamsburg and pass them over with a brief comment or two. They do say that "Even colonial towns of two or three thousand inhabitants, afforded more social amenities in the eighteenth century than American cities of many times their population today."[4]

Nichols and Nichols do not treat colonial towns directly and
fail to even list them in their index under that title or related
headings, and a search for specific treatment of them in the body
of the text fails to reveal anything definite about them.

The order of treatment of texts chosen from more than twenty
which were investigated for this study, will be dealt with in the
following pages alphabetically, according to authors.

The first to which attention is called is *Provincial Society,
1690-1763,* by J. T. Adams.

In describing "The Structure of Society" between 1690 and
1700, the author says:

> South of the Delaware River the unit of settlement was
> the solitary farm or large plantation, and that section contained
> not a single town, with the exception of Charleston which may
> have numbered two hundred and fifty families by 1700. Phila-
> delphia . . . . had but a few hundred houses some years later
> and is said to have had not over seven hundred at the close
> of the century. New York was slightly larger . . . . but it was
> the only community in that colony larger than a hamlet . . . .
> Newport could count less than two thousand, and Boston . . . .
> not over seven thousand inhabitants.
>
> The Townsman or village dweller of today has difficulty
> in realizing the extreme narrowness and provinciality of out-
> look which resulted from such conditions . . . . . Actually,
> beyond limited economic contacts, there was little to enlarge the
> minds of the vast majority of the settlers. There was, indeed,
> more or less traveling by horseback between villages, and more
> rarely between the larger centers of different colonies . . . . .
>
> Under such conditions it is evident that the local interest
> would be the supreme interest . . . . .
>
> Heterogeneous as the population of the colonies always
> was even from the beginning, it was to become far more so in
> the course of the eighteenth century . . . . .
>
> At the opening of our period [the eighteenth century]
> we thus have to deal with a widely scattered and mainly agri-
> cultural population leading a hard-working, narrow, parochial
> life—in solitary farms, tiny hamlets, or at most in what would
> now be considered small villages . . . . . It was a society in

which all the conditions tended greatly to emphasize the solidarity of family life and that of the smaller political units.[5]

He then concludes the chapter by saying:

> The young American society . . . . was closely articulated with others over-seas. Indeed, these connections with other communities across the water were in many cases closer than those which bound the several continental colonies to one another . . . . .[6]

In his chapter on "The Life of the Spirit," he summarizes the content of the chapter with this statement:

> In the brief survey which we have made of some aspects of colonial life at the opening of the eighteenth century we have also seen that its culture was more or less uniform and evenly spread throughout the entire length of the seaboard.[7]

Finally, in his concluding chapter, "The Mid-Century," he summarized his picture thus:

> In the two generations which we have covered from 1691 to 1763, the growth of the colonies had been most extraordinary . . . . . Instead of the scattered settlements . . . . there was now almost continuous settlement from Maine to Georgia, connected by a network of roads . . . . when our story began, there was not a single newspaper in America and no public means of conveying letters from one isolated settlement to another. At the end, there was a score of . . . . journals carrying the news of all the colonies, and a post which brought even the most remote settlements into fairly economical touch with one another. In most of the colonies . . . . there had developed not only a local public opinion but some glimpse of a larger life and destiny.[8]

The next work under consideration is C. M. Andrews's *The Colonial Period of American History.*

Of all writers on colonial history of the United States, perhaps the average student would expect to find the fullest and clearest account in the writings of Charles M. Andrews. On examining the present text for information on the question in hand, the present writer was not surprised to find the picture given here fully in keeping with the reputation of the author for accuracy and clearness, and although not directly or completely presenting the cosmopolitan concept of this paper, he is to a very considerable extent inclined toward this point of view.

A few quotations will indicate the character of the picture given in this text. From the chapter on Rhode Island, pages 58-60, I quote:

As long as Rhode Island, island and mainland, remained isolated from commercial contact with such centers of trade as Boston and New Amsterdam, each of which was extending its activities and reaping benefits of overseas intercourse, its people were veritably dwellers in the wilderness far removed from the world. Newport . . . . took the lead not only in Rhode Island but in some respects also of all other colonial seaport towns, except Boston and Philadelphia . . . . . Newport . . . . like Venice depended on her ships for a place in the sun. She ploughed the sea.[9]

In the chapter on "The New Haven Colony," the author says: "The simple truth is that despite ambitions of the founders, the towns of the New Haven jurisdiction never were more than small agricultural communities . . . . ."[10]

Again, in the chapter entitled "Far Flung Barbados," the author makes his most significant statement tending to picture colonial towns as cosmopolitan. In speaking of Barbados and the Leeward Islands, he says:

Many an inhabitant of Newport, Boston, and Philadelphia owned plantations in one or other of the islands . . . . . From New Hampshire to Georgia, ships with provisions and other supplies sought these British West India islands . . . . .[11]

The fullest discussion of this concept is given in the chapter on "Aspects of Early Massachusetts Life." He first gives a picture of the physical appearance of a typical New England colonial town.

Then he proceeds to discuss the extent and character of colonial
towns, particularly those of New England.

The following quotation reveals the essence of the picture:

> After 1640, shipbuilding and commerce became the leading
> activities of Boston, Charleston, Dorchester, and Salem . . . . .
> Voyages covered a wide area of profitable trading enterprise.
> During this period vessels went coastwise to Piscataqua, Isles
> of Shoals, and the Maine coast, to Plymouth, New Haven,
> New Amsterdam, and Virginia, quite frequently to Ferryland
> in Newfoundland . . . . . Overseas they went to and from
> England, Ireland, Holland, France, Portugal, Spain, and Italy
> —to London, Bristol, Dublin, Amsterdam, La Rochelle, Bor-
> deaux, Superdevecha, 'Oury,' Marseilles, Bilbao, Lisbon, Ma-
> laga, Barcelona, Leghorn, and Malta. [In a footnote he refers
> to a "Scanderone" voyage, stating that the only Scanderoon
> or Alexandretta known was in Syria, with which port he thinks
> Massachusetts merchants also traded]. They went occasionally
> to the Barbary States and Guinea . . . . and to the Wine Islands
> very frequently, particularly to Madeira and the Canaries, for
> wines. But their most important overseas trade was with the
> West Indies, chiefly Barbados, but also St. Kitts, Antigua, and
> Nevis.[12]

It will be noted that nothing is said of the effects of these
economic activities on the class of people participating in them
or of their impact upon the thought and culture of the townspeople.
It should also be noted that little or no attention is given to any
colonial southern town except Charleston, thus leaving the impression that they were unimportant or did not exist. On the contrary
many of the towns in the South equaled or excelled many of those
of the North which he mentions. Norfolk, for instance, Falmouth
and Fredericksburg combined, and several others which will be
described in a later chapter of this study carried on a volume of
trade comparable with that of most northern cities of that day.

We now look at Bassett's *A Short History of the United States*.
In this text as in others, the most that is said about colonial towns
is in connection with trade, and no definite point of view with
respect to their provincialism or cosmopolitanism is expressed.

Bassett speaks of Boston's being the center of rum manufacture for all the colonies, the largest amount of which he says was exported to Africa. He goes on to say, concerning fisheries, that New England made "every ocean the hunting ground" for the whaling interests.

In discussing colonial trade, he states further that:

> In the northern colonies trade established itself in much the same way as in England, that is, trading towns on shore and river supported a merchant class which distributed merchandise to, and collected the products from, the people around them. Also, there arose such large importing centers as Boston, Providence, New York, Philadelphia, and Charleston. The growth of these places was rapid, for each was the commercial metropolis for a large and rapidly developing back country. In 1760 Boston and Philadelphia each had a population of 20,000. New York came next with 10,000; Charleston, whose merchants exported rice to many ports of Europe, had 9,000 and was the home of much wealth and luxury . . . . . Boston's size was not what might be expected from the oldest city of the group, located in a large commercial colony. The New England trade was shared by a number of smaller towns, as Salem, Marblehead, Gloucester, Newport, Providence, Portsmouth, Falmouth, New Haven, New London, and Hartford.[13]

Of trade in Maryland and Virginia he says:

> No town of importance was established. In Maryland the rise of Baltimore begins with the settlement of the Susquehannah Valley in the first decades of the eighteenth century, and in 1760 it had less than 5,000 inhabitants. The planters of this region dealt directly with London or Bristol commission agents . . . . . Under these circumstances, competition in trade was difficult, and towns could not develop . . . . In 1760 the largest Virginia town was Norfolk, whose prosperity arose chiefly from the trade which came to it from the Albemarle section of North Carolina . . . . Rice grew in the Cape Fear section which . . . . had a thriving export trade from Wilmington.[14]

This is the extent to which this text treats colonial towns. If the content of the text is taken as a whole the general impression is that they were provincial in character. The statement that "No town of importance was established" in Virginia, totally ignores the several places which compared favorably with the northern towns both in extent and volume of the trade which they carried on.

Next to be considered is the text of Carman and McKee, *History of the United States.*

In Chapter VII, "The Colonial Mariner and Merchant," the authors give a rather full treatment of the intercolonial and foreign trade of the colonies. They do not, however, discuss the provincialism or cosmopolitanism of colonial towns. They do, however, give a map of "Colonial Oceanic Trade," inserted between pages 148 and 149, which shows clearly the trade routes, commodities and ports which were included in colonial trade.[15]

A few statements from this chapter will indicate that the authors have made some effort, at least by implication, to show that colonial towns, particularly seaports, in some respects were cosmopolitan. The following quotation is of interest here:

> Intercolonial trade . . . . was carried on almost entirely by water . . . . . By far the greater portion of continental intercolonial commerce and, indeed, of all colonial shipping was in the hands of enterprising Northerners who, with hundreds of small craft, penetrated every harbor, bay, estuary, and navigable river . . . . .[16]

Almost as interesting is the following:

> Yankee vessels laden with grain, livestock, liquors, hardware, fish, and imported cloth anchored in southern ports . . . . . Hundreds of sloops, piled high with goods collected at the larger commercial centers of Boston, Newport, New York, and Philadelphia, visited the smaller ports and river towns to trade with local merchants . . . . .[17]

Another statement is of similar character:

> Although the intercolonial trade was advantageous in that it furnished a source of capital . . . . it was not as important

as the oceanic commerce of the colonies, which long before the Revolution, rivaled that of European nations . . . . .[18]

After stating that Philadelphia, Boston, New York, Charleston, and Newport, ranking in that order, were the largest commercial centers in the colonies, the authors extend this concept further by saying that "Baltimore, Norfolk, Portsmouth, Salem, Providence, New London, and New Haven were promising commercial towns."[19] They continue: "With the increase of population during the eighteenth century a number of inland towns became industrially and commercially important."[20]

The authors state that colonial towns were important as "centers of wealth and communication,"[21] and as places where "the merchant aristocracy of the colonies lived";[22] that "During the early years the American settlements were in large measure cut off from the Old World and from each other";[23] and that "Under such conditions it was impossible to break down the barriers of provincialism or to develop anything like a common intellectual life."[24]

They continue further:

By 1750, however, there was marked improvement . . . . . There were enough roads as early as 1732 to warrant publication of the first American guidebook which . . . . gave the roads and distances between the more important towns. Regular lines of stagecoaches and stageboats were beginning to operate between such places as Boston and New York, and New York and Philadelphia . . . . Under the direction of Benjamin Franklin and William Hunter of Virginia, who were appointed deputy postmasters-general in 1753, the postal service was re-organized and expanded.[25]

After discussing towns as centers of colonial journalism, they go on to state that "Colonial culture and science centered in commercial towns."[26] Continuing under the topic of "Colonial Culture and Science Centered in Commercial Towns,"[27] they discuss scientific achievements in colonial America, colonial colleges, books and libraries, the learned professions of theology, medicine, law, and the fine arts such as architecture, furnishings, paintings, sculpture, music, and drama, all of which centered in and radiated primarily from colonial towns. It was these influences which contributed most to the creation and development of colonial political philosophy and to the unification of Colonial America. The colonial towns were the principal source of origin of most of these forces.

Channing in his *History of the United States* fails to give any definite picture of the character of colonial towns. They are mentioned in his chapter on "The March of Education, 1690-1760" in connection with the establishment of the "road between Boston and New York, Philadelphia, and Baltimore, and the road passing westward and southward from Philadelphia by York, Pennsylvania, Frederick, Maryland to the Valley of Virginia and thence southward to the 'upper regions' of the Carolinas."[28]

The author continues:

> South of Baltimore there were no intercolonial roads on the seaboard. Indeed, the transportation of those Southern colonies was almost entirely by water . . . . . Most of the transportation of goods from colony to colony was carried on by water in small vessels plying along the coast. To this fact was due the commercial importance of an inland town like Newport, which in the existing modes of communication was as well fitted for the distribution of goods as a mainland town like Boston. The export trade of Philadelphia was largely in the products within a radius of forty or fifty miles from that town . . . . .[29]

Then in the chapter on "Colonial Industry and Commerce," he mentions Philadelphia, New York, Newport, Boston, and Norfolk as carrying on most of the trade in rum and molasses, other direct West Indian trade, and the triangular trade with Europe, Africa, and the West Indies.[30]

This is the extent of Channing's treatment of colonial towns, a picture that is hardly cosmopolitan in any respect.

Craven and Johnson in their text, *The United States*, scarcely mention colonial towns. No description of them is included in the chapter on "Colonial Society" nor in the one on "The American Revolution." Although they devote some attention to such subtopics as "trade," "merchants," "The Economic Basis of Life," "New Blood and Expansion," "Religion and Colonial Culture," little is said about towns or their place in history. Under the topic "Religion and Colonial Culture," the authors make a single reference to towns: "Musical recitals and concerts were so well developed by 1750 that they were a regular feature of life in the larger towns."[31]

Faulkner's *American Political and Social History* gives no specific treatment of colonial towns. The urban factor in the history of colonial life is slighted. Mr. Faulkner deals with the towns only in a general way in relation to trade, and leaves the reader to draw his own conclusion or concept as to whether they were provincial or cosmopolitan. He does give a very interesting map entitled "The Domain of Colonial Commerce about 1750"[32] to illustrate his picture of the colonial triangular trade with England via southern Europe, England via the West Indies, and the West Indies via Africa. But he fails to point out the effects of such trade contacts upon the character of colonial towns and the people who engaged in this commerce.

Forman in *Our Republic,* in treating the colonies during the eighteenth century, refers to towns and cities in these words:

> Towns and cities were, indeed, few and far between . . . . .
> In Maryland, Virginia, and North Carolina life was almost entirely rural. Norfolk, indeed, had become a busy little seaport, but it was still a village. Charleston, however, had grown to be a place of considerable size.[33]

This is the extent of Forman's direct treatment of colonial towns, which are mentioned at different times in connection with trade and commerce but without any correct picture of the towns or townspeople.

A few quotations will suffice to illustrate. In one place the author says: "A ship loaded . . . . at Boston, with salt fish, staves, and lumber would sail to the West Indies, exchange her cargo for sugar and molasses and proceed to London . . . . ."[34] Under the topic "Commerce," the author makes a very interesting statement:

> To a great extent colonial commerce rested upon the trade with the West Indies, yet ships went out from American

ports to all ports of the world, to Surinam, to the Canaries, to the Levant, to Lisbon, and Madrid.[35]

Furthermore he states that, "In 1766 twenty-three hundred vessels, sailing from foreign shores, entered the ports of the thirteen colonies."[36]

In general the text leaves the impression that colonial life was scarcely more than isolated rural communities. His picture may be summed up in this quotation: "In every colony life was essentially rural. 'Some few towns excepted,' wrote a colonist, 'we are all tillers of the soil.' "[37]

In Greene's *Foundations of American Nationality,* in discussing "Intellectual Centers of the South," the author comes very near to presenting colonial towns as cosmopolitan rather than provincial places. The general impression left, however, is that these towns were more provincial than cosmopolitan.

The following quotation covers practically all that is said about colonial towns:

> The chief intellectual centers of the South were Williamsburg and Charleston . . . . . Here also were the provincial printing press, the principal book shop, and the College of William and Mary with its faculty recruited from the British universities. The drama, too, had its place; the Williamsburg theatre, built in 1716, was probably the first in America. Charleston had no college, but it was a real city, with perhaps the most cultivated society to be found anywhere in America. Here in the middle of the eighteenth century the South Carolinians had a chance to hear scientific lectures, good concerts, and some good English plays.[38]

A second book by Green, *Provincial America* fails to recognize the cosmopolitan characteristics of the society which he pictures. In his "Preface," in describing the colonial period, he says: "A second important feature of the time is the interaction of imperial and provincial interests . . . . . Finally, with due allowance for divisive forces, there was a growing unity of provincial life."[39] Later he states: "In all the colonies agricultural interests were predominant . . . . ."[40] The towns of this period he describes in his chapter on "Immigration," as follows:

As late as 1750 the South had scarcely any urban centers . . . . . Annapolis was hardly more than a village . . . . Baltimore had hardly a hundred inhabitants . . . . Williamsburg had been made the capital and had some public buildings which attracted attention, but its permanent inhabitants were few. Richmond was not laid out as a town until about the close of this period. Norfolk . . . . was described by William Byrd in 1728 as having most the air of a town of any in Virginia. The principal places of North Carolina were mere country villages. South Carolina, alone of all the Southern colonies, had a real urban centre in Charleston, which, more than any other town in America, concentrated in itself the economic, social, and political activity of the colony to which it belonged.

Philadelphia . . . . developed into a town of about thirteen thousand people . . . . . Germantown . . . . was a thriving settlement . . . . . The growth of New York was less rapid . . . . and during this decade it stood next to Boston and Philadelphia. There were no other large towns in the middle colonies; but New York, New Jersey, and Pennsylvania each had a few other substantial places.

In New England, town life had . . . . been relatively important from the first . . . . Boston held its place as the most considerable center of population and trade on the continent . . . . . Second in importance was Newport . . . . . Along the coast from New Hampshire to New York were such considerable port towns as Portsmouth, Salem, New London, and New Haven.[41]

Despite his general attitude the author makes a rather important statement for our point of view when he says in the chapter on "Culture," "Provincial society was growing richer, freer, more cosmopolitan in the eighteenth century . . . . ."[42]

Harlow's *Growth of the United States* does not deal in any specific way with colonial towns. They are mentioned only in connection with trade or as political units. The implied impression left by the general content of the book as it relates to towns and urban society is that they were much more provincial than cosmopolitan.

Harlow makes only two or three references which have any bearing one way or the other on the question in hand. In his chapter on "Economic Development of the Colonies," he speaks of Charleston thus:

Perhaps the most obvious result of the profitable rice and indigo trade was the growth of Charleston, the only flourishing commercial city of the South. Here the wealthy planters had their houses well furnished according to English standards, and well stocked with European wine. By 1750, Charleston had lost its primitive frontier aspects, and had become a center of aristocracy and culture.[43]

In connection with the Middle Colonies he writes:

The agricultural products of the Pennsylvania group included grain and live stock, especially hogs and cattle; these furnished much of the material for the export trade going out from Philadelphia. To the West Indies, the merchants of Philadelphia sent grain, flour, salt meat, and lumber. They had agents in all ports of the world, and Philadelphia ships were known in all the 'seven seas' . . . . . By the middle of the eighteenth century, Philadelphia, with a population of fifty thousand, had become the largest city of the English colonies. Between 1727 and 1766, the records show a total of about sixteen hundred fifty ships under Philadelphia.[44]

Of New England, he says: "New England merchants were famous for the well known triangular trade, from their own ports, to Africa, to the West Indies, and back again."[45]

Little else is given in this text which bears upon the question under consideration.

Hockett, in his *History of the United States,* devotes an entire chapter to "Provincial America," with sub-topics like "Urban Life," "Economic Development," "Country Life," "The Frontier," and "Relations of Frontier to Coast."

In discussing colonial urban life the author says that, "While the towns on the coast still lacked many of the pleasing features of the maturer culture of the Old World, they had far more in common with eighteenth-century Europe than with the United States of our own day."[46]

Of the South, he writes:

> Crossing the Potomac . . . . the inns became more intolerable, and the population more diffuse . . . . . Williamsburg, the provincial capital, had about two hundred dwellings, and while Norfolk, the center of trade with the West Indies, was larger, Virginia—in fact, the South in general—was distinctly a region of country life . . . . . In the absence of towns the country store, where almost everything could be bought, was becoming an important institution . . . . . A great planter, like a medieval lord, sought to make his establishment as nearly independent as possible, and trained his slaves as carpenters, coopers, blacksmiths, tanners, shoemakers, spinners, and weavers, as well as house servants and field hands. Lumber, fuel, meat, grain, fruit, vegetables, wool, cotton, flax, rough furniture, shoes, flour, brandy, cloth, casks, all these were often produced on the estate. Articles for the great house and the personal use of its occupants were generally brought from England . . . . .[47]

In referring to the economic development, he states:

> Boston, Salem, and Newport were the centers of New England's commerce. Hundreds of native-built ships cleared yearly from these ports laden with lumber, the products of the fisheries, or rum. The Catholic countries of southern Europe were the chief buyers of fish, the poorer grades going to the West Indies to feed slaves. Lumber was sold in the same markets, while most of the rum was exchanged on the Guinea coast for gold, or negroes to supply the slave market of the Spanish colonies. From the West Indies came in this round of trade goods of European manufacture, sugar and molasses, and cash in the form of Spanish silver coins. Little of the export trade was with the mother country.
>
> In contrast with commerce of the northern and middle colonies, the chief trade of the southern provinces was with England. The people of the back settlements at first lived as self-sufficing family units . . . . . By the end of the colonial era the back settlements were producing an agricultural surplus

which found a market in the tidewater for consumption or export.[48]

Clearly, in this text as in the others we have a very incomplete picture of the character of colonial towns and the society which made them up.

Marcus W. Jernegan's *The American Colonies, 1492-1750,* in discussing early New England towns, says that "the town . . . . was favorable to social progress, especially the development of the church and school."[49] Describing the origin, economic, and political aspects of New England towns he states that:

> The New England town was in part a product of inherited ideas and practices of local government; in part it was an indigenous institution arising out of the immediate needs of the people. The essential things to note are these. (1) The town was a distinct geographical entity covering about forty square miles. (2) In Massachusetts, after 1635, towns were established by the general court. (3) They arose through that body granting a tract of land for a town, sometimes only a 'plantation right,' authorizing settlements.[50]

The above description of New England towns, it might be noted in passing, fits southern towns almost equally well, particularly those of Virginia in 1682 and 1691, when the earliest colonial towns were established by acts of the House of Burgesses.

On succeeding pages Jernegan comments on the religious and intellectual character of early New England towns.[51] He is entirely silent on towns of the southern colonies with the single exception of Charleston. He describes the "Early trade of Pennsylvania and New Jersey"[52] in terms which almost perfectly describes the trade of various Virginia towns, but again he fails to even mention their existence.

Later Jernegan has a significant paragraph about early American towns but again applies the description to the northern colonies only. In commenting on those towns he says:

> Besides the landed aristocracy there were the merchants. These gentlemen advanced rapidly in the latter part of the

seventeenth century. Randolph reported in 1676, that in Massachusetts there were thirty merchants with from ten to twenty thousand pounds. Planters and speculators looked to the land for the source of their wealth. The merchants looked to the ocean. The merchant princes lived in commercial seaport towns of the northern colonies, sometimes in houses as pretentious as those of the great planters. The merchants and the growth of seaport towns greatly affected the structure of eighteenth century society. The eight leading towns of 1750 were Boston, Salem, Providence, Newport, New London, New Haven, New York, and Philadelphia. The only considerable commercial town in the South was Charles Town, South Carolina To these towns came ships which brought merchandise from many ports located on the seven seas.[53]

The foregoing description of northern colonial towns fittingly describes Fredericksburg in 1750, also Norfolk, Williamsburg, Alexandria, Petersburg, and other Virginia towns of that date. Each of the above-named Virginia towns contained more than 2000 inhabitants in 1750. Founded in 1727, Fredericksburg enlarged its boundaries four times by 1770, namely, 1742, 1759, 1763, 1769, certainly no mean growth.

Morison and Commager, in *The Growth of the American Republic,* give little attention to the place of colonial towns. Under "Industry and Commerce," they state that:

Baltimore was founded in 1729, largely because the local river bearing the humble name of Jones Fall afforded water power for mills which ground the wheat of German-settled Pennsylvania and up-country Maryland into flour, for which there was a brisk demand in the West Indies. Before many years the export of grain and flour from Chesapeake Bay was pushing tobacco for first place. Philadelphia remained the principal place of export for grain and provisions . . . . .

In the year 1731, over 200 vessels cleared from Charleston, carrying 42,000 barrels (or about 21 million pounds) of rice, 14,000 barrels of pitch, tar, turpentine, about 250,000 deer skins, and a large quantity of provisions . . . . .[54]

With these two exceptions—Baltimore and Charleston—no other towns of the South are mentioned.

Muzzey and Krout's *American History for Colleges* gives the impression that colonial towns were little more than isolated frontier communities with little contact with the outside world. Under the topic, "A Frontier Society," the authors state that:

> The economic and social life of the Colonists was that of a frontier community . . . . . Boston, the largest town of the seventeenth century, was a small fishing-port and mart of trade . . . . . The establishments of the town with its local domestic features of meeting-house and public school could not be realized in the Southern Colonies . . . . .[55]

Under "Mercantilism," they discuss the Navigation Acts, but without mention of the influence of colonial towns upon opposition to these acts or their influence in molding opinion into a nationalistic unity.

Pease, in *The United States*, devotes only two pages of his chapter on the "Evolution of Puritan New England," to the character of colonial towns. He introduces the subject of towns with the statement that "These first seacoast settlements have well been called the English frontier."[56] The discussion that follows deals with these towns as economic, religious, and political units:

> Towns were bound together not merely by a community of interest in religion but also by a common property of land . . . . . The town . . . . was the unit of representation in colonial legislature . . . . . A New England town was exclusive because admission to the town implied admission to valuable economic rights . . . . .
>
> The town . . . . might be the nucleus of a colony. It was for a hundred and fifty years the unit of the expansion of the New England frontier.
>
> In Virginia towns did not thrive. Williamsburg . . . . was a village . . . . . Norfolk had more the air of a town . . . . . At Charleston flourished the most sophisticated urban society in America; the city in that day was still on equal terms in population and trade with New York, Boston, and Philadelphia . . . . .[57]

Under the topic of "Mercantile Classes in the South," the author states that:

> Further to the south [speaking of Maryland and Pennsylvania] the export of the staple crops and the import of English goods was largely in the hands of British firms . . . . . In these colonies there were few large towns—Charleston was almost the only one south of Baltimore—and little local trade. The factor in his economic and political outlook was turned to the east; the planter without any distinctly colonial mercantile influence to supplement him was narrowly provincial.[58]

Comment on the commerce of the middle and New England colonies leaves an impression a little more favorable to the idea of cosmopolitanism in colonial towns. He says, "Philadelphia and New York thus became thriving trade centers with mercantile firms of pretensions."[59] Yet in referring to Connecticut Pease makes the statement that, "With her almost autonomous colonial charter, she was in some ways most remote of the colonies from outside influences."[60]

The implications in the title of Schlesinger's *The Colonial Merchant and the American Revolution* leads one to expect a near approach to the point under consideration in the present study. The text is, however, disappointing in this respect. It is true that the colonial merchant is given a significant part in the American Revolution, but his place in colonial history as a determining factor in molding the outlook of urban communities and colonial society is rather incompletely drawn. The subject matter is confined largely to the beginnings of the conflict and the War of Independence. The following quotations reflect the nature of treatment insofar as the text bears on the issue in hand. In dealing with the tobacco trade, he says:

> The exportation of tobacco was confined by law to Great Britain; and by the middle of the eighteenth century, two hundred sail of ships were employed in the trade . . . . . Sweet-scented tobacco from the region of the York River was highly esteemed by English epicures, and thus only the inferior varieties like the "Oronoac" were re-exported to Holland, Germany and Sweden.[61]

He goes on to say that "there were probably fifty foreign houses or companies and two thousand factors who had charge of trade in Virginia,"[62] and then continues:

It is not unreasonable to say, that every house or company makes fifteen thousand pounds a year, net gain, by the trade of this Colony; and consequently, fifty houses will annually export seven hundred and fifty thousand pounds sterling to Scotland and England; which will be just so much saved to the Colony, whenever its own citizens shall become its merchants.[63]

One or two texts on the economic history of America remain to be examined.

Kirkland's *A History of American Economic Life,* while not treating directly the cosmopolitan factor in colonial history, gives a very excellent chapter on "The Domain of Colonial Commerce." In his introductory paragraph to this chapter the author makes this statement: "In the case of the British colonies in North America, overseas trade probably played a greater part than domestic commerce."[64]

Under the topical heading "Internal Transportation and Commerce," in speaking of the coastal region he says:

Here there was a relative density of population. Boston, Newport, Providence, New York, Philadelphia, Charleston, and Baltimore furnished considerable markets and impressed observers with their settled air . . . . . The coastwise traffic between the thirteen colonies . . . . was the largest item in domestic commerce. Although its value never equaled that of the direct trade with Europe or the West Indies . . . . .[65]

Under the topic "Colonial Commerce, Commodities and Routes," the picture which the author gives is clearly cosmopolitan in subject matter and breadth of treatment. Here he mentions English entrepots, the Iberian peninsula, and the Mediterranean as market centers for colonial commerce. In this connection he says:

Southern Europe rivalled the British Isles . . . . as a trans-
atlantic market . . . . . Colonial vessels sailed directly to Portugal and Spain or, penetrating the Strait, stood off for Marseilles
and Leghorn, the distributing ports of the Mediterranean and
the centers of its numerous trade routes . . . . .[66]

He mentions Madeira and the Azores as mid-shipping points in
this trade. He then describes the West Indian and Caribbean trade
of the colonies, naming specifically the contacts made here with
the Spanish, Dutch, Danish, and French.

The most interesting feature of this chapter is the map, "The
Domain of Colonial Commerce about 1750."[67] The strongest impression one gets from this map is of the extent of colonial contacts
represented on it. Practically every point shown is mentioned in
the papers of William Allason, merchant of Falmouth, Virginia,
1757-1793.

Among the other topics discussed in this chapter are "The
Colonial Merchant Marine," and "Merchants: English and American." The author describes the significance of these factors in
American history, but without directly suggesting the character
of colonial population or culture resulting from such world-wide
economic contacts.

Fred A. Shannon, in his *Economic History of the People of
the United States,* makes some significant statements in analyzing
the population of the American colonies. His comments have a
bearing on the premise of the present thesis regarding colonial
towns.

He says that:

Before the Revolution most communities and every grade
of society contained a mixture of Old-World peoples . . . . .
Of fifty-six signers of the Declaration of Independence, nearly
a third were non-English. Eight were immigrants—three from
Ireland, two each from England and Scotland, and one from
Wales. Joseph Galloway calculated that half the revolutionary
army was Scotch-Irish, and only a fourth was English or
Scotch.[68]

This general description of colonial population suggests a relatively high cosmopolitan character.

The Shannon text goes on to describe more fully specific centers of population. The author says:

> Of population centers large enough to encourage wide diversification and specialization of employment among craftsmen there were only four of sufficient size to be classified as cities. Boston had a population of 7,000 before 1700 and about twice that number half a century later . . . . . The population on Manhattan Island in 1664 was about a thousand, but in 1700 the number had increased to 5,000 . . . . . A census of 1746 showed 12,000 people, of whom 2,400 were slaves. Philadelphia, though the youngest of the cities, outstripped the rest in population . . . . . A census of 1699 showed 4,500 inhabitants, which number had grown to 20,000 by 1740. A count of houses in 1776 showed 4,474 sheltering an estimated population of 26,000. Charleston, a city of the South, having a population of 10,000 in 1776, was nearly as cosmopolitan as New York or Philadelphia.[69]

The representative historians cited in this chapter have been shown to assume or imply that the descriptions which they give of colonial population, and particularly of colonial towns, applied primarily to northern and middle colonies. The facts point to the contrary, however. It might be interesting to note that Urbanna, Virginia, was founded the same year as Philadelphia, and was a thriving port of entry on the Rappahannock in 1700. It declined in importance with the receding frontier and the rise of new competing towns to the West. Tappahannock, Port Royal, Fredericksburg, higher up the Rappahannock River, became flourishing towns during the eighteenth century. Norfolk, Williamsburg, Petersburg, and Alexandria were also prosperous colonial towns, each having well over 3000 inhabitants in pre-revolutionary days. Norfolk and Fredericksburg were the largest towns in Virginia in 1750. All of these towns had large elements in their population who possessed broad world outlook and the towns themselves reflected an air of cosmopolitanism.

## NOTES

1. Oliver P. Chitwood, and Frank L. Owsley, *A Short History of the American People* (New York: Van Nostrand Co., 1945), I, 145, 164f.

2. John D. Hicks, *The Federal Union* (New York: Houghton Mifflin, 1937), p. 76.

3. *Ibid.*, p. 54.

4. Samuel E. Morison, and Henry S. Commager, *The Growth of the American Republic* (New York: Oxford Univ. Press, 1942), I, 108.

5. James T. Adams, Provincial Society, Vol. III of the *History of American Life Series*, ed. Arthur M. Schlesinger and Dixon Ryan Fox (12 vols.; New York: Macmillan, 1927-44), pp. 2-4, 23.

6. *Ibid.*, p. 23.

7. *Ibid.*, p. 165.

8. *Ibid.*, pp. 320, 321.

9. Charles M. Andrews, *The Colonial Period of American History* (New Haven and London: Yale Press and Oxford Press, 1934-38), II, 58.

10. *Ibid.*, p. 177.

11. *Ibid.*, I, 513-15.

12. *Ibid.*, p. 271.

13. John S. Bassett, *A Short History of the United States* (New York: Macmillan, 1930), p. 142.

14. *Ibid.*, pp. 142-3.

15. Harry J. Carman, and Samuel McKee, *A History of the United States* (New York: Heath & Co., 1931), insert between pages 148 and 149.

16. *Ibid.*, p. 145.

17. *Ibid.*, p. 146.

18. *Ibid.*, p. 147.

19. *Ibid.*, p. 159.

20. *Ibid.*, p. 159.

21. *Ibid.*, p. 160.

22. *Ibid.*, p. 160.

23. *Ibid.*, p. 161.

24. *Ibid.*, pp. 161-2.

25. *Ibid.*, p. 162.

26. *Ibid.*, p. 165.

27. *Ibid.*, p. 165.

28. Edward Channing, *A History of the United States* (6 vols.; New York: Macmillan, 1927-30), II, 473-4.

29. *Ibid.*, II, p. 473-4.

30. *Ibid.*, pp. 495-6.

31. Avery Craven, and Walter Johnson, *The United States* (New York: Ginn & Co., 1947), p. 72.

32. Harold Underwood Faulkner, *American Political and Social History* (New York: Crofts, 1937), facing p. 78.

33. S. E. Forman, *Our Republic* (New York: Appleton-Century, 1935), p. 30.

34. *Ibid.*, p. 49.

35. *Ibid.*, p. 49.

36. *Ibid.*, p. 96.

37. *Ibid.*, p. 48.

38. Evarts B. Greene, *The Foundations of American Nationality* (New York: American Book Co., 1922), p. 335.

39. Evarts B. Greene, *Provincial America*, Vol. VI of the *American Nation Series*, ed. Albert Bushnell Hart (28 vols.; New York and London: Harpers, 1904-18), p. XX.

40. *Ibid.*, p. 9.

41. *Ibid.*, pp. 243-4.

42. *Ibid.*, p. 321.

43. Ralph V. Harlow, *The Growth of the United States* (New York: Henry Holt, 1925), p. 99.

44. *Ibid.*, p. 100.

45. *Ibid.*, p. 102.

46. Homer C. Hockett, *Political and Social History of the United States* (New York: Macmillan, 1931), p. 62.

47. *Ibid.*, pp. 75-6.

48. *Ibid.*, pp. 77-9.

49. Marcus W. Jernegan, *The American Colonies, 1492-1750* (New York and London: Longmans, Green, 1939), p. 115.

50. *Ibid.*, pp. 166-7.

51. *Ibid.*, pp. 167-90.

52. *Ibid.*, p. 227.

53. *Ibid.*, p. 391.

54. Samuel E. Morison, and Henry S. Commager, *The Growth of the American Republic* (New York: Oxford Univ. Press, 1942), pp. 100-1.

55. David S. Muzzey, and John A. Krout, *American History for Colleges* (New York: Ginn & Co., 1933), p. 14.

56. Theodore C. Pease, *The United States* (New York: Harcourt, Brace, 1927), p. 66.

57. *Ibid.*, pp. 121-2.

58. *Ibid.*, pp. 121-2.

59. *Ibid.*, p. 122.

60. *Ibid.*, p. 123.

61. Arthur M. Schlesinger, *The Colonial Merchant and the American Revolution* (New York: Facsimile Lib., 1939), p. 33.

62. *Ibid.*, p. 601.

63. *Ibid.*, p. 601.

64. Edward C. Kirkland, *A History of American Economic Life* (New York: Crofts, 1933), p. 92.

65. *Ibid.*, pp. 93-4.

66. *Ibid.*, p. 110.

67. *Ibid.*, insert between pp. 110 and 111.

68. Fred A. Shannon, *Economic History of the People of the United States* (New York: Macmillan, 1934), p. 73.

69. *Ibid.*, pp. 73-4.

# 2

## INDIANS IN THE RAPPAHANNOCK VALLEY

One of the first bases for cosmopolitanism was trade with the aboriginal inhabitants. David I. Bushnell, noted anthropologist and archeologist who is an outstanding authority on the American Indian, states that the oldest known historical remains within the vicinity of the falls of the Rappahannock are the Indian fish traps, still to be seen in the river bed near Falmouth. He points out that "fish traps may have extended across the rocky bed of the river, below the island, in the year 1608 as some do at the present time . . . . . Traps similar to these had undoubtedly been made by the Manahoac, as well as by others who had preceded them in the region."[1]

These artifacts undoubtedly represent the oldest date in human history connected with the Fredericksburg vicinity and testify to the occupancy of the region by native tribes of Indians long before the coming of the first white men to these parts. The natives who were found here were "pursuing the manners and customs and practicing the arts of the Stone Age"[2] when Captain John Smith voyaged to this point in 1608 and recorded his observation as follows:

In the discovery of this River some call the Rappahannock we voyaged by many villages . . . . . Between Secobeck and Massawoteck is a small Isle or two, which causeth the River to be broader than ordinary . . . . . The next day sayled so high as our boat would float there setting up crosses and graving our names in trees.[3]

45

The principal tribes of Indians who dwelt in the vicinity of the Falls of the Rappahannock River and those along other nearby rivers, as well as those with whom the English settlers in the vicinity of the falls had extensive trade relations, included the Rappahannocks, Potowomecks, Nantaughtacunds, Cuttatawomens, Mattaponies, Pamunkies, Chickahominies, and several others.

The Mannahoac, Monacan, Conoye, and Nanticoke Indians originally lived partly within the Rappahannock Valley and immediately on its periphery and just across the Potomac on the Bay in Maryland and on the Eastern Shore. Farther to the northwest, west, and southwest were the great Cherokee tribal groups and the Shawano and Delaware Indians, situated in and to either side of the paths traversed by the numerous trails and colonial roads which led westward from the falls country of the Rappahannock. Falmouth and Fredericksburg became the pivotal point and junction of these roads.

The Powhatan Confederacy was surrounded by the Manahoacs, Monacans, Tuscaroras, Nottoways, Meherrins, Conoys and Nanticokes. The latter tribal groups were not so friendly toward the frontier white settlers as the Powhatans, but they were of great economic interest to them. But of even greater economic importance were the tribal groups to the west, including the Cherokees, the Catawbas, the Shawnees, and the Delawares.

To the Indians the rapids of the Rappahannock River were favorite fishing places and the region about the falls choice hunting grounds and attractive sites for villages, according to Captain John Smith. His map[4] shows no fewer than 16 Indian villages along the banks of the Rappahannock River between Leedstown and the falls, and at least 13 above the falls, all within a distance of 20 miles each way from the falls.

Rivalry for control of the vicinity adjacent to the falls led to constant wars between the Powhatans who occupied the lower part of the Rappahannock Valley and the Manahoacs who dwelt in the upper part.

While the Powhatan Indians were alternately friendly and hostile toward the English settlers of the Rappahannock Valley, the Manahoacs, who were kinsmen of the warlike Sioux Indians, held no love for the invading white settlers and bitterly contested the latter's right to penetrate and take possession of the upper Rappahannock and the falls country. Consequently the settlers in the lower part of the valley petitioned the House of Burgesses and by an Act of 1676 secured the building and garrisoning of a fort near the falls for protection against the frequent incursions of the Manahoac Indians. The Act, "for the safeguard and defense of the country against Indians," ordered that "One hundred and eleven men out of Gloster county to be garrisoned at one ffort or place of defence at or near the ffalls of Rappahannock river of which Major Lawrence to be captain or chiefe commander . . . . . "5

The Powhatans made attacks on the white settlements in Virginia on a number of occasions, killing many of the settlers. The worst attacks occurred in 1622 and 1644. After the 1644 attack, the settlers declared war on them, reducing the tribe to impotency by 1676 and subjecting it to white supremacy by the treaty of Albany in 1685. They gave no further trouble. Moreover, by 1682 the fear of hostile invasions by the Indians had practically disappeared from the Rappahannock frontier, so that the House of Burgesses ordered "that the severall forts and garrisons be abandoned . . . . . "6

Various estimates of the number of tribes and the Indian population of the Virginia colony have been given by early writers and historians. Robert Beverley lists the Indian villages and estimates their population in his *History of Virginia* as follows:

| | |
|---|---|
| Chickahomanians | Nearly 16 families, |
| Appamatucks | Not above seven families, |
| Nandsamunds | 20 families, |
| Mattapaments | 20 families, |
| Pamunkees | Nearly 40 fighting men, |
| Rapahanocks | A few families, |
| Wighcocomoco | 3 families.7 |

Governor Alexander Spotswood in a letter written in 1711 states that there were only nine tribes of Indians in Virginia at the time, while Thomas Jefferson in his *Notes on Virginia* enumerates only six tribes. Burke adds three8 which he states were not listed in Jefferson's notes.

The Jesuits established a mission among the Powhatans on the Rappahannock River, in 1570, perhaps in the very vicinity of the falls, as indicated on the map of "Exploration and Settlement of Northern New Spain." The Father Segura Mission was destroyed and the missionaries were killed by the Indians, probably the warlike Manahoac tribe.

The English first came into contact with the Powhatans in 1607 at the settlement of Jamestown. The Powhatan territory or confederacy embraced the region lying between the present Virginia-North Carolina line and the Maryland-Virginia line and extended westward to the fall line, "comprehended about 8000 square miles, 30 tribes, and 2400 warriors,[9] according to Jefferson. He writes that:

> Capt. Smith tells us, that within 60 miles of Jamestown were 5000 people, of whom 1500 were warriors. From this we find the proportion of their warriors to their whole inhabitants, was as 3 to 10. The Powhatan Confederacy then would consist of about 8000 inhabitants, which was one for every square mile . . . . .[10]

Burke estimates the original number of Powhatan Indian warriors in 1607 to be 2385, reduced to 528 by 1669.[11] Captain John Smith lists 160 Powhatan villages on his map of Virginia. Interestingly enough, there were 29 Indian villages along the banks of the Rappahannock River within 20 miles of the Falls, while many others were located a short distance back from the river.

A map of Indian trails of the Rappahannock Valley would resemble a huge spider web whose pivotal point would be in the region of the present sites of Falmouth and Fredericksburg, from which the lines of the network would lead out in all directions until they linked with those from other regional centers.

Falmouth and Fredericksburg were the junction also of an eight-way road system which linked the towns with all parts of the country. These colonial roads, in the main, followed the earlier Indian trails of the Valley. They served as important links in trade among the various Indian tribes and confederacies and served as such in the later English trade with the Indians of the Rappahannock Valley and with the regions beyond the Blue Ridge Mountains.

Along the old Indian trails, which later became colonial roads, following the courses of the rivers and their tributaries winding through the mountain passes, went the immigrants and new home seekers of the Rappahannock Valley, adventurous spirits interested in cultivating friendly relations with the native Indians for their wealth in furs, or in appropriating their land for colonial estates. Many a zealous missionary followed these routes to the west country. Over these primary routes of water and land moved the wagons, ox carts, sleds, canoes, rafts, boats, bateaux carrying furs, hides, and other commodities obtained from the Indians, and in return supplying the frontiersmen, back settlers and native tribes with necessary items in exchange for their products. These "large quantities of tobacco and other commodities . . . . every year [were] brought down to the upper landings [Falmouth and Fredericksburg] on the said river [Rappahannock], to be shipped off and transported to other parts of the country . . . . ."[12] greatly enhancing the importance of these two towns.

In the seventeenth century, John Lederer in the *Journal* describing his expedition in 1670, to discover the sources of the Rappahannock River, forecast the volume and the significance of the trade between the English and the Indians:

> If you barely designe a home-trade with neighbor Indians, for skins of deer, beaver, other, wild-cat, fox, racoon, etc., your best truck is a sort of course trading cloth . . . . as also axes, hoes, knives, sizarz, and all sorts of edg'd tools. Guns, powder and shot, etc., are commodities they will greedily barter for . . . . .[13]

Virginians established trade with the Indians very early. They were the first colonists to organize trade with the natives "to the South West of the Colony." Acts concerning trade with the Indians passed by the House of Burgesses during the seventeenth century reveal the type and the extent of such commerce. Some of the laws referred specifically to the people of the Rappahannock Valley, while others were general laws applying to all tribes alike. In 1661/2 a law was enacted digesting earlier acts relating to the Indians but specifically showing a sympathetic regard for the native tribes by

making provision to supply "better reliefe of the poore Indians
whome the seating of the English hath forced from their wonted
conveniences of oystering, ffishing and gathering tuckahoe, cut-
tyemnions or other wild fruits . . . . .[14]

Acts furthering trade between the settlers and the Indians were
enacted by the House of Burgesses in June, 1676,[15] in 1677,[16] and
in 1679.[17] The act of 1677 established a "marte or ffaire" in Lancaster County, doubtless at the fort which had been erected at the
falls of the Rappahannock River in 1676. The act was intended
to encourage trade between the white settlers and the Indians, prin-
cipally for the exchange of dogs. It was called a Dog Mart and
continued as a regular event annually until the outbreak of the
Revolutionary War in 1775. In 1927 the Chamber of Commerce
of Fredericksburg revived the original Dog Mart, which was attended
by the Indian descendants of the once-powerful Powhatans, now
confined to a small reservation on the Pamunkey River in King
William County, where fewer than 100 remain of the once proud
tribe.

Cadwallader Jones, who served as Commander of Virginia
Rangers on the frontier, and was one of the first white men to
settle in the vicinity of the Rappahannock falls, perhaps on the
very site now occupied by the town of Fredericksburg, addressed
Governor Nicholson in 1698/9 on the matter of trade with the
Indians. Calling his treatise an "Essay about the Indian Trade,
with a MS or plat of Louisiana," Cadwallader Jones described the
rich trade with the Indians of the Ohio country which at that time
was flowing to the French of the Great Lakes region, the St. Lawrence, and to Pennsylvania and New York. He urged Virginia to
avail herself of the opportunity to share in this thriving business
by seeking to divert it from the northern course to Virginia—which
he thought could be done by erecting forts on the far frontier,
organizing a trading post for the purpose, and establishing trade
routes to the Northwest. His scheme was to channel the huge trade
through the passes of the Appalachian and the Blue Ridge Mountains and down the Rappahannock Valley.[18] He thus anticipated
by fifty years the Ohio Company and its efforts to exploit the rich
resources of the Northwest.

The Indians of the Rappahannock Valley engaged in extensive pottery, textile and weaving industries, besides hunting and
fishing, gathering wild fruits, quarrying flint and diabasic rock for
arrowheads, making their several weapons of warfare, constructing
canoes, manufacturing certain dyes, extracts, beads, pipes, tools,
moccasins, hammocks, medicines, cultivating Indian maize, vegetables, and certain other food crops, tanning furs and hides, and
making various kinds of coarse cloth and other commodities which
they exchanged with the various tribal groups in the Rappahannock Valley and with the English there and elsewhere.

The merchants and traders of the Rappahannock Valley, and
particularly those of Falmouth and Fredericksburg, carried on a
flourishing trade with the back country, much of which derived
from the Indians of the region. It consisted mainly of furs, skins,
pottery, basketry, rush mats, dyes, etc., for which the white traders
exchanged beads, glassware, axes, knives, scissors, coarse cloth, looking glasses, pictures, bracelets, toys and other trinkets. Brandy and
other liquors as well as guns, powder, shot, arms and ammunition
were often sold to the Indians, contrary to the laws of the time.

The map of "The Cherokee and Their Neighbors", presents
an enlarged perspective of the geographic position of the major
groups of the Indians whom the explorers, traders and trappers,
Virginia rangers, and later the adventurous merchants and settlers
of the Rappahannock Valley met as they pushed gradually westward
up the rivers and across the Blue Ridge Mountains, and poured
into the Ohio, Kentucky, and Tennessee countries. From these
remote Indian tribes in the West came the rich fur trade described
by Cadwallader Jones in his essay.[19]

By 1680 the back country was filling up rapidly with white
settlers. Trade in the region and with the Indians farther to the
west had become so important that Virginia became tremendously
interested in furthering these efforts by erecting ports and towns
throughout the colony. Definite steps were made by the Virginia
colony to encourage trade with the native tribes and develop her
economic interests on a more extensive scale. According to the
numerous acts of the General Assembly, authorization was made

for the establishment of bridges, ferries, landings, towns, ports and other facilities for this purpose.

Beginning as early as the act of the Assembly in June, 1641, when the establishment of ferries and bridges was authorized in the colony to facilitate travel and trade,[20] at least twenty separate acts were passed by 1779 pertaining to the establishment of ferries and bridges on the Rappahannock and nearby rivers. The act of 1748 alone authorized the establishment of twenty new ferries across the Rappahannock, as compared with forty for the James River, twenty for the York, fifteen for the Potomac, two across the Nottoway, and one each "From York, Hampton, and Norfolk towns . . . . ."[21] These bridge and ferry systems knit the region of the falls and the Rappahannock Valley into the economy of other areas of the Virginia Colony. Likewise, laws authorized the founding of towns and ports along the trade and communication routes of the Colony. In 1727, an act was passed to erect the towns of Falmouth and Fredericksburg "in some convenient place, near the falls of the said river [Rappahannock], for the cohabitation of such as are minded to reside there . . . . whereby the peopling of that remote part of the country will be encouraged, and trade and navigation may be increased . . . . ."[22]

Falmouth and Fredericksburg, like other colonial towns, became centers of trade, culture, and social contact for the settlers. The Indians of the region, as well as those of the Northwest, influenced the trend of the economic and political development of other colonies along the Atlantic Seaboard besides Virginia. Their impact on these two river ports was significant.

The diffusion of Indian cultures through various avenues of intercourse and interchange of commodities, migrations, warfare, travel, and intermarriages took place on an extensive scale. Mr. Bushnell points out the international and inter-tribal character of Indian beads which he discovered at Leedstown, stating that "Similar beads [have been found in] Tennessee . . . . Alabama . . . . Georgia . . . . Pennsylvania . . . . North Carolina . . . . Florida . . . . Maryland . . . . New York . . . . California . . . . Louisiana . . . . Mississippi . . . . and in various parts of Virginia . . . . ."[23] He also found a number of Folsom points in the Valley of the

Rappahannock, "one in the vicinity of Orange, another a short distance below Fredericksburg in King George County . . . . a specimen of a different form . . . . but equally old . . . . about a quarter of a mile north of Elys Ford . . . ."[24]

Comparing the beads found in the Rappahannock Valley with the blue glass beads in the National Museum in Washington, also found in California, Mr. Bushnell concludes that "All are thought to be of the same age and to have come from the same source, some glasshouse in Spain."[25]

Thus, long before the introduction of European culture into the Rappahannock Valley, the groundwork for cosmopolitan society here was laid by the American Indians with their industries and culture. Furthermore the sources of origin and the makes of the various articles constituting the stock-in-trade of Indian and white inhabitants of the Rappahannock Valley were widely scattered over America, Europe, Asia, and Africa. Indians, Spanish, English, Scotch, Irish, Welsh, French, Dutch, Germans, Italians, Jews, Bohemians, Swiss, and Negroes shared in producing them, a fact which illustrates the interdependence and inter-relationships of peoples in, near, and remote parts of the globe. Indians, the presence of Europeans and Africans, in varying numbers in the population of the Rappahannock Valley, was primarily responsible for cosmopolitanism of race, religion, culture, and outlook represented by the people of the region in the seventeenth and the eighteenth centuries.

## NOTES

1. David I. Bushnell, *The Manahoac Tribes in Virginia, 1608* (Washington: Smithsonian Institution, 1935), p. 17.

2. *Ibid.*, p. 44.

3. Captain John Smith, *True Travels and Observations* (London, 1629), I, 186.

4. *Ibid.*, I, 148.

5. William Waller Hening, ed., *The Statutes at Large* (13 vols.; Richmond, Philadelphia, New York: Virginia Commonwealth, Gray, Desilver, etc., 1814-1823), II, 326.

6. *Ibid.*, p. 498.

7. Robert Beverley, *The History and Present State of Virginia* (London, 1705), p. 134.

8. John Burke, *History of Virginia* (Petersburg, Va., Dickinson & Pescund, 1804), III, 88-89.

9. Thomas Jefferson, *Notes on the State of Virginia* (Philadelphia, 1788), pp. 97-99.

10. *Ibid.*

11. Burke, *op. cit.*, III, 88-89.

12. Hening, *op. cit.*, p. 234.

13. *Discoveries of John Lederer* (London, 1672), cited in Alvord and Bidgood, *First Explorations of the Trans-Alleghany Region* (Cleveland: Clark, 1912), pp. 169-70.

14. Hening, *op. cit.*, II, 140.

15. *Ibid.*, p. 350.

16. *Ibid.*, pp. 410-12.

17. *Ibid.*, p. 448.

18. Cadwallader Jones, *An Essay about Indian Trade with a MS or Plot of Louisiana*, British Transcripts, No. 1310, MS Division, Library of Congress; cited in Fairfax, *Landmarks of Old Prince William*, as Doc. 5: 1315, in the Colonial Office, London.

19. *Ibid.*

20. Hening, *op. cit.*, I, 269.

21. *Ibid.*, I, 17.

22. *Ibid.*, IV, 234-39.

23. David I. Bushnell, *Indian Sites Below the Falls of the Rappahannock River* (Washington: Smithsonian Institution, 1937), p. 31.

24. David I. Bushnell, *The Manohoac Tribes in Virginia, 1608*, p. 35.

25. Bushnell, *op. cit.*, *Sites Below the Falls*, p. 34.

## ◆§ *3* ෂ◆

FREDERICKSBURG, FALMOUTH, AND THE RAPPAHANNOCK RIVER
AS SEEN BY EARLY TRAVELLERS, EXPLORERS, AND WRITERS

Perhaps one of the most objective appraisals of the strategic importance of the Fredericksburg-Falmouth neighborhood in the annals of the American nation may be found in the neutral observations recorded by travelers, writers, and explorers of the Eighteenth Century who included these towns in their North American itinerary. The very fact that such a large number of these world travelers took note of the Rappahannock Valley and visited the twin towns situated on its river indicates that these were centers of commercial, economical, cultural and political significance in an era of expanding world colonization.

More than a century before the Virginia General Assembly authorized the erection of Fredericksburg and Falmouth in 1727 "for the cohabitation of such as are minded to reside there . . . . ."[1] Captain John Smith in 1608 explored the Rappahannock River to the falls on either side of which Fredericksburg and Falmouth are now located. As an explorer and traveler seeking objective data, Smith noted that "the third navigable river is called the Tappahannock [Rappahannock]. This is navigable for 130 miles [from its mouth at the Chesapeake Bay]."[2] This was about one hundred years before the first white man settled here, but Smith recorded that "at the top inhabit the people called Mannahoaks . . . . ."[3] While visiting in the New World around 1610-12, William Strachey concurred with Captain John Smith's observation of the river and the native tribes inhabiting the region. He added that

the "river by the Naturalls of old was called Opiscatumeck, of late
Tappahannock, and we the Queen's River . . . . ."[4] The name Rappahannock was originally applied to a tribe of the Powhatan
confederacy.

But it was the German traveler and explorer, John Lederer,
who gave a detailed description of the flora and fauna he encountered in the Rappahannock River region, while on an expedition
in 1670 exploring this waterway to its source. He was undoubtedly
the first white man to leave a written observation testifying to that
wealth of natural resources found in this area which contributed immeasurably to the development of Fredericksburg and Falmouth as
important cosmopolitan and commercial centers of colonial America.
In addition to his descriptive brochure, Lederer made "A General
Map" of the whole territory he explored. Travelling with the aid
of "nine English horse and Five Indians on foot . . . ."[5] this German explorer, in company with "Colonel Catlett of Virginia . . . ."[6]
found this virgin country rich in animal life, vegetation and natural
resources. Lederer wrote one of the most complete descriptions of
the Rappahannock River region recorded by man as follows:

> The ground is overgrown with underwood in many places
> . . . . and that so perplext and interwoven with vines, that who
> travels here, must sometimes cut through his way . . . . . These
> thickets harbour all sorts of beasts of prey, as wolves, panthers,
> leopards, lions, etc. . . . . and small vermine as wilde cats, foxes,
> racoons . . . . . The parts inhabited here are pleasant and fruit-
> ful, because cleared of wood, and laid open to the sun. The
> valley feed numerous herds of deer and elks larger than
> oxen . . . . . Beaver and otter I met with at every river that
> I passed; and the woods are full of Grey foxes.
> They [the Indians] plant abundant grain, reap three crops
> in a summer, and cut their granary supply all adjacent parts.
> From these mountains or hills the Indians draw great
> quantities of cinobar, with which they colour their faces . . . .
> this mineral is of a deeper purple than vermillion, and is the
> same which is in so much esteem amongst physitians, being
> the first element of quicksilver . . . . find hard cakes of white
> salt amongst them; but whether they were made of sea water,
> or taken out of salt-pits, I know not, but am apt to believe the

latter, because the sea is so remote from them. Many other rich commodities and minerals there are undoubtedly in these parts.[7]

There are numerous primary sources giving descriptions and impressions of the Rappahannock Valley settlement from the beginning of Virginia history. These consist of travelers' records, legislative acts, land grants, church records and diaries. More than a score of world travelers left their written observations of the "magnitude, opulence, trade and elegance"[8] of the eighteenth century Fredericksburg-Falmouth community.

Fredericksburg may be said to have had its beginning in 1676, for it was in that year that the Virginia House of Burgesses recognized the strategic position of a "place . . . . at or near the ffalls of Rappahannock River . . . ."[9] by directing that "one ffort or place of defence . . . ."[10] be erected there as a "safeguard . . . . of the country against the Indians . . . . ."[11] The fort that was built here a hundred years before the signing of the Declaration of Independence (to which ideas and principles espousing human rights were contributed by men born and/or living in this neighborhood) served as a sentinel at this intersection of the East-West and the North-South trans-seaboard routes by safeguarding against enemy encroachments the embryonic English settlements along the lower Rappahannock River.

However, records show that it was approximately a quarter of a century later that the first white man settled on the site now embraced by Fredericksburg.[12] William Levingston [Livingston] had a lease from John Buckner and Thomas Royston to whom Sir William Berkeley executed a patent on May 2, 1671, for 2,000 acres of the land upon which Fredericksburg stands today.[13] Because this was a wilderness country well into the beginning of the Eighteenth Century, no special designation was given officially to what later became Fredericksburg, but for several decades the site was known as "Lease Land" because "William Levingston is possessed of a lease under the said Thomas Royston . . . . ."[14]

Early explorers and travelers recognized the advantageous position of the site at the falls of the Rappahannock River. Waterways formed the principal transportation system in colonial days. The

Rappahannock and its tributaries, the Rapidan, Conway, Robinson and Massaponax, constituted the principal artery for commerce and travel in this region. These were supplemented by the Potomac River and the Mattapony, since Falmouth and Fredericksburg were so near these waters. Moreover, in that day smaller streams such as Hazel Run, Fall Run, Potomac Run and others afforded additional water power and transportation facilities accommodating these twin towns.

Prior to and including the eighteenth century and the early part of the nineteenth, the Rappahannock River was more than twice as wide and deep as it is today, according to the testimony of numerous writers, travelers and published data of that period. Although Captain John Smith made his initial voyage on the river in 1608 "in an open barge near three tons burthen . . . ."[15] the Rappahannock waters accommodated ships of 140 tons[16] drawing 10 feet of water, and few vessels in the eighteenth century exceeded this size or tonnage. Writing in 1705, Robert Beverley named this one of the "four great Rivers"[17] of Virginia. The list included the James, York and Potomac.

In colonial days the Rappahannock at Fredericksburg had a normal depth of 12 feet with a tidal rise of four feet, giving a maximum depth at high tide of 16 feet, which accommodated the largest sea-going vessels of the eighteenth century. Jefferson in his *Notes* estimates the width of the navigable part of the river at from half a mile at Fredericksburg to four miles at its mouth.[18] Other writers, observers and gazetteers, including John F. D. Smyth[19] and John Davis Schopf,[20] give these same depth and width estimates. In more recent years, however, the original bed and the channel have been narrowed and made shallow by the alluvial deposits and the diversion of water to other purposes.

With such a natural transportation system as the Rappahannock and its tributaries offered, early colonists, adventurers and planters soon flocked to its shores, especially to the region about the Falls. Court records and land books reveal the vast acreage patented by these early colonizers, looking to the promising future in commerce, trade and social activities that later developed in the Falmouth-Fredericksburg neighborhood.

Oddly enough, the first person to receive a patent for a large tract of land comprising the site of present-day Fredericksburg was the feminist of colonial times, Margaret Brent, to whom Governor Francis Moryson granted one thousand acres in 1658.[21] Significantly, today, an institution of higher learning for women, the Mary Washington College of the University of Virginia, is located on part of this tract acquired by a woman in an era when few of her sex challenged the rule of men.

Eight years later Robert Taliaferro, who became one of the first permanent settlers of the Rappahannock country, and Lawrence Smith, received a grant of 6,300 acres of land six miles below the falls of the Rappahannock.[22]

From these beginnings, vast tracts of virgin land were patented by seventeenth and eighteenth century men to whom many of the plantations with colonial mansions throughout this region stand as memorials today.

Harry Beverley was granted 1020 acres in 1705;[23] Henry Willis obtained 3277 acres in 1727;[24] while others received similar or smaller grants. However, it was Governor Alexander Spotswood and Lord Fairfax who held patents for the largest tracts granted within the Virginia Colony. Spotswood held title to 125,000 acres in Spotsylvania County,[25] while Lord Fairfax owned the entire territory designated as the Northern Neck, consisting of 5,282,000 acres[26] and embracing 8,253 square miles lying between the Rappahannock and the Potomac rivers. It extended from the Chesapeake Bay to the head waters of the Potomac in the Alleghany Mountains, and covered nearly one fourth of the area of the colony. Falmouth and Fredericksburg were located at the heart of this vast Fairfax estate.

Gradually the wilderness country that was the Rappahannock Valley in the seventeenth century was being peopled, so that in 1727 Falmouth and Fredericksburg commanded the attention of the Virginia General Assembly, which in that year authorized their establishment. Documentary evidence indicates that these frontier towns thrived, progressed and reached significant magnitudes in the commercial, economical, political, cultural and social cognizance of the eighteenth century America and the world. From the time

Captain John Smith paid it literary tribute by noting the Falls in the Rappahannock, having explored it one year after the first permanent English settlement was made in America at Jamestown in 1607, a host of travelers and writers from England and Europe, as well as the American colonies, journeyed to Fredericksburg, leaving posterity written descriptions of this cosmopolitan center in the New World.

Five years after the incorporation of Fredericksburg, Colonel William Byrd visited the town in 1732. He found that:

> It is pleasantly situated on the South Shore of Rappahannock River, about a Mile below the Falls. Sloops may come up and lye close to the Wharf, within 30 yards of the Public Warehouses, which are built in the figure of a Cross. Just by the Wharf is a Quarry of White Stone . . . . . Besides that there are several other Quarries in the River Bank, within the Limits of the Town, sufficient to build a great City. The only Edifice of Stone yet built is the Prison . . . . . Tho' this be a commodious and beautiful Situation for a Town with the advantages of A Navigable River, and wholesome air, yet the Inhabitants are very few. Besides Colo. Willis, who is the top man of the place, there are only one Merchant, a Taylor, a Smith and an Ordinary keeper; though I must not forget Mrs. Levingstone, who acts here in the Double Capacity of a Doctress and Coffee Woman, and were this a populous city, she is qualified to exercise 2 other callings.[27]

In the next quarter of a century, Fredericksburg was a flourishing town. Visiting the port in 1759 while on "Travels through the Middle Settlements in North America," Rev. Andrew Burnaby observed that the town "is regularly laid out . . . . in parallel streets. Part of it is built upon an eminence, and commands a delightful prospect; the rest upon the edge of the water for convenience of warehouses. The town . . . . is at present by far the most flourishing one in these parts."[28]

Then he adds that Falmouth at the Falls "is a small mercantile town . . . . whose inhabitants are endeavouring to rival the Fredericksburgers in their trade . . . . . It . . . . consists of eighteen or twenty houses."[29]

Travelers noted that the two towns were thriving on trade and commerce, and more settlers were making their homes in the centers or in the surrounding country. From the original 50 acres upon which the town was established in 1727, Fredericksburg grew, requiring four enlargements by legislative acts between the date of incorporation and 1769.

How well the people of the Fredericksburg-Falmouth neighborhood lived in the mid-Eighteenth Century is told by a traveler who noted his observation in the *Journal of an Officer who Travelled in America and the West Indies in 1764 and 1765*. Visiting the major towns of the Virginia colony, he wrote:

> This . . . . would be my choice in preference to any, I have yet seen; the country in general is more cleared of woods, the houses are larger, better and more commodious than those to the Southward, they all drive Six horses, and travel generally 8 to 9 miles an hour . . . . going frequently Sixty Miles to dinner . . . . you may conclude from this their roads are extremely good.
>
> Their provisions of every kind are good, their Rivers supply them with a variety of Fish . . . . their pastures afford them excellent Beef and Mutton, and their Woods are stocked with Venison, Game and Hogs. Poultry is as good as in South Carolina, and their Madeira Wine is Excellent, almost in every house; Punch and small beer brewed from Molasses is also in use, but their Cyder far exceeds any cyder I ever tasted at home.
>
> In the back country there are Mines of Lead and Iron . . . . . All manners of European fruits, roots, and Garden Stuff do well here . . . . .[30]

Drawing on the ample natural resources and provisions manufactured in the area and imported from other colonies and countries, Falmouth-Fredericksburg supplied the needs of people who ventured beyond the Rappahannock Valley region during mid-1700's to found homes in the western lands beyond the Blue Ridge Mountains. The petition of Jost Hite, et al, who trekked their westward way through Rockfish Gap, Swift Run Gap and Ashby's Gap to

settle in the Shenandoah Valley cites the fact that the frontier
settlers there are "so far distant from any settlement . . . . as
could supply them with any provisions or necessairies that they
could scarce procure any one thing necessary than from Pennsylvania or Fredericksburg . . . . ."[31]

James Burket visited America in 1750-51 and while in Halifax,
Nova Scotia, observed that "I do not find there is any iron works
in this Province for in the last year they paid a most intolerable
price for iron which they chiefly have from Maryland, Virginia
& Pennsylvania, not only for Shipwork but for all other uses."[32]
A great part of the iron from Virginia came from the iron works
near Falmouth and Fredericksburg.[33]

Joseph Hadfield saw Fredericksburg in 1765 and noted that
it "is a considerable town of trade, furnishing the country around
. . . . ."[34]

It was almost the eve of the Revolutionary War when John
F. D. Smyth came to Fredericksburg in 1772. The town was, for
the time, a flourishing metropolis, a veritable hotbed of republican
ideas, according to this traveler, who reported that:

> After passing through a small town named Falmouth . . . .
> we crossed that river in a ferry-boat and arrived at Fredericks-
> burg, putting up at an inn or public house kept by one Weedon,
> who is general officer in the American Army, and was then
> very active and zealous in blowing the flames of sedition.
> It [Fredericksburg] is a very handsome town, considerably
> larger than Suffolk . . . . . Above Falmouth there is a very
> valuable forge, and iron works, belonging to a Mr. Hunter.[35]

In 1775, when the town was yet unmarked by the ravages of
the Revolutionary War nor impoverished by that conflict, Nicholas
Creswell stopped at Fredericksburg and found it "is a pretty large
town . . . . . Great quantities of tobacco is shipped from this
place . . . . . The land is pretty good in this neighborhood and
produces a great deal of Wheat. Saw a machine for threshing wheat
with horses . . . . ."[36]

Although Fredericksburg, along with other Tidewater Virginia
towns, suffered population loss and a decline of trade, industry and

commerce as the frontier moved westward, this was not too evident at the close of the Revolutionary period. Schopf visited the area in 1783 and 1784 and noted the following:

> This town of middling size . . . . public buildings . . . .
> churches, market house, courthouse lie at this time in ruins
> . . . . for reason . . . . that during the war there was no use
> for them and were neglected . . . . . [Mr. Schopf seems in
> error about the condition of the buildings, for the Minutes
> of the City Council of Fredericksburg for 1780-1800 make a
> number of references to the damages done to the Market House
> and other places during the Revolution.]
> Above Falmouth near the falls of the Rappahannock, is
> one of the finest and most considerable iron works in North
> America. More than 6-800 tons are worked there yearly . . . . .
> These works are distinguished besides a rolling and a slitting
> mill, and of this there are only two or three in America . . . . .
> The hills close about Fredericksburg and on the river
> consisted of sand-stones of divers colors. Fragments of fine gran-
> ites also appeared, which species of rock indeed make up the
> ridge causing the falls of the Rappahannock. These fragments
> of quartz, feldspar, and mica sprinkled now and again with
> sharl.[37]

Two years after Cornwallis surrendered at Yorktown, Count Luigi Castiglioni observed that in 1785 "Fredericksburg like Alexandria enjoys the privileges and is by law styled a City . . . . ."[38] Traveling southward to Richmond from this port on the Rappahannock, Castiglioni saw "many plantations large and small . . . . along the road. The houses are generally built with a porch, and the outbuildings ranged on either side . . . . ."[39] He noted that Alexandria had some 300 houses and around 3,000 inhabitants, and that Richmond had only 4,000 people living in some 400 houses. Another traveler recorded that in 1790 Fredericksburg "contains upwards of 300"[40] houses.

Judging from estimates given by these and other writers, Fredericksburg had a population of 3,000 to 4,000 inhabitants in 1785. Prior to this, however, when the town was in its prime, Fredericksburg must have had a population of 4,500 to 5,000 people. This is a conservative estimate, reckoning the damages the houses incurred and the loss of population suffered during the Revolution, after which many migrated from the region.

Just before the turn of the century, William Loughton Smith recorded in his *Journal* that Fredericksburg in 1790 was "a pretty town, consisting of one long street, containing several good houses. This place . . . . appears to be thriving and carrying on a large business; there are a great many stores in it, and the houses are generally neat and in good repair . . . . ."[41]

By the turn of the century, the Westward Movement was a fact that affected every city, town and community in America, including a reduction of population and industries in the region of Falmouth and Fredericksburg. However, these two centers had not lost their eighteenth century grandeur, according to Baron de Montlezum, who saw it about this time. He recorded the following:

> A large avenue of poplars, lined with houses, constitutes its [Fredericksburg] principal street. This city communicates to the north with Washington with a road . . . . . To the south a stage route leads to Richmond . . . . . Two roads lead to the west, one terminating in Orange County, where is the residence of the present President of the United States.
>
> Fredericksburg is rather pleasantly situated. Its principal street parallels the Rappahannock at a distance of a hundred yards; from there the land slopes gradually upward towards the west to a very pretty plateau on which the streets are laid out. There are some isolated houses which appear very nice, although built of wood. They are embellished with gardens . . . . .
>
> The Rappahannock is navigable as far as Fredericksburg . . . . . Right now there are fourteen or fifteen schooners anchored in its port.[42]

At the beginning of the nineteenth century, Fredericksburg had only 4,000 residents, but continued to be a "prosperous commercial port."[43] Its staples were grain, flour and tobacco, with an annual average sales of $4,000,000.

The town continued to lose population and business, however, until after the War of 1812, which contributed further to its decline.

## MARGARET BRENT
### (c. 1601-1671)

No portrait is known to have survived of Margaret Brent of "Peace" Stafford County, Virginia, first American feminist. She was the first white person to own the site now occupied by Fredericksburg, 1658, and the first to recognize the location as a site for a town.

## GENERAL
## GEORGE ROGERS CLARK
### (1752-1818)

Known as the "Conqueror of the Old Northwest," he was born near Fredericksburg.

## PRESIDENT JAMES MONROE
### (1758-1831)

Monroe settled in Fredericksburg in 1787. He was a member of the Town Council and was admitted to the bar here. He was subsequently delegate to the General Assembly from the town and later became the fifth president of the United States. He was author of the Monroe Doctrine.

*Courtesy of Laurence G. Hoes*

### GOVERNOR
### ALEXANDER SPOTSWOOD
### (1676-1740)

Known as the "First Citizen of Spotsylvania County," he founded the German colony at Germanna, 1714; led the transmontane expedition, 1716; and from his seat at "Newpost" near Fredericksburg acted as Deputy Postmaster General of the British Dominions in North America and the West Indies, 1730-1739.

### COMMODORE
### MATTHEW FONTAINE MAURY
### (1806-1873)

Universally known as the "Pathfinder of the Seas," Maury was born near Fredericksburg. He was instrumental in founding the United States Naval Academy, the Naval Observatory and the Weather Bureau.

COLONEL FIELDING LEWIS
(1725-1781)
and his wife
BETTY (WASHINGTON) LEWIS
(1733-1797)

Colonel Lewis was a leading planter and industrialist and in 1752
built "Kenmore" and resided there with his wife, the only sister of
General Washington who was often a visitor.

*Courtesy Kenmore Association*

**GENERAL GEORGE WASHINGTON**
(1732-1799)

The "Father of His Country" spoke of Fredericksburg as "the place of my growing infancy." This original portrait by Gilbert Stuart is one of the prized possessions of Fredericksburg Masonic Lodge No. 4.
*Courtesy Masonic Lodge No. 4*

KENMORE

This handsome brick mansion was built in 1752 by Colonel Fielding Lewis upon his plantation adjoining Fredericksburg and is now 1201 Washington Avenue. Handsomely furnished with many original pieces, it is maintained as a shrine by the Kenmore Association.

ADMIRAL
JOHN PAUL JONES
(1747-1792)

Fredericksburg was the only home in America of Admiral Jones. He came here in 1773 upon a visit to his elder brother, William Paul, a tailor. William Paul died late in 1774 and in 1775 John Paul accepted a commission in the Continental Navy.

### GENERAL GEORGE WEEDON
#### (1734-1793)

The tavern of General Weedon in Fredericksburg was the popular meeting place of the Revolutionary Patriots of this neighborhood. He and Doctor (later General) Hugh Mercer married sisters, the only daughters of John Gordon, early tavernkeeper to whose business Weedon succeeded.

### GENERAL HUGH MERCER
#### (1726-1777)

Mercer was a pre-Revolutionary physician in Fredericksburg and closing his apothecary shop entered the Continental Army and was killed at the Battle of Princeton. A handsome monument to his memory stands on Washington Avenue and his Apothecary Shop is maintained as a shrine.

### GENERAL
### WILLIAM WOODFORD
### (1734-1780)

Woodford lived at "Windsor" in
nearby Caroline County, and commanded the Virginia troops at the
Battle of the Great Bridge, December 9, 1775. He was a prominent
leader in the Revolutionary War
and died a British prisoner in
New York City.

### GENERAL THOMAS POSEY
### (1750-1818)

Posey participated in Dunmore
War, fought in the battle of Point
Pleasant, and was with General
Washington in New Jersey and
Pennsylvania where he was en-
gaged in several battles.

## DR. HUGH MERCER'S APOTHECARY SHOP

This pre-Revolutionary building at the corner of Caroline and Amelia
Streets is said to be the "Oldest Drug Store in America," and is
maintained as a shrine in memory of its owner.

## JAMES MONROE LAW OFFICE

This quaint building at 908 Charles Street was the law office of James
Monroe and is now maintained as a museum. Here is displayed an
interesting collection of his personal belongings, furniture and portraits.

## MARY WASHINGTON HOUSE

Here at 1201 Charles Street is the "Home of Mary, The Mother of George Washington;" it was her residence from 1772 until her death here, 1789. Furnished with period furniture, it is maintained as a shrine by The Association for the Preservation of Virginia Antiquities.

## SURVEYOR'S OFFICE OF GEORGE WASHINGTON

This little building at "Ferry Farm," opposite Fredericksburg, is said to have been used by the youthful Washington as a surveyor's office. Here, too, tradition holds he cut down the cherry tree and threw the dollar across the Rappahannock River.

## MASONIC LODGE BUILDING

Standing at the corner of Princess Anne and Hanover Streets is the building occupied by Masonic Lodge No. 4. This is "The Mother Lodge of George Washington" and into which he was initiated November 4, 1752, in the Old Town Hall where the Lodge held its first meetings. The building contains many interesting Masonic relics and is open as a shrine.

## THE RISING SUN TAVERN

This pre-Revolutionary house at 1304 Caroline Street was built by Captain Charles Washington *circa* 1760 and was long operated as a tavern by various persons. It is quaintly furnished with period furniture and is maintained as a shrine by the Association for the Preservation of Virginia Antiquities.

## FEDERAL HILL

This handsome residence on Hanover Street, was the home of the Honorable Robert Brooke, Governor of Virginia 1794-1796, and later of Thomas Reade Rootes, Esq:, attorney at law of Fredericksburg. It is now the residence of Doctor and Mrs. Richard N. Lanier.

## DOCTOR LAWRENCE BROOKE'S HOME

This pre-Revolutionary house at 303 Caroline Street was the home of Doctor Brooke, surgeon on the "Bon Homme Richard," and is now the residence of Miss Lavinia Adams.

SMITHFIELD

Three miles below Fredericksburg near the banks of the Rappahannock
River stands Smithfield, home of the Brooke family. The plantation
is believed to have taken its name from Major Lawrence Smith who
commanded the first fort built at the falls of the Rappahannock River,
1676. The property is now the quarters of the Fredericksburg Country
Club.

CLEAR VIEW

Overlooking Falmouth and the Rappahannock River from an eminence
on the Stafford heights is Clear View, the home of Major Andrew
Buchanan (17—- 1804), prominent attorney at law, and now the residence of Mrs. Michael Wallace.

## HOME AND OFFICE OF DOCTOR JAMES CARMICHAEL

These properties at 305-309 Hanover Street were occupied by Dr. James Carmichael (1771-1831) as a residence and office and until recently by his descendant the late Miss Frances Tucker Carmichael. Dr. James Carmichael, his two sons, his grandson and a great-grandson, all physicians, have added lustre to the medical profession in Fredericksburg.

## THE KITCHEN AND SMOKEHOUSE AT STANSTEAD

About a mile above Falmouth is Stanstead, the pre-Revolutionary plantation of Colonel Charles Carter (1707-1764) later of Cleve in King George County. The mansion house of Colonel Carter is destroyed and the only original buildings are the kitchen and smokehouse. The farm is now owned and occupied by Mr. and Mrs. Spencer Berry.

*Courtesy of Mr. Spencer Berry*

## THE CHARLES DICK HOUSE

This house at 1107 Princess Anne Street is said to be one of the oldest houses in Fredericksburg now standing. It was the pre-Revolutionary residence of Charles Dick, Esq: (1715-1783) and is now the residence of Mr. and Mrs. Edwin A. Gibson.

## CHATHAM

This handsome brick mansion house overlooking the City of Fredericksburg from the Stafford Heights across the Rappahannock River was built *circa* 1769 by the Honorable William FitzHugh (1741-1809) who resided here 1769-1797. It is undoubtedly the handsomest pre-Revolutionary residence now standing in the vicinity of Fredericksburg and it was here FitzHugh had his famous race track and lavishly entertained his numerous company. Chatham is now the residence of Mr. John Lee Pratt.

## BIRTHPLACE OF THE HONORABLE JOHN FORSYTH

This ancient house at 1301 Prince Edward Street was the pre-Revolutionary residence of the Hon. Robert Forsyth, later of Georgia, whose distinguished son, the Hon. John Forsyth (1780-1841), was born here. It was demolished in 1926 and the residence of Messrs. George H. S. King and Francis M. King now stands here.

## CHIMNEYS

This large frame house now standing at 623 Caroline Street was the residence of John Glassell, Esq:, prominent merchant of Fredericksburg. To the rear of this house near the river stood the Public Tobacco Warehouses.

## THE HOME OF JOHN FRAZER, ESQ:

The large frame house now standing at 1112 Charles Street, opposite The Mary Washington House, was the home of John Frazer, (*circa* 1756-1793), Revolutionary officer, and is now operated as the Betty Washington Inn by its owner Miss Frances Mason Williams.

## THE QUARTERS

These brick buildings at 303 Amelia Street were built *circa* 1820 by Carter Littlepage Stevenson, Esq: (1780-1840), attorney at law, and by him sold in 1827 to Dr. John Hall. Dr. Andrew C. Doggett acquired the property in 1888 from Doctor Hall's heirs, and until recently The Quarters was the home of his daughter the late Mrs. Kate Doggett Boggs.

By 1830 it had begun to experience a revival of prosperity and regained some of its former prestige as a thriving commercial port. At this time Joseph Martin's *Gazetteer* recorded the following:

> This [Fredericksburg] is a prosperous port: vessels of 140 tons can be navigated to the foot of the falls . . . . . The public buildings are a C.H., clerk's office, and jail, neat brick market house . . . . . There are 5 houses of public worship, 1 Episcopalian, 1 Presbyterian, 1 Methodist, 1 Baptist, and 1 Reformed Baptist, 5 male and 7 female schools, besides 2 free schools, 1 male and 1 female, which are incorporated and endowed, the former having 40 and the latter 18 pupils, and to each of the above churches is attached a Sunday School. There are 1 orphan asylum, 4 taverns and 97 licensed stores, 2 printing offices, the Virginia Herald and the Political Arena, each issuing a semiweekly paper. [The Virginia Herald is the second oldest newspaper in Virginia.] The principal mechanical pursuits are 3 tanners and 3 saddlers, besides house carpenters, iron founders, cabinet makers, tailors, boot and shoe makers, house, sign and ornament painters, stone cutters, brick layers, blacksmiths, watch makers, tallow chandlers, tin plate workers, coppersmiths, gunsmiths, hatters, butchers, bakers, machinists, coach makers and trimmers, carvers and gliders, stucco workers, plasterers, lumbers, turners, and confectioners . . . . . There are annually exported from this town 75,000 barrels of flour, 500,000 bushels of Indian corn, 499 hogsheads of tobacco, 150,000 bushels of wheat, 500 tierces of flax seed, and between 65 and $70,000 worth of gold, etc. . . . . . Population, whites 1797 persons, of whom 16 are resident physicians, and 6 regular physicians; slaves, 1124; free blacks, 387—Total, 3,308.[44]

The same gazetteer describes Falmouth as:

> Rapidly improved, containing 70 dwelling houses, 12 general stores, 1 house of public worship free for all denominations, 1 common school, 1 masonic hall, 1 druggist shop, 3 merchant mills, manufacturing about 30,000 barrells of flour annually, and inspecting 60,000, 3 grist mills . . . . (one of which is situated on the site of an old forge at which was the largest manufactory of arms during the revolution) . . . . . Population of

about 500 persons, of whom 2 are attorneys and 3 regular physicians.[45]

Visiting Fredericksburg in 1825, Mrs. Anne Royall found it "a handsome little town . . . . ."[46] Her description suggests the character of the city in colonial days.

It [Fredericksburg] possesses two great advantages, viz: that of rich fertile soil, which extends some distance on both sides of the river; and secondly, the advantages of navigation; vessels of one hundred and thirty tons ascend to the town. The amount of exports annually is estimated at four million of dollars. The surrounding country is in a high state of cultivation, and exceeded by none in fertility or beauty; I never expected to see such a country as this in the worn-out east . . . . . The soil produces corn, wheat, tobacco, and almost every thing necessary for man . . . . . The houses are mostly of brick, and some of them are handsome and commodious There are two bridges over the river. It is an incorporated town; contains four churches, . . . . a courthouse, jail, collectors office, a post-office, an academy, and about 4000 inhabitants. For several miles after leaving Fredericksburg you pass through a country of unequaled beauty; the scenery is beyond description, rich and picturesque. Handsome buildings, and highly cultivated farms are in constant view . . . . .[47]

## NOTES

1. Hening, *op. cit.*, IV, 234-39.
2. Captain John Smith, *True Travels and Observations* (London, 1629), I, 117.
3. *Ibid.*
4. William Strachey, *The Historie of Travaile into Virginia Britannia* (London: Hakluyt Soc., 1849), ed. by R. H. Major, pp. 33, 38.
5. John Lederer's Brochure, The Discoveries of John Lederer, C. W. Alvord, and Lee Bidgood, eds., *The First Explorations of the Trans-Alleghany Region by Virginians* (Cleveland: A. H. Clark, 1912), pp. 163-66.
6. *Ibid.*, p. 141.
7. *Ibid.*, pp. 148, 156, 158.
8. John F. D. Smyth, *A Tour in the United States of America* (London, 1784. 2 vols), II, 96.
9. Hening, *op. cit.*, II, 326.

10. *Ibid.*

11. *Ibid.*

12. Letters of Lord Fairfax, 1739-1751, *Relating to the Dispute over the Boundary of Northern Neck,* "depositions of John Taliaferro, Francis Thornton, and Wm. Russell," MSS., Library of Congress.

13. Land Office, Richmond, Va., Patent Bk. No. 4, p. 16.

14. *Ibid.,* Bk. 4, p. 234.

15. Smith, *op. cit.,* p. 117.

16. *Commercial Directory* (Philadelphia: Kayser & Co., 1823), p. 218; Richard Brooks, fl. 1750, *General Gazetteer Improved; or, A New and Compendious Geographical Dictionary* (Richmond, 1806), p. 335; Joseph Martin, *A New and Comprehensive Gazetteer of Virginia and the District of Columbia,* (Charlottesville: Editor, 1835), pp. 281-82; Mrs. Anne Royall, *Sketches of History, Life and Manners in the United States* (New Haven: The Author, 1826), pp. 117-18.

17. Robert Beverley, *History of Virginia* (London, 1705), pp. 93-94.

18. Jefferson, *Notes on the State of Virginia* (Brooklyn: History Printing Co., 1894), pp. 4, 24.

19. Smyth, *op. cit.,* II, 96-97.

20. John David Schopf, *Travels in the Confederation, 1783-1784* (translated by Alfred James Morrison, Philadelphia: Campbell, 1911, 2 Vols.), II, 41.

21. Land Office, Richmond, Patent Book 4, p. 425.

22. *Ibid.,* Bk. 5, pp. 287-88.

23. *Ibid.,* Bk. 10, p. 260.

24. *Ibid.,* Bk. 13, p. 214.

25. *Sainsburg Abstracts,* IX, 132, Transcripts in the Virginia State Library.

26. Lord Fairfax Letters, 1739-1751, *op. cit.*

27. William Byrd, *The Writings of Col. Wm. Byrd,* "A Progress to the Mines," (ed. by John Spencer Bassett, New York: Doubleday, Page, 1901), pp. 373-74.

28. Rev. Andrew Burnaby, *Travels Through the Middle Settlements in North America, in 1759 and 1760* (ed. by John Pinkerton, London, 1912, 3 Vols.), III, 718.

29. *Ibid.,* p. 719.

30. *Journal of an Officer [Lord Adam Gordon] Who Travelled in America and the West Indies, in 1764 and 1765,"* (ed. by Newton D. Mereness under the title of *Travels in the American Colonies,* New York: Macmillan, 1916), pp. 404-07.

31. Lord Fairfax Letters, 1739-1751, p. 4.

32. James Burket, *Some Cursory Remarks Made by James Burket in his Voyage to North America, 1750-51* (New Haven: Yale Press, 1916), pp. 12-13.

33. Smyth, *op. cit.,* II, 96-97, 112-13, 127.

34. Joseph Hadfield, *An Englishman in America, 1785, Being a Diary of Joseph Hadfield* (ed. by D. S. Robertson, Toronto: Hunter-Rose, 1933), p. 11.

35. Smyth, *op. cit.,* p. 151.

36. *The Journal of Nicholas Creswell, 1774-1777* (New York: Dial, 1924), p. 56.

37. Schopf, *op. cit.,* II, 41-46.

38. Count Luigi Castiglioni's *Travels in the United States* (Milan, 1790), II, 266-68.

39.  *Ibid.*

40.  Wm. Loughton Smith, *Journal, 1790-91* (Cambridge: Univ. Press, 1917), p. 64.

41.  *Ibid.*

42.  "A Frenchman Visits Norfolk, Fredericksburg, and Orange County, 1816," in the *Virginia Magazine of History and Biography*, Vol. LIII, Part I, No. 2 (April, 1945), pp. 114-15.

43.  Brookes, *op. cit.*, p. 335.

44.  Martin, Joseph, A New and Comprehensive Gazetteer of Virginia, Charlottesville, 1836.

45.  *Ibid.*, p. 284.

46.  Mrs. Anne Royall, *Sketches of History, Life, and Manners in the United States* (New Haven: The Author, 1826), pp. 117-118.

47.  *Ibid.*, p. 118.

# *4*

## Falmouth and Fredericksburg as Geographic, Communication, Commercial and Trading Centers

Geography was a major factor in the development of Falmouth and Fredericksburg into important cosmopolitan communication, commercial and trade centers of colonial America.

Time and circumstance together were largely responsible for locating in this area the first communication headquarters for the British Dominions in North America and the West Indies. It was established in 1730 at Newpost, outside Fredericksburg, with Alexander Spotswood, of nearby Germanna, as Deputy-Postmaster-General for the British Dominions in North America.[1]

The same factors contributed immeasurably toward making the two towns on the Rappahannock River rank twentieth among the forty-three ports and areas of North America handling the greatest volume of trade in the colonial period. Excluding the nine ports located outside the thirteen English colonies, the Rappahannock port held fifteenth place among the thirty-four towns in the colonies, according to the listings of the Customs House Records.

Reckoning the South Potomac and the Rappahannock together, since their traffic concerned the same region, the two areas combined exceeded in tonnage all but ten of the forty-three ports listed. This placed Falmouth and Fredericksburg as the tenth largest shipping center in all North America, following the lead, in descending order, of Philadelphia, Charleston, Boston, Hampton-Norfolk, New York, Salem, Baltimore, Falmouth (Mass.), and Providence. Quebec, Halifax and Newfoundland had less grand total tonnage than Falmouth-Fredericksburg.[2]

Located strategically for domestic, continental and world commerce and trade, Falmouth and Fredericksburg sent out ships of cargo to more than one hundred and twenty-five ports and areas of the world where merchants and business men of the Rappahannock area conducted their import-export trade. The Naval Lists of the Customs Records of London report that, between 1727 and 1773, Falmouth and Fredericksburg traded with these ports and areas, extending from Quebec in Canada to the Gold Coast of Africa:

Aberdeen, Amsterdam, Accomac, Anguila, Antigua, Ayr, (Ayre), Azores, Bahama, Barnstaple, Barbados, Basseterre, Beaufort, Bermude, Bideford, Boness (Borrowstoness), Bonny, Bordeaux, Boston, Bremen, Bristol, Brunswick, Brussels, Burgundy, Burlington, Cadiz, Calabar, Cette (Cetti), Ceyenne, Charleston, Chester, Coasting, Cork, Curacoa, Dublin, Dunbar, East Florida, Eustatia, Exeter, Falmouth (in England and Mass.), First Entry, Florence, Gambia, Geneva, Gibraltar, Glasgow, Gold Coast, Grenados, Greenock, Guadeloupe, Halifax, Hamburg, Harve de Grace, Hull, Ireland, Irvine, Isle of Man, Isle of May, Jamaica, James River, Kinsale, Kirkcudbright, Leeds, Leedstown, Leghorn, Leith, Leven, Limerick, Lisbon, Liverpool, London, Lynn-Regis, Madeira, Madrid, Martinque, Maryland, Mobile, Nantucket, Nevis, New Castle, New England, New Haven, New Jersey, New London, New Orleans, New York, Norfolk, North Carolina, Old Calabar, Oporto, Patuxent, Pensacola, Perth Amboy, Philadelphia, Piscataqua, Port Glasgow, Port Hampton, Port Lewis, Portroyal, Port York, Potomac River, Quebec, Rappahannock River, Rhode Island, Roanoke River, Rotterdam, St. Augustine, St. Croix, St. Johns., St. Kitts (St. Christopher), St. Petersburg, St. Thomas, Salem, Saltatudas, Savannah, Scarsborough, Silesia, Southhampton, Surinam, Teneriff, Topsham, Turks Island, Vigo, Urbanna, Weymouth, Whitehaven, York River, Yorktown.

Commercial interests of the merchants and planter industrialists of the Rappahannock River area kept the people of this cosmopolitan center in constant contact with forty different countries of Europe, Turkey, the Eastern Mediterranean and other sections. At the same time trade was carried on between Falmouth-Fredericksburg and some 43 major towns and regions in North America, extending from Quebec to Bermuda. This coastal and overseas trade of the two Rappahannock ports had its counterpart in the inland trade with the back country, including the Shenandoah, the Monongohela, the Ohio, the Great Lakes, Kentucky and the Tennessee regions of the western frontier.

It may be said that fate decreed that the Rappahannock area be the commercial and cultural center of colonial America by locating it at the crossroads of the Western hemisphere. Like all important colonial towns, Falmouth and Fredericksburg were situated on or near good navigable bodies of water. Each was at the head of navigation of the Rappahannock River, about one hundred and thirty miles inland from the Chesapeake Bay; hardly ten miles from the Potomac River, which makes its nearest approach to the Rappahannock in this vicinity; and almost equidistant from the Mattaponi and North Anna rivers.

From the early days when Powhatan and Manahoac chieftans and warriors held their powwows at the falls of the Rappahannock down to the present day, this area has maintained its importance as a communication center not only for a wide section of Tidewater and Piedmont Virginia, but for a vast hinterland which in colonial times included parts of territories now embraced by several other states. Growing consciousness of this fact led the Virginia House of Burgesses to order in 1671 that "garrisons . . . . be erected and built at the heads of the ffouer great rivers . . . . Potomac . . . . Rappahannock . . . . Mattopony . . . . and the James."[3]

The fort was erected here in 1676, indicating a great strategic value of the area to the first English colony. Moreover, the statute directed that two forts be erected in the neighborhood of the Rappahannock River, one "at or near the falls," and the other on the Mattapony River, which geographically and historically belongs with the Fredericksburg area, as does the South Potomac. The rank in importance of the regions is indicated further by the Burgesses in the wording of the 1671 act, which names the Potomac, Rappahannock and Mattapony in the lead, followed by the James, Pamunkey and the Appomattox, whose strategic significance was secondary to the colony in its effort to maintain clear lines of communication along the Atlantic Seaboard. This act, as well as many subsequent statutes passed by the colonial legislature, indicates the direction in which the major interests and thinking of Virginians was being conditioned preliminary to the settlement of the Rappahannock area, and even through the Nineteenth Century, served as a springboard for the Westward movement across the Blue Ridge Mountains and on to the West Coast.

By 1680 the Falls area was made comparatively free from the threat of Indian incursions and the forts were abandoned. But the importance of this region in the colonization of the Eastern Seaboard increased because Falmouth and Fredericksburg were regarded as the main gateway to the West, being significantly situated in relation to the three great passes across the Blue Ridge Mountains: the Ashby Gap to the northwest, the Swift Run Gap directly west, and the Rockfish Gap to the Southwest.

Friendly contacts, communications and trade relationships with the Cherokees and other Indians to the West were established and maintained through the post at the falls of the Rappahannock. The rich fur trade derived from the Indians induced further efforts to extend settlements and trade relations westward. The trading post at the Falls soon became the principal, and for some time the only, entrepot for the whole western and northwestern Virginia. This position was maintained for nearly a hundred years. Eventually, however, its monopoly was relinquished to newly rising towns on the frontier, such as Winchester, Woodstock and Staunton, which siphoned off much of the resources formerly enjoyed by the Fredericksburg area. This development was one of the main reasons for the decline of Fredericksburg from its colonial superiority.

With the cessation of Indian hostilities by 1680, the upper parts of the Rappahannock Valley were rapidly settled. Large grants of land were conveyed to individuals who became leaders of the commercial, cultural, economic and political life of this region. The Fitzhughs, the Brents, the Fairfaxes, the Carters, the Taliaferroes, the Thorntons, the Robinsons, the Beverleys, the Lewises, the Masons, the Brookes, the Willises, the Smiths, the Buckners, the Roystons and many other large planters, colonial officials, merchants and enterprising individuals secured vast acreage by availing themselves of "head-right" to land through the privilege granted for importing settlers. So many squatters had settled in the Valley of the Rappahannock that a new frontier county of Spotsylvania was authorized in 1720. Seven years later Falmouth and Fredericksburg were laid out as towns.

By 1730 the region was considered one of the most important in the Atlantic seaboard. As stated previously, the colonial head-quarters for the British Dominions in North America and the West Indies were established at Newpost, outside Fredericksburg, with Spotswood as the third deputy postmaster-general for the entire British dominions in the Western Hemisphere. Spotswood's post office stood on the west bank at the junction of the Massaponax with the Rappahannock River just below Fredericksburg. From this point postal communications were carried on with all parts of the world.

In 1753 the responsibility of distributing mail and postal information and managing the British postal system in America became the joint responsibility of Benjamin Franklin of Philadelphia and William Hunter of Williamsburg. Spotswood had been primarily responsible for promoting Franklin to this position. In the intervening years, however, Spotswood resigned his office in 1739 to undertake the Cartagena Expedition. John Lynch, of Caroline County, succeeded him, serving until 1743 when a Scotchman, Elliott Benger, of Spotsylvania County, brother-in-law of Spotswood, became the third successive man from the Rappahannock country to be appointed deputy postmaster general of the English colonies. These three men served in this capacity from 1730 to 1753; upon the death of Benger in 1753, Benjamin Franklin and William Hunter were jointly assigned the responsibility, 1754.

For more than twenty years all the political, commercial and personal communications of a continent centered at Newpost, just outside Fredericksburg. This was the beginning of what today is a national postal system serving the forty-eight States of the union, its territories and possessions. However:

Post offices were established in the colony of Virginia in 1657, the system established at the time being merely a requirement that every planter should furnish a messenger to carry the mail to the next plantation under the penalty of forfeiting a hogshead of tobacco in default. The General Assembly of Virginia authorized a post office in the colony, 'believeing such an office to be of general concernment and of great advantage for the increase and preservation of trade and commerce therein, for thereby speedy and safe dispatch may be had' . . . . .

Fredericksburg was a stop on the first 'main post road' that was operated from Scoodic in Maine to Saint Mary's in Georgia . . . . . Fredericksburg was a gateway to the South. In 1810 seven mail routes emanated from the office, which was a considerable number for that time. There also passed through this office the mail route between New York and New Orleans.[4]

The location, in practice, of the headquarters for colonial communication system at Fredericksburg was not a mere accident of history. Geographically this center was favorably situated on the two main trans-colonial routes from the northern to the southern colonies: the Trans-Seaboard Route and the Old Carolina Road. It was the principal Cis-Monte point from Williamsburg to Winchester, to Pittsburgh and to the Northwest. Falmouth and Fredericksburg were the conjunction points of roads from Middle Peninsula and Northern Neck in Virginia, being the only doorway to and from the latter area. They were points of departure and the eastern terminus of the roads to the West via Swift Run Gap and the Rockfish Gap. The great North-South road and the Williamsburg-to-Winchester road crossed at Fredericksburg. An eight-way road system fanned out from these two towns on the Rappahannock, linking them with every important trade and population center of the Atlantic Seaboard and with the frontier in the West.

Furthermore, the Rappahannock River, with tributaries, was a highway to the world. Ocean-going vessels of nearly all types of that day could come up to the Falls, while smaller craft could go higher up the Rappahannock and the other waterways within the vicinity.

The Potomac River makes its nearest approach to the Rappahannock River for some distance above and below Falmouth and Fredericksburg, with the two rivers being scarcely six miles apart at the closest point and the average being about ten miles for a considerable distance. The South Potomac area has always accounted for a great portion of the prosperity and importance of these twin towns. They are situated at the waistline or apex of two cone-shaped land masses, then known as the Greater Northern Neck of Virginia, and the Lord Fairfax Domain. The eastern cone is still known as the Northern Neck. The two areas comprised over five million acres of land, covering nearly ten thousand square miles and embracing about one-fourth of Virginia. Geographically the whole area belonged to the Falmouth-Fredericksburg trading sphere, for they were the principal commercial centers of the whole realm.

The same holds true for the Mattaponi Valley, particularly above the confluence of the Mat, Ta, Po, and Ni Rivers. The areas drained by these rivers and their tributaries have always been attached geographically, historically and economically to Falmouth and Fredericksburg.

Both of these towns early were designated ports of entry for the colony of Virginia. The large plantations in the valleys of these rivers, the vast hinterland richly endowed with a great variety of natural resources, and the large export-import commerce conducted by the twin towns accounted for their growth and commercial importance in the colonial era.

From the standpoint of geographic and topographic position, perhaps few other areas in the English colonies had advantages superior to Falmouth-Fredericksburg. Added to the natural advantages provided by the waterways and the position as a crossroad of overland highways, the area was richly endowed with fertile soil, forest, scenic beauty, valuable mineral deposits, mineral springs, various kinds of builders' clays, sandstone, granite, slate, salt and potash.

Maps of the early colonies show that Falmouth and Fredericksburg were in the main currents of travel, trade and communication traffic. The Jefferson-Fry map of Virginia and Maryland published in 1751 shows Fredericksburg and Alexandria as the most important frontier towns of that period. Recognizing this fact and wishing to encourage the flow of trade into the colony, the Virginia House of Burgesses decreed in its act of 1766 that a road be opened through its frontiers to Fort Pitt on the Ohio. Accordingly "Thomas Walker, Thomas Rutherford, James Wood and Abraham Kite, gentlemen . . . . are hereby appointed, authorized and empowered, to view, lay out, and direct, a road to be cleared from the north branch of Potomac river to Fort Pitt on the Ohio, by or near the road called Braddock's road."[5] This was enacted because "a very advantageous trade might be carried on with the Indians . . . . ."[6]

Commerce and trade with coastal towns of America, the inland centers and the world at large conducted by the merchants and industrialists of Fredericksburg area were facilitated by the communication system of the post office which was located prior to and during the Revolutionary War at Weedon's Tavern, in Fredericksburg. George Weedon was the town postmaster at the opening of the war. The position was the second most important one of its kind in the colony. Weedon was responsible for forwarding by stage and post-riders the mail for both the North and the South, and the East and the West, and for all local mail, which frequently involved considerable distances beyond the immediate environs.

Geographic factors affecting favorably the establishment of trade, commerce, and communication centers at Fredericksburg also helped to widen the interests and contacts of the people within the area. All phases of their lives were influenced by this world contact, which not only imported new ideas, philosophies and forces, but sharpened their desire for luxuries and necessities of everyday living that only a successful import-export trade conducted by the businessmen of that day could satisfy.

The William Allason papers, the Customs Reports and Naval Lists for the period provide an alphabetical list of 175 common items that were imported by the Falmouth-Fredericksburg merchants for sale and distribution to the people in the neighborhood and for reshipment to the hinterland and the frontier centers of Virginia and beyond the Blue Ridge Mountains. At the same time at least 125 items, ranging from apple brandy, beaver skins, chemicals, corn, and lumber, to teeth, were exported from the area.[7]

Trade reports show that the greater portion of overseas commerce of the Rappahannock ports was with the West Indies. Barbados, Caracoa, Surinam, Cayenne, St. Croix, the Leeward Islands and Jamaica are the places most frequently mentioned in the Order and Invoice Books of the merchants. Although nearly every important port and trading center in Europe was in direct contact with the Falmouth-Fredericksburg merchants during the eighteenth century, the largest volume of commerce was handled with London, Bristol, Whitehaven, Liverpool, Dublin, Glasgow, Edinburgh, Aberdeen, Kinsale, Sligo Kilmarnock, Ayre, Barnstaple, Cork, Exeter, Falmouth, Greencock, Hull, Irvine, Kirkcudbright, Topsham and Leeds.

Jamaica and other West Indian ports and New England supplied the bulk quantity of rum handled by the merchants of the Rappahannock. Madeira, Cape Verde, Canaries, Teneriff, Oporto (Spain), Bordeaux (France), Geneva (Switzerland) and other continental European ports were the principal sources of finer wines, brandies, whiskeys and other alcoholic beverages.

Merchants of Fredericksburg frequently refer in their reports and books to trade contacts with Mediterranean ports of Florence, Leghorn, Marseilles, Cadiz; the northern European towns of Amsterdam, Brussels, Hamburg, Stockholm; and to points on the African coast.

Coastal towns of North America most frequently mentioned in the trading of the two towns included Port Royal, Leedstown, Hobbs Hole, and Urbanna on the Rappahannock; Yorktown on the York River; Norfolk on the lower James; Yocomoco, Nomini Hall, Port Tobacco, Marlborough, Aquia, Dumfries, Colchester and Alexandria on the Potomac River. Annapolis and Baltimore were the principal ports on the Chesapeake Bay which did a large volume of business here. Philadelphia, New York and Boston were the most important towns of the northern colonies trading with the merchants and businessmen of Falmouth and Fredericksburg.

Counties of eastern Virginia, and back parts of the colony and the countries specifically mentioned trading with the Rappahannock ports, were Northumberland, Hanover, Accomac (Eastern Shore), Shenandoah Valley, Ohio country and Kentucky. Chains of ordinaries and stores extended from Falmouth to these back parts of Virginia through which the merchants traded. Wagons and teamsters from the frontier population centers were a common sight in these two towns. William Allason's wagons and drivers kept up a regular business for him with centers in the Shenandoah and as far west as the Kentucky meadows. "Wagoners Lots" and grounds were provided for these tradesmen who came to town, and to the present day numerous "wagoners lots" are pointed out to visitors in Fredericksburg.

Imports consisted of all sorts of supplies for the wealthy planters, their homes and estates: artisan's tools; general merchandise; European goods; drugs and medicines; carpenters tools; cutlery; pottery; dye stuffs; mine and furnace equipment; glassware; hardware; tinware; chinaware; silverware; jewelry; watches; saddlery; leather goods of all kinds; pewterware; firearms; fruits; nuts; olives; raisins; rope; wines and spirits; thoroughbred horses and jennies; sugar, tea and coffee; musical instruments; pictures-paintings; bricks for ballast; Negroes; servants; molasses; wood products; textile and fiber products; books.

Although books are not ordinarily the chief interests of immigrants and settlers in a frontier country, the orders of Allason & Company reveal a surprisingly large number of books of a scholarly type, indicating a wide selection in reading. Single orders for importing books frequently amounted to several hundred pounds English sterling. An order of August 15, 1757, was for £206.13.0 worth of books. Often two or three orders for books were made in the same year, and never for less than £40 each—indicating a large demand for reading, which was generally supplied by the James Knox Bookstore of Glasgow.

Chief commodities of export trade from Falmouth and Fredericksburg were tobacco, wheat, corn and other grains, food stuffs, bread, meat, pork, cherry rum, wines, cider, liquors and whiskey, furs, leather, skins, lumber, staves, planks, boards, casks, hoops, masts, scantlings, barrels, kegs, iron mongery, mineral and metal products, hemp, fish, fruits, eggs, vegetables, drugs, chemicals, dye stuffs, textile and fiber products, walnuts, wool, tanned leather, flax, potash, tallow, cotton, military stores, flaxseed, livestock, sugar and molasses.

Appended to this chapter are sample statistical tables of exports and imports of the Fredericksburg area, showing the volume of trade handled in 1727, when the two ports were erected, and compared with the trade handled in the years prior to the outbreak of the Revolutionary War. Several tables in the appendix show the ports and towns of the world with which the merchants of Fredericksburg and Falmouth traded, as well as the commodities most frequently imported and exported between these centers.

Some of the statistical tables of "Exports" and "Imports" of the Fredericksburg area for various years are given on the following pages:

## N O T E S

1. See Spots. Co. Records, Order Bk. K, p. 405.
2. See Appendix on Imports.
3. Hening, *Statutes*, II, 433.
4. Post Office Dept., Correspondence, Washington, D. C., July 3, 1914, 14707-C z-AC.
5. Hening, *op. cit.*, VIII, 252.
6. *Ibid.*
7. The William Allason Papers, State Library, Richmond.

## TABLE I

### PORT RAPPAHANNOCK*[1] .... 1727 .... IMPORTS
### SOURCE OF ORIGIN, COMMODITY, QUANTITY

| Source | | | | | | |
|---|---|---|---|---|---|---|
| *Bristol:* | Teeth—10 1 lbs. | Skins—352 | Rum—17 Casks | Staves—6,000 | Goods, Sundry Euro—3 Shipments | Linen—16 Bales |
| *Dunbar:* | Goods, Sundry Euro—1 Shipment | | | | | |
| *Exeter:* | Goods, Sundry Euro—1 Shipment | | | | | |
| *Glasgow:* | Goods, Sundry Euro—4 Shipments | Wine—3 Pipes | | | | |
| *Irvine:* | Goods, Sundry Euro—1 Shipment | | | | | |
| *Levin:* (Leven) | Wine—7 Casks | | | | | |
| *Liverpool:* | Teeth—50 | Skins—265 | Wine—6 Pipes | Goods, Sundry European—2 Shipments | | |

## TABLE I Continued

| | | | | | | | |
|---|---|---|---|---|---|---|---|
| *London:* | Goods, Sundry Euro— 2 Shipments | | | | | | Silk Mfg.— 2 Cases |
| *Whitehaven* | Goods, Sundry Euro— 1 Shipment | | | | | Hops— 5 Bags | |
| *Accomac, Va.:* | Goods, Sundry Euro— 1 Shipment | | | | | | |
| *Boston:* | Molasses— 5 hhds. | Sugar— 18 Casks | Rum— 37 Casks | Wine— 2 Pipes | Salt— 472 bu. | | |
| | Woodenware— 1 Crate | Calico— 3 Pieces | Ozenbrig— 3 Pieces | | | | |
| *Maryland:* | Goods, Sundry Euro— 1 Shipment | | | | | | |
| *New England:* | Rum— 6 Casks | Wine—Madeira 4 Pipes | Wine—Port— 3 Pipes | | | | |
| *N. Car.:* | Household Goods— 1 Shipment | Furniture— 1 Shipment | | | | | |

## TABLE I Continued

| | | | | | | |
|---|---|---|---|---|---|---|
| **Philadelphia:** | Goods, Sundry Euro—1 Shipment | | | | | |
| **Topsham:** | Goods, Sundry Euro—1 Shipment | | | | | |
| **Barbados:** | Wine—1 Pipe | Rum—22 Casks | Sugar—11 Casks | | | |
| **Bermuda:** | Salt—1500 bu. | Rum—7 Casks | | Teeth—10 | Negroes—108 | Goods, Sundry Euro—1 Shipment |
| **Other Listings:** | Furs, Leather, & Skins | Household & Husbandry Goods | Misc.: | Goods, Sundry European | Negroes, Servants, Passengers | Provisions & Food Stuffs: Hops Salt Madeira Wine |
| | Sugar & Molasses | Textile & Fiber Products: Calico Linen Ozenbrig Silk mfg. | Wines & Spirits: Rum Wine—Madeira Port | Wood Products: Staves Woodenware | | |

¹ Transcripts, Customs 16/1, MSS. Library of Congress.

• (After the erection of Falmouth and Fredericksburg in 1727, they were referred to in the Customs Reports as the "Port of Rappahannock")

## TABLE II
## IMPORTS, 1769-1770
## VESSELS

| PORTS | TOTALS EXTRA CONTINENTAL | | | TOTALS WITHIN THE CONTINENT | | | GRAND TOTALS | | |
|---|---|---|---|---|---|---|---|---|---|
| | Topsails | Sloops, etc. | Tonnage | Topsails | Sloops, etc. | Tonnage | Topsails | Sloops, etc. | Tonnage |
| *South Potomac* | 22 | 4 | 3066 | 16 | 10 | 2319 | 38 | 14 | 5385 |
| *Rappahannock* | 23 | 14 | 3774 | 5 | 25 | 1284 | 37 | 40 | 5058 |
| (Lower Part) | 125 | 83 | 17502 | 5 | 68 | 2141 | 130 | 151 | 19643 |
| James | | | | | | | | | |
| (Upper Part) | 60 | 6 | 7320 | 7 | 26 | 1923 | 67 | 32 | 9243 |
| Charles Town | 185 | 78 | 24199 | 20 | 150 | 4927 | 205 | 228 | 29126 |
| Patuxent | 119 | 32 | 16739 | 13 | 58 | 3045 | 132 | 90 | 19784 |
| Philadelphia | 307 | 94 | 29910 | 45 | 253 | 12425 | 352 | 347 | 42333 |
| New York | 157 | 121 | 14918 | 26 | 429 | 11959 | 183 | 550 | 26877 |
| Boston | 150 | 129 | 20057 | 27 | 573 | 20426 | 177 | 702 | 40483 |
| York River | 27 | 15 | 4092 | 2 | 26 | 1005 | 29 | 41 | 5097 |
| Salem-Marblehead | 50 | 115 | 10824 | 4 | 123 | 5124 | 54 | 238 | 15948 |
| Rhode Island | 65 | 106 | 6599 | 20 | 437 | 11926 | 85 | 543 | 18525 |
| New London | 28 | 101 | 5080 | 5 | 269 | 6857 | 33 | 370 | 11931 |
| Falmouth (Mass.) | 34 | 28 | 7952 | 4 | 54 | 2068 | 38 | 82 | 10020 |
| Brunswick | 56 | 25 | 7530 | 11 | 38 | 2099 | 67 | 60 | 9629 |
| Savannah | 48 | 39 | 6272 | 8 | 48 | 1976 | 56 | 87 | 8248 |
| North Potomac | 38 | 5 | 5145 | 9 | 27 | 2191 | 47 | 32 | 7336 |
| New Haven | 14 | 54 | 2965 | — | 159 | 3628 | 14 | 213 | 6593 |
| Roanoke | 22 | 37 | 3064 | 5 | 91 | 3254 | 27 | 128 | 6318 |
| Beaufort | 16 | 24 | 2547 | 1 | 77 | 2246 | 17 | 101 | 4793 |
| Newfoundland | | | | | | | | | 11652 |
| Quebec | | | | | | | | | 7687 |
| Halifax | | | | | | | | | 7006 |
| Piscataqua | | | | | | | | | 15446 |

Rank: Philadelphia (1), Boston (2), Charleston (3), James (4), New York (5), Patuxent (6), Rhode Island (7), Salem (8), Piscataqua (9), New London (10), Newfoundland (11), South Potomac and Rappahannock (12).

## TABLE III
## EXPORTS, 1769-1770
## VESSELS

| PORTS | TOTALS EXTRA CONTINENTAL | | | TOTALS WITHIN THE CONTINENT | | | GRAND TOTALS | | |
|---|---|---|---|---|---|---|---|---|---|
| | Topsails | Sloops, etc. | Tonnage | Topsails | Sloops, etc. | Tonnage | Topsails | Sloops, etc. | Tonnage |
| Piscataqua | 96 | 119 | 14938 | 9 | 96 | 3874 | 105 | 215 | 18812 |
| Falmouth (Mass.) | 38 | 153 | 9706 | 4 | 50 | 2599 | 42 | 103 | 12305 |
| (Lower Part) | 106 | 90 | 14442 | 8 | 62 | 2604 | 114 | 152 | 17046 |
| James (Uper Part) | 98 | 7 | 12743 | 5 | 27 | 1640 | 103 | 34 | 14383 |
| Salem-Marblehead | 47 | 109 | 9634 | 7 | 108 | 4682 | 54 | 217 | 14316 |
| Boston | 140 | 95 | 17338 | 42 | 552 | 19707 | 182 | 647 | 37045 |
| Rhode Island | 76 | 128 | 7463 | 18 | 448 | 12665 | 94 | 576 | 20128 |
| New Haven | 21 | 63 | 3646 | 1 | 150 | 3413 | 22 | 213 | 7059 |
| New London | 34 | 116 | 6125 | 3 | 270 | 5165 | 37 | 386 | 11290 |
| New York | 150 | 135 | 15419 | 25 | 485 | 11640 | 175 | 620 | 27059 |
| Philadelphia | 312 | 96 | 30403 | 24 | 246 | 10468 | 336 | 342 | 40871 |
| Patuxent | 121 | 31 | 16504 | 10 | 61 | 2819 | 131 | 92 | 19323 |
| North Potomac | 41 | 5 | 5849 | 1 | 36 | 1352 | 42 | 41 | 7201 |
| *Rappahannock* | 40 | 12 | 5812 | 1 | 20 | 826 | 41 | 32 | 6638 |
| *South Potomac* | 28 | 4 | 5085 | 5 | 10 | 825 | 33 | 14 | 5905 |
| York River | 28 | 11 | 4629 | 1 | 30 | 966 | 29 | 41 | 5595 |
| Roanoke | 36 | 48 | 4591 | — | 88 | 2813 | 36 | 136 | 7404 |
| Brunswick | 58 | 26 | 7410 | 1 | 32 | 719 | 59 | 58 | 8129 |
| Charles Town | 200 | 78 | 26261 | 20 | 136 | 5006 | 220 | 214 | 31267 |
| Savannah | 52 | 46 | 6677 | 5 | 41 | 1173 | 57 | 87 | 7850 |
| Quebec | | | | | | | | | 7628 |
| Halifax | | | | | | | | | 7324 |
| Newfoundland | | | | | | | | | 10458 |

Rank:   Philadelphia (1), Boston (2), James (3), Charleston (4),
New York (5), Rhode Island (6), Patuxent (7), Piscataqua
(8), Salem (9), Falmouth (10), South Potomac and Rappahannock (11).

# 5

## Major Industrial Enterprises and Businesses

Records disclose that colonial Fredericksburg and its neighborhood community had practically every type of industry and business conducted in that period. Moreover, men here were pioneers in the development of several industries, such as iron mines and the manufactory of iron products. The list of businesses and industries developed and conducted with financial success by colonials of the Rappahannock Valley covers the entire range from large scale farming on vast plantation estates, to shipping, iron works, merchandising, warehouses, printing and publishing, taverns, salt works and lumber industries.

Drawing upon the resources and products of the fields and forests of the wealthy plantations located in the region and utilizing the natural advantages afforded by the navigable Rappahannock River, enterprising men early flocked to this area and soon developed Falmouth and Fredericksburg into a major colonial metropolis, whose commerce and trade ranked fifteenth among the thirty-four leading towns in the British colonies in America.

This area had some of the largest and wealthiest plantations in Virginia. Many of its citizens conducted businesses that made them among the richest men in colonial America. Their land holdings spread throughout northern Virginia and extended to the southwestern parts of the colony and into the Ohio, Kentucky and Mississippi territories. Throughout this vast domain, industries were established whose products not only found market in the Rappahannock Valley and the Virginia Colony, but furnished food, clothing and shelter to consumers all along the Atlantic Seaboard, the frontier of the West, and the major towns and ports of the colonial world at large.

Early in the eighteenth century the foundation was laid for a permanent iron industry in Virginia by Governor Alexander Spotswood, who built a furnace at Germanna on the Rappahannock River in 1715. This "was not only the first [regular blast] furnace in this country, but the first in North America"[1] to be built and successfully operated. Spotswood built and operated four furnaces in the area located on a 45,000-acre tract of land which abounded in rich iron ore deposits. By 1732, the Spotswood Iron Mines Company expended 12,000 pounds for land, Negro labor and cattle used in the operation of the enterprise. Spotswood annually earned 5,000 pounds[2] from his iron works, producing casting for chimneys, iron for fenders, plates for hearths, pots, skillets, mortars, rollers for gardens, boxes for cart wheels and other items. These were sold in the colonies and also shipped to England, Scotland, Ireland, the West Indies and other countries.

In the Rappahannock region also was the headquarters for the Principio Company with which Captain Augustine Washington, father of General George Washington, was connected. This was the largest exporter of iron in the American colonies.

These early and successful developments of the iron industry at Fredericksburg led to the establishment of the Hunter Iron Works, about a mile above Falmouth, the Gunnery Plant at Gunnery Spring near the city limits of Fredericksburg, and the Old Bloomery-Foundry and Iron Works located in the southeast corner at the intersection of Princess Elizabeth and Sophia Streets in Fredericksburg.

In the making of the American nation, Fredericksburg has been a major factor through its contribution of men of ideas, men of action, and materials. In a literal sense, this area was the arsenal and breadbasket of the Revolutionary War. It was the recruiting and training center for and the rendezvous of armies. It was here that several hospitals and prison camps of the Revolutionary War were located.

With the outbreak of the Revolutionary War, a gunnery plant for the manufacture of small arms was established at Gunnery Spring, with Fielding Lewis as manager.[3] Authorized by the General Assembly of Virginia in July, 1775, this plant was located on the Dixon Mill Tract on the left side of Hazel Run "within 200 yards of Fredericksburg and convenient to the landing, where sea vessels may quickly load."[4] It consisted of the main manufactory; a powder magazine managed by Charles Washington, brother of George Washington; cartridge works; repair shops; the Roger Dixon Mill; vegetable garden, etc. During the war, the manufactory turned out 100 stands of arms a month, repaired large quantities of salvaged arms, and prepared thousands of cartridges and other ammunition supplies for the Continental Armies.[5] This was the first public gunnery used in the Revolution.

The Hunter Iron Works above Falmouth were considered "one of the finest and most considerable iron works in North America,"[6] being one of two or three of a "rolling and slitting mill" type found in the country. Working more than "6-800 tons"[7] of iron annually, this establishment played a vital role in the prosecution of the American Revolution.

"It is from Mr. Hunter's Works that every camp kettle has been supplied for the continental and all other troops employed in this State, and to the southward . . . ."[8] wrote James Mercer to Thomas Jefferson on April 14, 1781:

> All the anchors for this State and Maryland and some for the continent have been produced from the same works; that without the assistance of the bar iron made there, even the planters hereabouts and to the southward of this place [Fredericksburg] would not be able to make bread to eat.
>
> As to the Town itself, I need not inform you that the public manufactory of arms is here, that without it, all our arms, however, so little injured, would be useless to us; besides the number of new muskets and bayonets made there, renders that an object worthy of our preserving and the enemies destruction. To this, however, I may add that there is not one spot in the State so generally useful in our military operations. Full one-third of all new lines rendezvous here; all the troops from

North to South and South to North must pass through this
Town, where wagons are repaired, horses shoed and many other,
etc., which it could not proceed without. The troops get provisions here to the next stage and no place is so convenient to a
very extensive and productive country for the reception of
grain and other articles of provision.[9]

In other words, the Hunter Iron Works and the Gunnery Plant
were considered indispensable and of prime importance by the officials prosecuting the Revolution. No other Virginia plant or town
excelled Fredericksburg in this regard.[2] On July 29, 1776, the House
of Delegates "Ordered, that the Muskets in the Magazine, which are
not fit for use, and cannot be immediately repaired in this city
[Williamsburg] be sent up to the Manufactory at Fredericksburg
to be put into the best order with all possible dispatch."[10]

Another iron works establishment in this area was the Old
Bloomery-Foundry and Iron Works founded prior to 1764 and
converted into a brewery in 1772 under the management of William
Fitzhugh, of "Chatham" in Stafford County. This plant covered
nearly a block in the lower part of Fredericksburg, employed some
100 persons and was valued at between 25,000 and 50,000 pounds
sterling.

An advertisement for the sale of the Hunter Iron Works was
carried in the *Fredericksburg Herald* for May, 1798, and described
the property as follows:

> The Iron Works and Mills . . . . consisting of a Forge
> 128 feet by 51 feet, eight fires and 4 hammers, a coal house
> 80 feet by 40 feet, a merchant mill 70 feet by 36 feet with two
> pairs of French burnstones . . . . a grist mill 20 feet by 18
> feet . . . . a saw mill 55 feet by 11 feet . . . . Contiguous
> thereto are a stable 54 feet by 27 feet . . . . a nailery, a tan-
> yard, coopers, carpenters, and wheelwright shops . . . . and
> houses for the managers, and workmen.[11]

These were gigantic enterprises for colonial times. One or two
of these factories could make thousands of kettles, traveling forges,
anchors and other supplies; turn out "immediately 1000 muskets;"

had the capacity to make "1½ tons a day of bar iron, and manufacture in a year 23 ships, 6 snows, 13 brigs, 31 Schooners, and 12 Sloops, besides turning out 113½ tons of bar iron and 364 tons of pig iron."[12]

There were numerous other industries and businesses in the Fredericksburg area of significance similar to the iron works.

Here were located some of the leading mercantile establishments of colonial America. William Allason, of Falmouth, not only owned the largest mercantile business in town but conducted a large scale trade through a chain of stores which he owned in part or whole throughout the Shenandoah Valley and the western frontier. He also traded with foreign nations in America and Europe.

Other large mercantile establishments in Fredericksburg were operated by Roger Dixon; John Allan; John Glassell; James Ritchie & Co.; Mitchell, Lenox and Scott; George McCall, Mitchell, Freeland & Co.; Dekar Thompson & Co.; Richards, Hall & Co.; Jackson & Co.; Heslop and Blair Co.; Fitzhugh, Brent and Leitch Co.; Joist Hite & Robert McKay Co. Basil Gordon amassed a fortune from merchandising business and warehouses in Falmouth, and is said to have become the first millionaire in America.[13] Michael Gratz was another prosperous merchant, with establishments in Fredericksburg and also in Philadelphia. He gave financial assistance to a number of Virginia delegates attending the Continental Congress in Philadelphia, including Thomas Jefferson, James Madison, Arthur Lee, Mercer, Randolph, Monroe and Theodore Bland.

Ship building, ship dealers and shipping constituted another major industry of Fredericksburg-Falmouth. Among these were Fielding Lewis & Co.; Roger Dixon; John Allan; James Maury; Fontaine Maury; Eliezer Callendar; David London; Wm. Proctor; John Legg; James Hunter. Jefferson's letter indicates the extent of this activity when he speaks of a yearly building capacity of 23 ships.

Manufacturing of various commodities was a thriving industry. There were factories making stockings, ink, tobacco and snuff, potash, cloth, and soap. The Potash Plant at the foot of Amelia Street shipped large quantities of soap to England prior to the Revolutionary War. During the war, it manufactured soap for the colonists and later made fertilizer.

Between 1729 and 1781 there were at least one hundred twenty-five ordinaries or taverns in Spotsylvania County and Fredericksburg, with fifty of them in the latter town. Although the number of such establishments varied from decade to decade, records show that for the period between 1750 and 1780 a score or more were flourishing in Fredericksburg at any given time. Among the famous taverns which served as meeting places for groups whose ideas made a permanent imprint on the American republic were the Weedon Tavern,[14] kept by George Weedon on Caroline Street, the Julian Tavern, Susanna Livingston's Ordinary and Coffee House, John Allan's Ordinary, the Long Ordinary, the Indian Queen Tavern, and the Willis Ordinary. It was at the George Weedon Tavern that the Committee to Revise the Laws of Virginia met after the Declaration of Independence and drafted more than 100 bills, including those for the establishment of religious freedom, for creating elementary school system and for the abolition of primogeniture.

Having more than its quota of physicians, Fredericksburg also had a large number of apothecary shops. The Hugh Mercer Apothecary is said to be among the oldest drug stores in America and was one of more than 30 such establishments located in this town on the Rappahannock. Many of the keepers and doctors accumulated handsome fortunes and built beautiful and spacious mansions some of which are still standing today.

As tobacco exporting centers, the two Rappahannock ports required a large number of public warehouses, which constituted a very important and prosperous business in colonial times. Fredericksburg had at least eleven public warehouses, with a comparable number located in Falmouth. How vast the shipping interest was in these towns is indicated by the salaries paid to the inspectors appointed for the public warehouses. First established in 1730, public warehouses had become leading concerns in Fredericksburg by the time of an act of the legislature in 1734, which authorized storehouses in forty-four different places in Virginia. In only eight of these forty-four was the salary of the inspector, which was based on the volume of business transacted, as much as 40 pounds per annum. These eight were Fredericksburg, Falmouth, Shoccoe, Warwick, Appomattox, Capital Landing, Aylett and Todd. At Norfolk the inspector received only 30 pounds.

Throughout the eighteenth century the salaries of the inspectors of these public warehouses were adjusted to pay for the increase or decrease of responsibility, according to the volume of business conducted. In 1748 only Shoccoe and Warwick with a 50-pound annual salary topped the 45 pounds paid to the inspectors at Fredericksburg, Falmouth, Conway's and Roy's,—all on the Rappahannock. All other ports had less volume of business. In 1762 Rockbridge and Osborne paid the inspectors 70 pounds, while four places paid 60: Fredericksburg, Shoccoe, Byrd and Crutchfield. Falmouth paid 50 pounds at each warehouse.[15]

There were also public warehouses for hemp and flour storage at Fredericksburg and Falmouth. Furthermore, in addition to the mercantile establishments there were such businesses as lumbering, sawmills, lumber yards, staymaking, coopers; mining and quarrying; flour and grist mills; powder factory; real estate concerns; insurance businesses; building and construction; printing and publishing; salt works; tanneries; counting and clearing houses; brickmaking.

Printing, publishing, bookbinding, and engraving were regular enterprises in colonial Fredericksburg. It was one of the first three towns of Virginia to establish a printing press and publish a newspaper. Only Williamsburg and Norfolk preceded Fredericksburg in this respect.

John Buckner, of Gloucester County, was the first man to use a printing press in the Virginia colony, in 1682.[16] John Buckner, the patentee with Thomas Royston of "Leaseland" (Fredericksburg) in 1671, was most probably the John Buckner of printing press fame. It is interesting to note that Fredericksburg founders were connected with the first printing in Virginia and that the future citizens of this town were also to play a significant role in printing.

Fredericksburg had at least four different newspapers before the end of the eighteenth century. They were the *Virginia Herald*, established in 1787 by Timothy Green, and continued until 1819; the *Republican Citizen* founded in 1793 by Lancelot A. Mullen and discontinued after a year's publication; the *Genius of Liberty* started in 1797 by Robert Mercer and George Carter. This paper passed into the hands of James Walker after Mercer's death in 1800. It was published later under the name of the *Courier* and was suspended in 1801.

Timothy Green was a direct descendant of a long and famous line of American printers which began with Samuel Green of Cambridge, Massachusetts, the first printer in America. Timothy Green of Fredericksburg was a great-nephew of Jonas Green of Annapolis, Maryland, who had once been connected with the printing houses of Bradford and Franklin of Philadelphia. Timothy Green was a staunch supporter of the Federalist cause, a friend and admirer of George Washington. He was a champion of the liberal movement as his forebears had been, and exerted a great influence over state and national affairs of his day.

William Hunter, editor of the *Virginia Gazette* of Williamsburg from 1751 until his death in 1761, printed the report of George Washington concerning his trip to Ft. Duquesne in 1751. He no doubt had printing connections and interests in Fredericksburg.

There were a number of printing and engraving establishments and bookbinding concerns in Fredericksburg. Roger Dixon and Thomas Nicolson owned a printing concern in Fredericksburg as early as 1780, located at the corner of Sophia and Hanover Streets.

References to book-binders, engravers, and printers of Fredericksburg found in the Spotsylvania County Records earlier than 1780, indicate that some binding and engraving, and perhaps printing of books at Fredericksburg was done prior to the Revolution. At least work of this type was being done here as early as 1778, as evidenced by a letter of George Webb, dated September 15, 1778, and addressed to the Treasurer of Virginia, wherein the business of engraving and copperplate printing at Fredericksburg is discussed.[17]

At about the same time Robert Scot was engaged in printing in Fredericksburg, as is shown by the records in the Journal of the Council of Virginia.[18] This Robert Scot may have been the first to engage in printing in Fredericksburg, about 1778.

Printing and newspapers helped the residents of the Rappahannock Valley to keep in touch with the affairs of the world. These mediums aided in developing their cosmopolitanism, for the newspapers of that day devoted considerable space to foreign news and activities. Intercolonial news was of secondary importance and local affairs were given the least space in colonial publications. Advertisements were a large part of the newspapers of colonial days. Foreign wares to be sold and services of doctors, lawyers, teachers and other practitioners were published in the newspapers. Books and newspapers were vital forces in the life of colonials, especially with the upper classes who had relatively easy access to them.

Large plantations and real estate holdings constituted another major enterprise of colonials in the Fredericksburg area which had the wealthiest plantations in the entire colony. Many of the land holdings ran into hundred thousands of acres. The largest, of course, was that of Lord Thomas Fairfax, whose domain contained 5,282,000 acres. His agent, Robert ("King") Carter, of "Corotoman," held some 1,000,000 acres. Spotswood owned an estate of 125,000 acres, stretching from Massaponax Creek to the Rapidan, while his grandson and namesake of "Nottingham," had 150,000 acres. George Washington's estate exceeded 130,000 acres.[19] William Fitzhugh, of "Chatham," Stafford County, had 100,000 acres. Other large estates were held by Henry Willis, Mann Page, Francis Thronton, William Dangerfield, Joseph Herndon, the Beverleys, the Baylors, the Holladays, the Woodfords, the Brents, the Wallers, the Masons, the Lees, the Corbins, the Walkers, the Mauryes, the Wallaces, Dr. Adam Stephen, Edmund Pendleton. Many of these also held titles to vast tracts of land in the Ohio Valley, ranging from 800,000 acres claimed by John Lewis and others in 1749, to 100,000 acres each, held by Thomas Lewis, granted in 1749, and by John Willis, Richard Corbin, and others, granted in 1753.

## NOTES

1. Col. William Byrd, *op. cit.*, p. 139.

2. Francis T. Brooke, *Narrative of My Life* (Richmond: Macfarlane, 1849), p. 66.

3. *Journals of the Council of the Colony of Virginia* (Richmond: State Printing, 1931), I, 248.

4. *Virginia Gazette* (Williamsburg: Purdie & Dixon), July 10, 1770.

5. John T. Goolrick, *Fredericksburg and the Cavalier Country* (Richmond: Garrett & Massie, 1935), p. 56.

6.  Johann David Schopf, *op. cit.*, II, 41-46.

7.  *Ibid.*

8.  *Executive Papers*, April 1781, *Calendar of State Papers*, II, 39-40; also in *Wm. & M. Quart.*, XXVII, 75.

9.  *Ibid.*

10.  *Official Letters of the Governors of Va.* (Richmond: State Library, 1929), I, 19.

11.  *Fredericksburg Herald*, May 18, 1798.

12.  *Thomas Jefferson Letters*, 1769-1786, in Library of Congress, 1770, Virginia.

13.  It is doubtful that Basil Gordon was the "first millionaire in America." He was not born until 1768 and died in 1817. Several colonialists possessed wealth which exceeded two million dollars at lowest estimate, Wm. Beverley had an estate valued at £250,000 to £300,000, Gen. Alexander Spotswood's fortune exceeded a million dollars in value, also Robert ("King") Carter and others.

14.  Smyth, *op. cit.*, II, 151.

15.  Hening, *Statues*, VII, 532.

16.  Isaiah Thomas, *History of Printing in America* (Worcester, Mass.: Thomas, 1810), II, 544-46.

17.  Auditor's Papers, State Library, Richmond, MS. Division, Letter of George Webb to the Treasurer of Virginia, Sept. 15, 1778.

18.  *Journals of the Council of Virginia*, II, 257.

19.  Smith, *Journal, op. cit.*, p. 64.

## 6

### POPULATION

While the population of colonial Fredericksburg and its neighborhood was predominantly English in all respects but number, there were numerous non-English groups living in this community and contributing a certain cosmopolitanism rather than provincialism to this area.

At the peak of its prosperity about 1780, Fredericksburg had a population of approximately 6,000 residents.[1] Although the English outnumbered all other white national-racial groups living here, the Negroes—Africans and mulattoes—constituted the largest single group of residents. These were greater in number than all other groups combined, with the English being the second largest group. The heavy slave industry of the eighteenth century accounted for the large Negro population.

Primary historical sources such as deeds, wills, land patents, letters, petitions, grants and tombstones reveal the prevalence of nearly a score of various national and racial groups living in the Rappahannock Valley in colonial times. Following the English lead, the Scotch, French, and German, in this order, were the next largest national groups. There were also the Irish, Welsh, Jews, Swiss, Dutch, Flemish, Bohemian, Italian, Russian, Polish, Scandinavian and Spanish residents. The aboriginal Indian was also present.

Each of these national groups contributed immeasurably to the cosmopolitan nature of the Fredericksburg neighborhood and had its influence on the development of a domestic society in this "Athens of America," that undoubtedly affected the ideas and philosophy of its leaders who also became founders of the American republic.

111

At Germanna, a few miles above the falls of the Rappahannock River, Governor Alexander Spotswood settled a German colony in 1714. Coming in several ship loads, these immigrant groups included not only Germans from Alsace, the Palatinates and Hesse, but also natives of Switzerland, Holland, France, Bohemia and Tyrol. Later, in 1717, a settlement of Germans and other nationalities was made at Germantown on the opposite side of the Rappahannock River in what is now Fauquier County, formerly Stafford County, a few miles above the Falls.[2]

Colonel William Byrd encouraged French Huguenots to settle in Virginia. Several shiploads of these arrived in the colony between 1698 and 1700, settling at Manakin Town on the James River just above the present site of Richmond, and in other parts of Virginia, particularly at Marlborough in Stafford County, and around Fredericksburg. In addition to the French, there were other nationalities among the settlers of this area.[3]

Several names of descendants of non-English groups are outstanding in the history of colonial Fredericksburg and its neighborhood. These include Hugh Mercer, a noted Scotch apothecary and physician of Fredericksburg; John Lederer, a German traveler, who explored the Rappahannock River to its source in 1670; Augustine Herman, a Bohemian geographer and explorer, who made a map of Virginia and Maryland in 1673; James Maury, a French Huguenot, was America's first ambassador to the Court of St. James, London; Matthew Fontaine Maury, the pathfinder of the seas, was of Huguenot descent, as was the Reverend James Marye, rector of St. George's Episcopal Church in Fredericksburg and teacher of George Washington, and perhaps of Madison and Monroe; General George Weedon perhaps of Scotch ancestry; the Reverend, later, General Peter Muhlenburg was a direct descendant of Germans at Spotswood's Germanna; and Christopher Gist (or Gest) of German stock, was Washington's personal guide on the mission to Ft. Duquesne in 1753, and was one of the colonials active in organizing settlements in the Ohio Company project; Van Braam, interpreter with Washington on his mission to Ft. Duquesne in 1753; and many others of importance.

The most prosperous and populous era of Fredericksburg was between 1750 and 1780, when the number of residents ranged from about 2,500 to 6,000. Authorized to be erected in 1727, this town on the Rappahannock River began its major expansion in size and population about 1738 when the House of Burgesses permitted the holding of annual fairs in Fredericksburg.[4] Within the next thirty years, the town grew so rapidly that its boundaries were officially enlarged four times, in 1742, 1759, 1762, and 1769.[5] In 1759 the Virginia Assembly authorized the town's enlargement by prefacing the act with the words: "Fredericksburg daily increases."[6] It is estimated conservatively that the number of people living in Fredericksburg in 1755 was 2,500; in 1769, there were 3,000; in 1773, there were 2,900; and a total of 6,000 in 1782.

In the years following 1750 when the great western trek began, instigated by the numerous land scheme projects, many people from the Rappahannock Valley moved into the pioneer lands sponsored by the Ohio Company, the Mississippi Company, the Vandalia, the Transylvania, the Indiana Scheme, the Georgian Colony, Franklin's Plan, Charlottiana, Hazard's Plan, and others. Many of these projects were initiated by citizens of Fredericksburg neighborhood who composed the majority of stockholders in several of these schemes to settle the western territories.

This loss of population was temporarily checked by the outbreak of the Revolutionary War. During this conflict the population of the town increased tremendously, doubling in number between 1773 and 1782. In the latter year the population of Fredericksburg reached a peak which it did not attain again for nearly a century and a half.

After the end of the war, great hordes of citizens from the Rappahannock Valley moved westward, depleting the population of Fredericksburg which continued to hold its own importance in other far-reaching ways affecting the affairs of the new republic. Visiting the town in 1785, Castiglioni observed that Fredericksburg, like Alexandria, was a "city."[7] William L. Smith saw the port in 1790 and noted that it had "upwards of 300 houses."[8] Both of these travelers estimated the town's population on these dates to be 3,000 citizens.

But the loss Fredericksburg sustained in population after the Revolutionary War was only numerical. These citizens who migrated westward spread the ideas, philosophies and social and civic leadership of the Rappahannock Valley into the frontier settlements that contributed so much to the development of American democracy in the formative years of the new republic.

## NOTES

1. See Appendix on Population.
2. Spotswood, *op. cit., Patents*, 14:381; *Spotswood Letters, op. cit.,* II, 66, 70, 78, 217; Spotsylvania County Records, Will Bk. A, p. 69; Rev. P. Slaughter, *History of St. George's Parish; Virginia Magazine of History and Biography,* Vol. XII, pp. 364-67.
3. Byrd, *Writings, op. cit.*
4. Hening, *Statutes,* V, 82.
5. *Ibid.,* V, 197-99; VII, 314-15; VIII, 418-19.
6. *Ibid.,* VII, 314.
7. Castiglioni, *Travels in the United States, 1785, 1786, 1787* (Milan, 1790), p. 211.
8. Wm. Loughton Smith, *Journal, 1790-1791* (Cambridge: University Press, 1917), p. 64.

## Amusement and Cultural Entertainment
## in Colonial Fredericksburg

The well-to-do planters, merchants, lawyers and officials of Colonial Virginia were resourceful in providing for themselves and their families numerous amusements and cultural entertainment in towns, at homes and even in frontier communities. No special effort, however, was exerted to provide similar activities for the masses of the people, or even the artisans, the small farmers or the middle classes.

Amusements were varied and numerous. Many of these, like the annual fairs, horse races, travel, theater, musical concerts and balls were an intricate part of colonial life, combining business activities with the social, religious and political phases of everyday living. Colonials of the upper class had leisure time which they used advantageously not only to further their economic interests at home and abroad, but to cultivate a taste in the art of living. Whatever else may be said about the privileged few of colonial times, it may be conceded that members of this group established a society which, in time, learned how to enjoy the best fruits of human civilization. Some of the by-products created by this leisure class benefited humanity at large through contributions in the fields of art, literature and philosophy.

Because much wealth was concentrated in the town and on the plantations in and around Fredericksburg, this neighborhood had access to practically every kind and type of amusement and cultural entertainment available in the eighteenth century.

Typical of the times were the fairs held twice a year, "on the first Tuesday in June, and the first Tuesday in October."[1] Later the day was changed to Wednesday because this suited the convenience of the majority of the residents. Designed to benefit the inhabitants of the town, the fairs were institutions of business and pleasure. The primary purpose, as authorized by the Virginia Legislature, was to establish a seasonal market where planters, traders and homemakers could display and sell their wares. The fairs were designed to encourage "the sale of cattle, provisions, goods, wares and all kinds of merchandise whatsoever."[2] First authorized in 1738, fairs were held in Fredericksburg throughout the greatest part of the eighteenth century. Colonial officials were eager that people attend these marts. Privileges and immunity from arrests while at the fair were granted to those who attended the events.

Fredericksburg fairs, which attracted rich and poor alike from the town proper and all nearby hamlets, plantations and farms, were held in the Market Square, at Kenmore Farm, in the neighborhood of Princess Anne Street between Charlotte and Hanover, where the post office stands today, and in other places in the community. It was here that various produce of the countryside was displayed, sold and bought. Farm products and handwork was sold and exchanged. Entertainment was offered to please the most discreet taste. There was music, dancing, gambling, horse racing, theater and other amusements.

The fairs of colonial Fredericksburg and Virginia were constructive institutions whose many creditable features have been lost through commercialization in modern times. They were integral parts of the social fabric of life, sponsored and supported by the most influential citizens of the community, who were concerned that the fairs be maintained on a high economic, social and cultural level.

The keen sense of social values possessed by the citizens of Fredericksburg and its neighborhood in this respect is demonstrated in the 1782 petition presented in the interest of repairing the town Market House, which was damaged during the Revolution. Signed by forty-two citizens and thirty-one Masonic members, the petition declared that:

We the subscribers having a due sense of the great Utility afforded the County in general as well as the Inhabitants of the Town of Fredericksburg by the commodious situation of the Town House in said Town, which rendered accommodation, not only to polite, and numerous Assemblies, by which youth were greatly benefited, but also to all sorts of Ancient and Modern Sociaties of Fellowship . . . . Do oblige ourselves to pay on demand the sum affixed to our names towards repairs of that useful building . . . . .[3]

Subscribing a total of £372.14 for the cause were such individuals of the town and its environs as Dr. Charles Mortimer, Dr. Charles Dick, Dr. John Julian, James Taylor, George Weedon, Dr. George French, John Lewis, Dr. Thomas Walker, James Maury, James Mercer, John Minor, Mann Page, John Robinson, John Tayloe, William Fitzhugh, William Dangerfield, Dr. Landon Carter, Alexander Spotswood, Dr. Lawrence Brooke, John Taliaferro, Fontaine Maury, and Francis Thornton.

Horse-racing was another major attraction which brought crowds to Fredericksburg. Some of the most famous horses of Virginia turf were run in races here, and for large purses. In the town and in the outlying area were several of the finest race tracks of colonial times. William Fitzhugh of "Chatham" had perhaps the finest. William Johnson had a track near his tavern that was considered superior. Another was maintained on the west edge of the town at the foot of Marye Heights, while others were scattered throughout the adjoining neighborhood.

Leaders in the horse-racing activities were General Alexander Spotswood, of "Nottingham," Spotsylvania County; Col. John Tayloe, of "Mt. Airy," Richmond County; Francis Thornton, of King George County; Philip Lee, of "Stratford"; Col. John Baylor, John Holmes, Col. Landon Carter, Mann Page, William Fitzhugh, Thomas Minor and General George Washington. These men imported thoroughbred horses and spent much time improving the breed. Blooded stallions were imported from England, Spain, France and other parts.

Washington imported fine horses, mules, cattle, sheep, swine and other animals. He is credited with introducing the mule into the American colonies. From the King of Spain he received a "Royal

Gift"—a jack and lighter animals from Malta; he also received a jack
and two jennies from Lafayette.[4]

Several jockey clubs were organized in Fredericksburg and this
was the Derby center of colonial times. General Alexander Spotswood, who owned "Fearnaught," tried to form a syndicate of Virginians in an attempt to win the Derby races.

Love for thoroughbred horses is closely associated with the
sport of fox hunting in which colonials of Fredericksburg participated extensively. It was one of the favorite pastimes of the gentlemen of this vicinity.

Men also played cards and gambled for pleasure and for money.
Betting on horse races was a favorite sport. Even Washington
indulged in cardplaying. Recording an evening at the Rising Sun
Tavern, he wrote: "Lost money as usual. The boys of Fredericksburg are too smart for me."[5] Cock-fighting was another popular
sport. Dancing was perhaps the favorite social entertainment of the
upper classes of Fredericksburg neighborhood. Several schools in
town taught dancing to the young and the old, preparing them for
the numerous balls at planters' mansions.

Colonials indulged freely in luxurious balls and banquets of
private and official origin. The Peace Ball held at Fredericksburg
immediately following the British surrender at Yorktown is an
example of social entertainment in which the colonials excelled.

The great Peace Ball was held on November 11, 1781, with
the most prominent of the officers and statesmen present . . . . .
Washington reached Fredericksburg the morning of November
11. The leading officers and statesmen were already present.
The great houses were ready, the candelabra placed, the wood
fires ablaze, the town crowded. The streets became a pageant
of brilliant uniforms, stylishly dressed men and women, and
gilded coaches splashed through the streets. Guests gathered
from far and near. Richard Henry Lee, and Lighthorse Harry;
George Mason of Gunston Hall and his daughter, Anne;
Thomas Nelson, Governor of Virginia, and Mrs. Nelson;
Colonel James Monroe; General Gustavus Wallace; General
William Woodford; and dozens of belles and beaux. Besides
these were the General Baron von Steuben; the Count de Es-

taing; General Anthony Wayne; Admiral the Count de Grasse;
the Count Deux Pont; General the Duc de Choisey; Field Mar-
shall Batiste Donatin de Vim; Colonel John Laurens; Mrs.
Hugh Mercer and Miss Mercer; Miss Mildred Washington;
Mrs. Willis and Miss Willis; Colonel Torbert Lewis and Miss
Lewis; Marshall de Campe, the Baron de Voiminel.

. . . . Lafayette reached the town in the forenoon, dined
(with Washington) at Kenmore, and after that Washington
'alone and on foot' walked to the home of his mother where
he remained for some time . . . . .[6]

Lotteries were legal and were common means of raising money
for worthy purposes, including churches and schools.

Travel in the colony, the West Indies and Europe was popular.
Local visiting was a favorite popular practice with planters, traders,
and officials, whose families extended their stays with relatives or
friends for weeks at a time.

Church activities of the Episcopal denomination, the established church in Virginia, were part of the social fabric of the leisure
class, whose membership was largely of this faith. Many of the educational, cultural, social as well as the religious programs were
sponsored by the established church located in the community.

Theater and music concerts attracted many in Fredericksburg.
This town was on a par in such entertainment with Williamsburg,
Richmond, Alexandria and Norfolk.[7] The Harmonic Society of
Fredericksburg gave vocal and instrumental concerts in the Concert
Room in the Market House every "third Wednesday evening in each
month."[8] Schools giving instruction in instrumental and vocal music
were conducted by John Victor, and others. Concert balls were frequent. Invoices, records and wills show that musical instruments
were not rare in the homes of Fredericksburg residents. Their cultural entertainment also included reading of plays and other literature. As early as 1752, stock companies presented plays at the
Fredericksburg fair.[9]

Colonials cultivated taste in finer living and in those accoutre-
ments and objects surrounding them daily. They imported household furnishings, paintings, clothes, statuary, tapestries, china, glassware, costly pieces of decorative and useful furniture, jewelry, and

other items. Many of the homes reflected the preferred architecture of the colonials. Some of these are standing today, reflecting the exquisite beauty and elegance of an era when men spent much time in the enjoyment of the cultural and artistic achievements of the human race. Some of these Eighteenth Century examples of the Georgian, Gothic, Renaissance and other classical styles of architecture were "Chatham," "Fall Hill," "Kenmore," "Willis Hill," "Belmont," "Nottingham," "Belvidere," "Mansfield Hall," "Forbes House," "St. George's Church," "Glassell Home," "Maury House," "Carmichael House," "Sentry Box," "Charles Dick Home," "Wellford Home."

Needless to say, the so-called lower classes had certain amusements of their own devising. Frequently their enjoyment consisted of watching their "betters" dance, banquet, race and travel. But within their own closely knit family unit, the poorer colonists had their family gatherings, dancing in the old barn-yard style, banjo-picking, folk singing, attending church, resting on Sabbath day, and attending the fairs, from which no one was excluded. There were market days, numerous holidays, fishing, hunting and swimming to be enjoyed by the less privileged of the Fredericksburg area, as by their fellows throughout the Virginia colony.

### NOTES

1. Hening, *op. cit.*, V, 82.
2. *Ibid.*, VI, 300.
3. Council Minutes of the City of Fredericksburg, 1782-1801, in City Hall, Fredericksburg, pp. 33-36.
4. George Washington Bicentennial, Honor to George Washington Series, *Pamphlet No. 4: Washington the Farmer* (U. S. George Washington Bicentennial Commission: Washington, Government Printing, 1931), p. 29.
5. John C. Fitzpatrick, *George Washington: Colonial Traveller* (Indianapolis: Bobbs-Merrill, 1927), p. 239.
6. Goolrick, *op. cit.*, pp. 37-39.
7. O. G. Sonneck, *Early Concert Life in America (1731-1800)*, (Leipzig: Breitkopf & Hartel, 1907), p. 57.
8. *Ibid.*, p. 57.
9. *Virginia Gazette*, April 17, 1752.

## 8

## The Church and Religion in
## The Fredericksburg Neighborhood

A variety of religious sects and faiths existed in Virginia from the very beginning of the English settlement at Jamestown, even though the Episcopal or the Anglican Church of England was the established or state church in this colony until Thomas Jefferson's Bill of Religious Freedom disestablished it in 1786.

But before this law inaugurated a state of complete religious liberty, numerous dissenting sects and groups throughout the colony fought for more than one hundred and fifty years to extend this principle to all men so that each could worship according to the dictates of his conscience. In this battle for religious freedom in Virginia, the chief torchbearers were members of the Quaker, Presbyterian, Baptist and Methodist denominations.

The hardships and struggles encountered by men in establishing homes in a frontier territory have a leveling effect on all manner of men. This equalization of social, economic, religious and political opportunities is a foundation upon which a democratic society is built. Because Fredericksburg and the surrounding area constituted a frontier country in the eighteenth century, this community played a major role in the fight to establish religious freedom in Virginia.

Early in its history Fredericksburg appeared a cosmopolitan neighborhood. Its racial elements were numerous. Its religious membership included not only the dominant Episcopalians, but Quakers, Presbyterians, Baptists, Methodists, Catholics and Jews.

As in the Virginia colony at large, the Episcopal membership was the most powerful sect and outnumbered all others combined in the Fredericksburg area. This denomination, however, did not succeed in assimilating the minor religious elements, nor in preventing dissensions in matters pertaining to religious worship.

The struggle of Protestant dissenters in Virginia for recognition, toleration and freedom falls into three distinct periods. The period from 1607 to 1649 is characterized by a conflict between the Puritans and the followers of the Anglican Church of England which had become the State Church in Virginia. In a large measure this was a carry-over of the old struggle between the Puritans and the Anglicans in England.

The second phase of this struggle for religious freedom in Virginia extended from 1649 to 1763, during which time members of the Quaker sect waged almost single-handedly the battle for toleration. They ranged from people ordered to "be imprisoned without baile"[1] to those of position and influence in the colony. The Presbyterians joined this struggle for religious freedom in the first decades of the Eighteenth Century.

In the third and the final stage, lasting nearly a quarter of a century until the Jefferson Bill became a law in 1786, members of the Baptist denomination joined the conflict. In many respects this period was marked by the intensity of the struggle, especially in the Fredericksburg area, where many Baptist ministers were frequently imprisoned for their preaching and teaching. Such persecution, however, seems to have added increased determination and persistance to resist the domination of the Established Church. Toward the end of this long conflict, the Methodists became a part of the movement.

Although various religious sects or faiths were represented by people who first settled the Fredericksburg area, it is perhaps logical that the Episcopalians should have been the first to build a house of worship for their members. They were the largest single church-group and remained the dominant religious institution in the Rappahannock Valley, as well as in the Virginia colony, throughout the colonial era.

The earliest church in this vicinity was erected about 1720 at Germanna. This was shortly after the German settlers on the vast Spotswood estate appealed to numerous Protestant agencies in Europe for financial aid to build a church there. Assistance for the erection of the church and the minister's salary was given to these colonists by the Society for the Propagation of the Gospel in Foreign Parts. Prior to this, however, the colony of these immigrants was served by a 75-year-old pastor, Henry Hoeger, who came to Germanna with the first twelve families who settled there in 1714.[2]

As was frequently the case of many settlements in the frontier country, the colony at Germanna was composed of people belonging to more than one sect or faith. Evidence indicates that members of different Protestant and Catholic faiths composed this group. Among these German and Swiss settlers were families of Lutheran, Anabaptist, Calvinist, Hussite and Zwinglian affiliations. They merged their differences and united in worship with those of the Episcopal faith under the Rev. Henry Hoeger.

The same act which authorized the establishment of Spotsylvania County in 1720 also created St. George's Parish,[3] which was later divided in 1734 to form an additional parish, known as St. Mark's Parish.[4]

The St. George's Episcopal Church in Fredericksburg was erected sometime before 1726, with Rev. Theodosius Staige as the first rector. Rev. Rodham Kenner succeeded him, while Patrick Henry, the uncle of the orator, served as rector here from January, 1733, to April, 1734. Rev. James Marye, a Huguenot who conducted a parish school in Fredericksburg where Washington, and perhaps Madison, and Monroe were educated, ministered to the parishioners from 1735 to 1767. His son, James, Jr., followed him as minister from 1768 to 1780.

In 1754 there were seventy-four parishes of the Episcopal Church in Virginia. Twenty of these were located in the Rappahannock Valley below, in, and above Fredericksburg. Among the most noted of these were the Abingdon Parish in Gloucester; St. Margaret's in Caroline; Washington and Cople Parishes in Westmoreland; Overwharton and St. Paul's in Stafford; Hanover and Brunswick in King George; St. George's in Spotsylvania; and St. Mark's in Orange.

Besides those already named, the outstanding Episcopal ministers of this neighborhood were Daniel Macdonald, Bartholemew

Yates, William Yates, John Dixon, John Fox, John Burnskill, Hancock Dunbar, Charles Rose, John Moncure, Archibald Campbell, William Stuart, William Davis, Robert Innes and Musgrave Dawson. Rev. James Maury was the parson in the famous "Parson case" of colonial controversy. He served the Hanover Parish.

Besides ministering to their parishioners, many of these Episcopal rectors were scholarly gentlemen who conducted schools as private enterprises or in planters' homes. James Marye, Archibald Campbell and John Moncure were outstanding as teachers and tutors in this area.

The Quakers were among the early religious faiths of the Fredericksburg area. Members of this sect were in Virginia in 1657 or earlier. There was a Quaker settlement at "Croaton on the Rappahannock River,"[5] which was in the lower part of the valley in 1657. George Fox, the founder of the faith, visited Virginia in 1672 and held meetings in the Mattapony and Pamunkey sections of the colony. One of his meetings on the Mattapony was attended by "Capt. Clayborn and Dr. Walker."[6] Dr. Walker may well have been the ancestor of Dr. Thomas Walker, of Fredericksburg, who was born on the Mattapony, while "Clayborn" must have been William Claiborne, who once led an exploration to find the Northwest Passage, which journey brought him up the Rappahannock.

Records show that numerous persons and individuals of the Quaker faith settled in the Fredericksburg area, particularly in the eighteenth century. Among these was Amos Janney,[7] who settled near Waterford in 1733. He came from Pennsylvania, to which colony his ancestor, Joseph Janney, came with William Penn in 1683. Later members of this family settled in Fredericksburg, where they have been outstanding citizens to the present day.

From the early days of the Virginia colony, however, the Quakers suffered persecution. During the greater part of the seventeenth century they were forbidden by law to worship openly. In 1659 the law ordered "that all . . . . Quakers . . . . be imprisoned without baile,"[8] while that of 1662 forbade "assembling of Quakers to the number of five for purposes of religious worship."[9] Objections to Quakers in Virginia was not based on doctrine, but on the supposition that they were a menace to the stability of social life and civil government. By their persistent opposition to religious intolerance and to slavery they greatly annoyed the political leaders of that day. Their insistence upon democratic principles being applied not only to religion, but to the social, racial and political fabric of society, and their opposition to military service disturbed the privileged classes in the colony. This resulted in restricting the activities of the Quakers, against whom severe measures were sometimes taken. In the later colonial period, however, a more tolerant attitude toward this sect was developed. Quakers led the struggle for tolerance and religious freedom for more than one hundred and fifty years.

The first Quaker meeting house near Fredericksburg was founded by 1773.[10] Many of the leading colonial families in this area were Quakers or sympathizers of the sect. William Duff, who in 1717 settled in King George County where Falmouth was founded ten years later, was a Quaker. He was a member of a prominent mercantile establishment of the twin ports on the Rappahannock. John Mitchell, physician, botanist, author and mapmaker, and John Clayton, considered Virginia's greatest naturalist, were Quakers living at Urbanna. Dolly Madison, President Madison's wife, was of Quaker family. Madison himself, as well as William Byrd, Isham Randolph and George Wythe had Quaker leanings.

As a sect the Quakers exerted tremendous influence upon the political, social, intellectual and religious thought of colonial Virginia. They made an immeasurable contribution in obtaining for the colony such rights as religious tolerance, abolition of slavery and the extension of human rights to the masses. They helped develop the great western frontier, where, in the Ohio Northwest alone, of the 408 Quakers locating there, 269 came from Virginia, while 25 came from Maryland, 45 from Pennsylvania and 69 from New Jersey.[11]

The first Catholic colony in Virginia was established near Fredericksburg on Aquia, sometime around 1650. It was here that Col. Giles Brent from Maryland settled and built "Peace" in 1646. Col. George Brent, nephew of Col. Giles Brent, came to this colony, 1671, was a prominent lawyer and a partner with William Fitzhugh of "Bedford" in Stafford County.[12] The Aquia colony was enlarged

by immigrations of Catholics to this area following the issuance
by King James II of the Toleration Proclamation of 1686-7, which
permitted settlers in Virginia to practice their faith freely. Huguenot
refugees were encouraged to settle here, also. Among the prominent
Catholics were Col. Giles Brent, who led the Stafford men in the
Bacon Rebellion of 1676, and Margaret Brent, the feminist, already
referred to as the first patentee of the land on which Fredericksburg
now stands.

Virginia was perhaps the scene of the first Jewish settlement in
North America, for the first man of this faith settled in the colony
in 1621 when "the good ship Abigail brought Elias Legardo." Others
followed Legardo for several Jewish names are mentioned in a mus-
ter of inhabitants in 1633.[13]

As early as 1652, Silvedo and Manuel Rodriguez, of Jewish faith,
lived in Lancaster County, which territory extended to the falls of
the Rappahannock at that time. Many of the traders in the early
days of the colony and the settlement in the Rappahannock Valley
were Jews.[14]

In trade, in war and in finance, members of the Jewish faith
played an important role in the Fredericksburg area. In 1765 nine
Jews were among the signers of the Non-Importation Resolutions.[15]
Michael Gratz came from Philadelphia to Fredericksburg in 1776;
he established a thriving mercantile business, dealt in ships, became
a leading trader and aided in the exploring, surveying and settling
of the Ohio and Kentucky territories. He became a Virginia citizen
in 1783, and had business affiliation with numerous prominent Virginians, including Richard Graham, of Dumfries; Fielding Lewis;
Col. Thomas Marshall, father of Chief Justice Marshall; and John
Sevier, who helped lay the foundation for the State of Tennessee.
Gratz also conducted business with Stephen Austin and his son,
Samuel, in the settlement of Texas. His dealings were extensive in
the exploring and settling of the Western frontier.[16]

Other prominent Jews of the Fredericksburg area were Joseph
M. Myers, who managed the Gratz interests; Ezekiel Levy, who
was a brother member with Washington in the Masonic Lodge at
Fredericksburg; Jacob Myer, a soldier in the French and Indian
War; and Isaac Levy, who was a physician, merchant and financier.

It was Levy who helped furnish provisions for the Virginia Revolutionary forces[17] and aided in the winning of independence of the Northwest Territory.

Judaism exerted its potent influence upon the leaders who laid the foundation for this nation. Madison and Jefferson were students of Hebrew literature. Haym Solomon, a wealthy Jew of Philadelphia, gave financial assistance to Virginia Delegates Arthur Lee, Theodore Bland, Mercer and Randolph[18] while they were in attendance at the Continental Convention. James Madison pointed out that when "pecuniary resources of the members of Congress, both public and private were cut off, resource was had to Mr. Solomon for means to answer their current expenses and he was always found extending his friendly hand."[19] Solomon had lent the government more than $300,000 which was never repaid him.[20]

The first Separate Baptist Church in Virginia was established by Rev. Dutton Lane in 1760 on the lower James River. Seven years later Lewis Craig founded the first church of this faith in Spotsylvania County which was the first Baptist church erected north of the James River. A branch of this church was "near Fredericksburg." Representatives of this denomination, however, were present in the colony at the close of the seventeenth century, and a church of the faith was in existence in Virginia by 1714.[21] The first official entry of the Baptists into this neighborhood was around 1714. After the middle of the eighteenth century, the Baptists increased by leaps and bounds. Persecutions and suppressions seemed to add vigor and zeal to the faith, which grew most rapidly in the Rappahannock Valley after the establishment of the first Baptist Church here in 1767. According to Dr. Brydon, the Baptists had settled in this area by 1713 and had erected a "Chappelle" on Horsepen Run in Stafford County between 1713 and 1719.

Samuel Harris and James Read were Baptist converts who led the Baptist movement in the Fredericksburg area. Harris had once served as a Virginia Burgess and a colonel of militia. Both men were converted to the Baptist doctrine while in North Carolina. Fired with a missionary zeal, the two men came to Culpeper, Orange and Spotsylvania counties about 1765 and began laying the groundwork for the new church. Among their converts were Lewis Craig, who founded the first Baptist church in Spotsylvania; John Waller, who organized the Waller Church in 1769 and served as its pastor for 24 years, during which time he constituted 18 Baptist churches in the colony; James Childs and John Burrus, who became missionaries of the denomination.

Waller was a zealous Baptist, coming from a prominent Spotsylvania County family whose ancestry goes back to the Wallers of "Newport," England. For dissenting and preaching the Baptist doctrine he suffered persecution and imprisonment. His brother, William Edmund Waller, served as a Baptist minister for 50 years, while another brother, Absalom Waller, was pastor of the Waller Church for 30 years.

For preaching and spreading the Baptist doctrines, John Waller, Lewis Craig and James Childs, with others, were tried in the Fredericksburg Court House on June 4, 1768, on charges of "misbehavior . . . . running into private houses, and making dissentions."[22] Despite their defence by John Waller, one of the accused, the men were convicted and imprisoned. This was perhaps the first case of imprisonment in Virginia of dissenters other than Quakers.

The battles of the Baptists to practice their faith soon enlisted the sympathy not only of orator Patrick Henry, but others including Governor John Blair, who observed, in his letter urging tolerance, "that persecuting dissenters increases their numbers."[23] Councillor Carter of "Nomini Hall" soon renounced the Church of England and became a Baptist. Other prominent Virginians followed. From twenty-five original members who constituted the first church organized in 1767 by Lewis Craig, the Baptists increased in the Fredericksburg area until fifteen new churches were established by John Waller alone in the years between 1770 and 1793. In less than ten years, between 1768 and 1775, there were thirty-four imprisonments of Baptist ministers in the Virginia colony.

But the leaders appeared undaunted. In 1770 the Baptists presented their first petition to the House of Burgesses asking for religious freedom in the colony.[24] This was the beginning of a continued series of petitions by the Virginia Baptists to the General Assembly to abolish the Established Church and establish complete religious freedom in the colony. Moreover, the General Baptist

Association recommended that the colony abolish slavery and that the faith undertake the establishment of seminaries of learning. Their membership grew. At the outbreak of the Revolutionary War in 1775, Virginia had more than sixty Baptist churches, with twenty-nine of these north of the James River embracing the Fredericksburg area. Baptist missionaries spread the doctrine and founded new churches in Kentucky, South Carolina, and in numerous parts of Virginia.

Joining the fight for religious freedom that became a powerful movement by the middle of the eighteenth century, the Presbyterians wielded their strongest influence perhaps in the field of education. They were pioneers in Virginia, New Jersey, New York, and other communities, in the establishment of schools and institutions of higher learning.

There were Presbyterians in Virginia as early as the middle of the seventeenth century, when Thomas Harrison was chaplain between 1647 and 1649 to Governor Berkeley. Francis Doughty was an early apostle of Presbyterianism in Virginia and Maryland in 1659. Missionary societies of the sect existed in the colony prior to 1700. But Presbyterianism began its rapid spread in Virginia after 1730, with the first ordained minister of the denomination coming from Spotsylvania County. John Craig was the first ordained pastor of the American Synod in Virginia, ordained in 1737.

Perhaps the best-known Presbyterian minister of the Fredericksburg area was Rev. Archibald Alexander. He was a tutor in the home of General Thomas Posey, who lived at "Greenwood" in Spotsylvania County. Alexander later became the president of Hampden-Sydney College and founded the Princeton Theological Seminary at Princeton.

Philip Fithian, tutor in the home of Councillor Carter, was another Presbyterian divine whose missionary activities took him throughout the Rappahannock Valley, the Piedmont and the Shenandoah.

With the spread of settlements into the western counties of the colony, Presbyterianism also gained momentum. Representatives settled throughout the Shenandoah Valley and moved into the Kentucky territory before the Revolution. They established Liberty

Hall Academy (now Washington and Lee University) in 1749 and the Hampden-Sydney College in 1776. Later the foundation for Transylvania College was laid in 1780, that institution being the oldest college in the West.

Before Jefferson succeeded in having Virginia inaugurate an era of complete religious freedom by the passage of his bill in 1786, the Methodists joined other dissenting faiths and liberals in the interest of toleration. Methodism in Virginia dates back to about 1766 and the first Conference of the denomination was held at Leesburg in 1778.[25] Robert Williams was the first minister of the sect in Virginia, serving in Norfolk in 1772. Two years later Methodist churches were established in Petersburg and Norfolk and Portsmouth. The circuit was extended to Hanover by 1782.

The best known Methodist leader serving in Spotsylvania County was Bishop Asbury, who came to America in 1771 and was ordained one of the first two bishops of the Methodist Episcopal Church in America at the Baltimore Conference in 1784. He died at the George Arnold home in Spotsylvania County on March 31, 1816.

These different religious groups added to the intellectual and cosmopolitan character of the times. This was particularly true with the clergy of the various faiths and that spirit was partially disseminated to their followers. Each faith was inspired by a missionary zeal which was constantly being fed afresh with streams of European immigrants and thought and further stimulated by an evangelical enthusiasm to spread their beliefs to far and near parts of the world. This is exampled by the Society for the Propogation of the Gospel in Foreign Parts. There was a relatively highly educated leadership in the Episcopal, Presbyterian, Jewish, Quaker, Baptist, and Methodist churches of the Fredericksburg neighborhood. This characterization was perhaps truer of colonial clergy than it is of modern clergy.

## NOTES

1. Hening, *op. cit.*, I, 532; II, 180-81.

2. Wm. S. Perry, *Papers Relating to the History of the Church in Va., 1650-1776* (Hartford: Church Press, 1870), p. 247; also Willis M. Kemper, *Geneology of the Kemper Family* (Chicago: Hazlitt, 1899), pp. 22-23.

3. C.O. 5. 1387. Anno: 1720 (2), Public Record Office, State Library, Richmond, Va.

4. Hening, *op. cit.*, IV, 305.

5. Materials in the Friends Meeting House, Baltimore, Md., 1682-1701, VI, 3.

6. George Fox, *A Journal or Historical Account of Life, Travels, etc.* (Philadelphia: Friends, 1832).

7. Materials in the Friends Meeting House, Baltimore, *West River Quarterly, Half Yearly and Yearly Meetings, Minutes of 1680-1688*, p. 22.

8. Hening, *op. cit.*, I, 532; II, 180.

9. *Ibid.*, II, 181.

10. Spotsylvania County Records, Will Bk. E, 1772-1798.

11. Harlow Lindley, *The Quakers in the Ohio Northwest* (Cedar Rapids, Iowa: Torch, 1912), p. 11.

12. The Brent Family in *Va. Mag. of Hist. Biog.*, XVII, 308-11, 420-23; XVIII, 96, 321.

13. Paul Masserman and Maxwell Baker, *The Jews Come to America* (New York: Bloch, 1932), p. 87.

14. Leon Huhner, *The Jews of Virginia, from the Earliest Time to the Close of the 18th Century* (Baltimore, 1911); Philip A. Bruce, *Social Life in Virginia in the 17th Century* (Richmond: Whitter & Sheperson, 1907), p. 261; Robert Beverley, *History of Virginia* (London, 1705), p. 67; *Records of New Amsterdam*, ed. by B. Furnow, II, 401-02; *Publ. of the Am. Jewish Hist. Soc.*, No. 18, p. 57.

15. Hening, *op. cit.*, I, 499.

16. *Letters of Michael Gratz*, ed. B. and M. Gratz, *Merchants of Philadelphia, 1754-1798* (Jefferson City, Mo.: Stephens, 1916).

17. *Collections of the Illinois State History Library*, II, Va. Series I, ed. by Clarence W. Alvord (Springfield: Ill. Lib., 1903), p. 463.

18. Herbert B. Adams, *Pubs. of the Am. Jewish Hist. Soc.* (Baltimore: The Society, 1914), No. 2, p. 9.

19. *Madison Papers* (Gaillard Hunt, ed., N. Y., 1900-1901), p. 163.

20. Masserman & Baker, *op. cit.*, p. 94.

21. Robert B. Semple, *A History of the Rise and Progress of Baptists in Va.* (Richmond: Pitt & Dickinson, 1894), p. 346. Rare Books, Library of Congress.

22. Semple, *Ibid.*, p. 16.

23. *Ibid.*

24. *Journals of the House of Burgesses* (Richmond: State Printing, 1915), May 26, 1770. Vol. 1770-1772, p. 20.

25. Jesse Lee, *Short Hist. of the Methodists in the United States of America: Beginning in 1766 and Continued until 1809* (Baltimore: Magill & Clime, 1810), p. 60.

## 9

### EDUCATION, SCHOOLS AND TUTORS OF
### RAPPAHANNOCK VALLEY CITIZENS

In an age when education and the development of native abilities and talents were reserved to a selected few, Fredericksburg and its neighborhood was outstanding for the maintenance of a large number of private schools and tutors who gave instructions in the fundamentals of learning, especially languages and classics, to the youth who later became the leaders of their communities, the Virginia colony and the nation at large. This foundation in the rudiments of learning was considered by the upper class colonials to be a necessary beginning for the broad cultural life enjoyed by the well-to-do in the seventeenth and the eighteenth centuries.

During the greater part of the eighteenth century, between 1735 and 1795, there were at least fifty outstanding private schools within the Fredericksburg area. Moreover, there was twice this number of scholars and tutors who instructed the youth in the private homes of the planters, merchants, doctors and the well-to-do. Half of these schools and tutors were found in Fredericksburg proper, while the rest were in the areas closely associated with the town.

Having rather a broad concept of culture, the colonials were not satisfied with bare rudiments of learning in classics, arts and sciences offered the youth by the eminent scholars and tutors at the private homes, schools and academies located in the area. Majority of the young men were given opportunity to broaden their education and prepare for professional careers by advanced studies in colleges and universities abroad and in the colonies. To this broad concept of what constituted an educated man may be

132

attributed, in a large measure, the development of a cosmopolitan attitude and a certain world-mindedness of the citizens who lived in the Fredericksburg neighborhood.

Records reveal that no other region of colonial Virginia had more sons educated in universities and colleges abroad than the Rappahannock Valley. Coming from ten counties in this area, thirty-seven students attended schools of advanced studies in Great Britain at one period in the eighteenth century.[1]

Moreover, one study has disclosed that of the thirty-four Virginians admitted to the famous Inns of Court, London, twenty-four of these were from the Rappahannock area.[2] At the same time, only the colony of South Carolina exceeded Virginia in the number of its citizens who were admitted to the Inns of Court.

Of the twenty Virginia students who attended colleges and universities in the northern colonies prior to 1775, the majority came from homes and families living in the Rappahannock Valley or adjacent to these counties.[3] Of this total, twelve attended Princeton, six Pensylvania College, and one each Harvard and King's College.

Teaching the fundamentals, the classics, languages, arts, sciences and manners, the tutors employed in the private homes of colonials and at the various schools and academies conducted for the sons of the upper classes, wielded a permanent influence on the community and its citizens. These scholarly instructors gave youth fundamentals which helped to guide their thoughts and actions in adulthood. As men, many of them contributed ideas, philosophies and actions that aided in the formation of the new American republic.

Some of the leading schools and tutors of Fredericksburg and vicinity during the eighteenth century are listed below with the names of some of their pupils who later became persons of historical importance. It will be noted that most of the pupils were sons of the well-to-do planters, doctors, merchants, ministers and lawyers. Some, however, were artisans' children. A few of the schools, notably the McPherson Charity School in Fredericksburg, were devoted to the education of children coming from poorer families. On the whole though, the youth of lower classes had limited or no educational opportunities in colonial Virginia. Education for the girls of upper class families was more nominal than factual in so far as true schools were concerned. They received education after a certain fashion, but not to the same extent as their brothers.

Some of the schools and tutors were:

Master Hobby School, first school attended by George Washington.

Rev. James Marye School at Fredericksburg attended by George Washington, and perhaps by James Madison and James Monroe.[4]

The Ducking Hole School conducted by Rev. William Douglas in Louisa County and attended by Jefferson and others.

James Robertson taught in the "Ducking Hole School."

Rev. Archibald Campbell taught in Washington Parish, Westmoreland County, where Washington attended.

Rev. Donald Robinson in King and Queen County where James Madison was one of the pupils.

Rev. Matthew Maury in Louisa County where Meriwether Lewis was taught.

Rev. Thomas Martin in King and Queen County; he also taught Madison.

Walker Maury in Orange County, where Jefferson attended.

John Lowe, in Westmoreland, taught in the Washington home.

Mr. McPherson, Mr. Davidson and Mr. Constable were tutors in George Mason's home, father of George Mason of Gunston Hall.

Mr. Williams and Mr. Wylie also were tutors of George Mason of Gunston Hall.

Dr. Ebenezer Brooks and Rev. James Thompson taught at "Oak Hill" in Marshall home.

Rev. Archibald Alexander, in Spotsylvania County, taught numerous scholars in the home of General Thomas Posey. He later became president of Hampden-Sydney College and founded the Divinity School of Princeton.

Rev. Jonathan Boucher at Port Royal was minister of Mount Church and tutored numerous youths of Caroline County.

Charles Lewis was headmaster of Rappahannock Academy, considered one of the finest schools in Northern Virginia.

Col. Bernard Moore held the Tutorial School at "Nottingham," the home of Alexander Spotswood. The "Log College" was held here also.

Martin Healy taught advanced subjects to Spotswood children at "Nottingham."

Catholic Parish Schools were conducted at the home of William Brent, "Woodstock," and also at "Richland," both on Aquia Creek.

John Harrower School was conducted at "Belvidere," home of William Dangerfield, where many scholars were taught. The deaf and mute were taught here.

William Grove, nicknamed "Master Hobby," taught at Falmouth, where he was Washington's first teacher.

William Williams taught at Oak Grove School, where he was the second teacher of Washington.

English School conducted near Fredericksburg.

Grammar School in Fredericksburg where the Brooke children studied.

Mr. Lennegan tutored in the Brooke Home, "Smithfield."

Latin and Greek Schools were near Fredericksburg.

Rev. William Yates School in Gloucester was attended by children of numerous prominent Virginians, including students John Page, Lewis Willis, Francis Willis, Charles and Edward Carter and Thomas Nelson.

William Price conducted the "Willis Hill" school in Fredericksburg.

Low's Grammar School in Fredericksburg was one of the largest schools of its type in the colony.

McPherson Charity School, in Fredericksburg, had Benjamin Day as its president. Its trustees were Charles Yates, George French, William Lovell, Fontaine Maury and Elisha Hall.

Fredericksburg Academy had Judge James Mercer as its president. Many leading Virginians were educated here.

Mr. Curly's French and Dancing School was conducted in Fredericksburg.

Mrs. Hudson's Boarding School was held in Fredericksburg.

John Allan School was also in Fredericksburg.

Fielding Lewis School was in Fredericksburg, but he also held similar ones elsewhere.

The Dame School was in Fredericksburg. This was perhaps the Marye School at a later date. It is possible that this was the school George and Betty Washington attended while in this town. It was located in the old St. George's Parish House near the site of the church which is standing today. Here Betty and other upper class girls were taught English, French, embroidery, et cetera.

Bartholomew Fuller Mathematical and English School was conducted in Fredericksburg.

Joseph Jones School, Bartholomew Barrett School, French Language School, Maria Jones School, Mr. Arnaud's French School, Berry and Custis School, John Callender Singing School, John Victor Music School and John Goolrick School, were all held in Fredericksburg. The last named institution was conducted for more than forty-five years on Caroline Street and at "Bunker Hill" and was considered one of the finest schools in the area.

A Medical College was established in Fredericksburg prior to the Revolution through a cooperative undertaking of the town's prominent physicians and surgeons who conducted surgical operations and laboratory experiments here.

The Llangollen University, in Spotsylvania County, founded by John Lewis and conducted by him from 1811 to 1830 belongs to the century following that covered by the present study. It is significant to note that this short-lived institution had considerable influence on Jefferson's idea for the establishment of the University of Virginia.[5]

## NOTES

1. *William and Mary Quarterly*, XXI, 196-99.

2. Edward Alfred Jones, *American Members of the Inns of Court* (London: St. Catherine, 1924), Introduction, pp. ix-xxx, 11-13, 20-21, 28, 34, 40-42, 50, 53, 76-77, 91, 107-08, 122-27, 186.

3. *William and Mary Quarterly*, VI, 217-19.

4. *Youth and Manhood of George Washington,* Program Three, The United States George Washington Bicentennial Commission (Washington: Government Printing, 1931), p. 5; also Alvin T. Embrey, *History of Fredericksburg, Virginia* (Richmond: Old Dominion Press, 1937), p. 99.

5. See Appendix on Private Schools accompanying this study for detailed information on these schools and tutors. For sources of information on the schools mentioned here consult the *Virginia Gazette,* Spotsylvania County Records, *W. & M. Quart., Dictionary of American Biog.,* family papers of Washington, Madison, Jefferson, et al, and Hening's *Statutes.*

## ❦ *10* ❧

### LIBRARIES

Books were not rare in the homes of the planters, ministers, doctors, lawyers and merchants of colonial Virginia. Private libraries in the homes of typical planters and the well-to-do of the Fredericksburg area had from one to two thousand volumes. When this is compared with the largest library in Virginia, owned by Colonel William Byrd of Westover, which contained 3500 volumes, and with that of Thomas Jefferson having 931 volumes, the numerous libraries of planters, lawyers and merchants of the Rappahannock Valley take on an added significance.

Fredericksburg and Falmouth were the principal book centers of northern Virginia. They supplied the well-to-do of the Rappahannock Valley, the Tidewater, Piedmont and a great portion of the northwest hinterland with the books read in many of the colonial mansions and the smaller homes in the colony.

Philip Fithian, who worked as a missionary among the pioneer settlers of western Virginia and Pennsylvania and served as tutor in the home of Councillor Robert Carter of "Nomini Hall," observed that "There are here [referring to the Shenandoah] many useful and amusing books: The *Spectator,* Pope's Work, Shakespeare's Work, Gray's Work, etc., many single, valuable Books . . . . . It is charming to see Books in the Infancy of this remote Land . . . . ."[1]

Below is a representative list of planters, doctors, ministers, merchants and officials residing in the Rappahannock Valley who owned outstanding private libraries.

The library of Governor Alexander Spotswood, who left his books and mathematical instruments to the College of William and Mary.

John Mercer, of Marlborough, had one of the two or three largest and finest libraries in Virginia, containing more than 1500 volumes of the best selections of that day, written in many languages. These consisted of law books, histories, books on divinity, philosophy, mathematics, surveying, science, geography, travel, education, money and exchange; on Latin, Greek, French, and other languages, memoirs, biography, classics, military and practical arts and sets of special works and collections and magazines. George Mason obtained most of his education from this library belonging to his uncle.[2]

James Mercer and John Francis Mercer added many volumes to their father's collections and possessed libraries of their own.[3]

Rev. John Waugh of Stafford County settled in the colony before 1688 and had one of the earliest book collections in the vicinity.

William Fitzhugh of "Bedford," Stafford County, owned a remarkably good assortment of books.

James Marye of Fredericksburg had 444 volumes. Fielding Lewis of "Kenmore" had a modest library.[4]

Robert Beverley of "Newlands," Spotsylvania County, nephew of historian Robert Beverley, had one of the finest libraries in the county, containing more than 250 volumes.

Rev. William Douglas had an excellent library. He was tutor in the Monroe home and headmaster of the Ducking Hole School in Louisa County.[5]

Rev. Robert Buchan, a Scotch tutor in the Travers Daniel Home at "Crows Nest," and tutor in the home of Col. James Wood, had a fine library.

Dr. Henry Heath, of Fredericksburg, left a large library.

Joseph Brock, of Spotsylvania County, had over 100 volumes. Col. John Waller, of "Newport," Spotsylvania County, had several hundred volumes consisting of Latin books, Greek, Gaelic, history, medicine, law, Dryden, Pope, Shakespeare, magazines, etc.[6]

William Walker of Stafford County had 100 volumes. Richard Lee of "Stratford Hall" and the other Lees of "Stratford" and

"Leesylvania," had exceptionally good libraries. So did William Beverley, of "Blandfield," Essex County, son of the historian. Rev. William Key, of Richmond County, owned a library valued at more than £261.[7]

Councillor Carter, of "Nomini Hall," Westmoreland County, owned a collection of more than 1500 volumes. These were scholarly books such as Puffendorf, Grotius, Spinoza, Newton, Chaucer, Blackstone, Moliere, Addison, Montesquieu, Locke, Erasmus, and numerous texts on philosophy, science, history, politics, etc.

Francis T. Brooke of "Smithfield," Spotsylvania County, notes in his *Narrative of My Life* that "my father had an excellent library."[8]

George K. Smart in his study of private libraries of Virginia lists over 600 names, of which the Fredericksburg neighborhood had a goodly share. Examining 100 libraries, he observed that most libraries were concentrated in York County, with Prince George, Princess Anne, Northumberland, Brunswick, Spotsylvania, Middlesex, Stafford, Lower Norfolk, Chesterfield and Montgomery well represented. Four counties here listed by Mr. Smart are in the Rappahannock Valley, two each on either side of the river at Fredericksburg.

Below is a sample of the books read and found in the homes of the people in the Rappahannock Valley as revealed by the book lists in the orders of the merchants at Falmouth and Fredericksburg. The list represents the volumes handled between 1770 and 1775 by Allason Company of Falmouth. Invoices of Fredericksburg merchants show similar orders.

(Copied from original list, William Allason Papers, op. cit. Original spelling has been preserved).

| | |
|---|---|
| Additons Evidence | Balm of Gilead |
| Addisons Works | Battledore |
| Afflicted Mans Companion | Baxters Call |
| Alarm to Unconvinced Sinners | Beauties of Nature and Art |
| Allans Alarm | Bible |
| Arithmetics | Bland Day Books |
| Bailies Dictionary | Bollingbrooks Work |

Boston 4-fold State

Buckaneers of American

Bull Finchs Songs

Campbells Tryal

Campbells Trial for Elington

Christian Education

Christian Hero

Colo. Garners Life

Collo. Gardner (Collo. Gardiners Life)

Companion to the Altar

Compleat Songster

Crawfords Dying Thoughts

Cynthia

Cyrus Expedition

Dacius (Dacier) Plato

Day Books

Dictionaries { Bailies / Dyckes / Johnsons / Postlewhites

Duty of Man

Dyckes Dictionary

Dyers Golden Chain

Esther Gift (Easter Gift)

Easops Fables (Aesop's Fables)

Elizabeth West

Erskins Gospel Sonnets

Explanation of Plain Catechism

Fairy Tales

Fillotsons Sermons

Food for the Mind

Fool of Quality

Free Thinker

Gays Fables

Gentle Shepherd

Gentleman { Instructed / Library

German Syntax

Gill Blass

Golden Toy

Gospel History of Sanctification

Gospel Sonnets

Grace Abounding

Grays Works

Haddingtons Poems

Harriot Stewart

Havies (Harvey's) Meditation

Harwoods Cheerful Thoughts

History of King David

Histories

Humes History of England

History of the Bible

History of China

History of England

History of Goody two Shoes

Horn Books

Ink Powder

Introduction to Reading & Spelling

Jests

Jockeys Master Piece

Johnsons Dictionary

Journals

Ledgers

Letter Cases

Letters Between Tommy & Miss Nanny

Lilliputian Magazine

Linnetts Songs

McAuley History of England

Marshall on Sanctification

Masques Songs

Memorandum Books

Memo. book Covers

Merry & Wise

Midnight Spy

Montesquieus Persian Letters

Museum

New Years Gift

Newtonian System of Philosophy

Nine Worthies

Pilgrims Progress

Pockett Herald

Poems { Hadingtons / Rochesters

Popes Essay on Man

Popes Homer in 2 Vols.

Popes Homers Iliad & Odyssey

Prayer Books

Prayer Book Com.

Present for Children

Postlewhites Dictionary

Pretty Books for Children

Pretty Books of Pictures

Pretty Pockett Books

Pretty Poems

Primers

Principles of Virtue & Morality

Psalters

Quarto Books

Ramsays Songs

Reading Made Easy

Religious Books

Religious Courtship

Renard the Fox

Robbers

Robertsons History of Scotland

Robinson Crusoe

Rochesters Poems

Royal Calendar

Royal Primers

Russells 7 Sermons

Sacramental Dictionary

Satans Invisible World

Scotch Magazines

Scots Magazines for 1770

Senecas Works

Shakespeares Works

Sherlock's Discoveries

Sherlock on Death

Short Histories

Six Penny Worth of Witt

Smolletts History in 16 Vols.

Songs { Compleat Songster / Linnett / Masque / Ramsays Songs / Songs

Song Books { Ramsays / Bullfinchs

Spectators

Sterns Sermons

Sterns Work

Testaments

Tissotts Advice

Tom Thumb folio

Treatise on Sanctification

Turkish Spy

Twelfth Days Gift

Valentines Gift

Virginia Laws

Voltaires Force of Education

Wassers

Watts {Hymns / Psalms / on Prayer

Whitefields Sermons

Whitsunday Gift

Whole Duty of Man

Willson on, etc. {Sabbath / Sacrament / Catechism

Wise Masters & Mistresses

Youngs Works

Youths Companion

The foregoing is a sample of a book order in almost original form taken from the Order Book of William Allason, merchant of Falmouth. It contains many of the finest books of that day: the works of Addison, Pope, Shakespeare; Macauley's, Hume's, and Smollett's histories; the writing of Seneca, Montesquieu, Newton, Voltaire to name only a few of the more scholarly ones. There are copies of the Spectator, diaries, journals, travel, and copies of works on many other subjects.

The typical library of the better colonial homes of this area consisted of law books, the classics, histories, books on divinity, politics, medicine, philosophy, mathematics, surveying, science, geography, travel, education, business, money and exchange, languages—Latin, Greek, Hebrew, German, Spanish,—, biography, memoirs, gazetteers, dictionaries, military and practical arts, besides collections and sets of special works, magazines, and miscellaneous subjects.

The merchants of Falmouth and Fredericksburg supplied the greater portion of the large demands for these books not only for the Rappahannock area but for the back country. They were the principal buying and distributing book centers for half of eastern Virginia and a large portion of the frontier regions. These literary interests built up broad outlooks and established wide cultural contacts of planters, ministers, lawyers, doctors, merchants, and other professional groups of the vicinity who made up a considerable portion of the colonial population of the area. These factors indicate a cosmopolitan character of outlook of the upper classes. The society of this class was marked by elegant homes, scholarly and literary tastes, broad education and wide reading which were stimulated by private tutors, superior intellectual attainments, study and extensive travel abroad, and by wide correspondence which contributed much toward making them world-minded.

## NOTES

1. Philip Fithian, *Journals and Letters, 1775-1776*, ed. by Robert G. Albion (Princeton: University Press, 1900-34), pp. 15, 49, 86, 177, *et passim*.
2. *Virginia Gazette*, Aug. 29, 1771, A Catalogue of John Mercer's Library, offered for sale in Fredericksburg.
3. The Mercer Papers in the Virginia History Association, Richmond, Virginia.
4. Spotsylvania County Records, Will Book E, p. 457.
5. Catalogue of Books in Will Book No. 7, Albemarle County.
6. Spotsylvania County Records, Will Book, Feb. 5, 1755.
7. *William and Mary Quart.*, LX, 164-68.
8. Francis T. Brooke, *op. cit.*, pp. 57-58.

## ~§ *11* §~

### FREDERICKSBURG NEIGHBORHOOD AS A
### LITERARY AND INTELLECTUAL CENTER

Fredericksburg neighborhood in colonial days was a center of a cultured and refined society with literary and intellectual achievements that made Francis T. Brooke apply to it the ambitious title "The Athens of America." Its literary contributions compare favorably with other cultural centers of the American colonies like Charleston, Philadelphia, New York and Boston. Men ascribed to this area produced writings of statesmanship and historical works of great significance and influence.

The upper society of the Eighteenth Century Virginia produced a leisure class with intellectual inclinations which flowered into a rich social heritage. This class built broad outlooks and established world contacts. Members of this favored group early developed a cosmopolitan approach to problems at home and abroad.

The character of the early writings of these colonials is aptly described by Tyler in his *History of American Literature*:

> In the early schools of the colonies the American mind was soon educated to a point in the science of politics much in advance of the contemporary culture of Europe, and it produced along with the intellectual progress, a literature the vigor and even sometimes elegance of which became the admiration of some of the first publicists and statesmen of England . . . . . Elaborate letters, or epistles . . . . men were wont to compose long dissertations in communications to their friends . . . . .[1]

### BELMONT

Overlooking the Town of Falmouth is Belmont which was built *circa* 1761 by John Richards, Esq: (1734-1785), prosperous merchant of Leedstown and Falmouth, for his daughter Mrs. Horner. Upon the death of William Knox, Esq: of "Windsor Lodge," Culpeper County, in 1805 it became the residence of his widow, Mrs. Susannah Stuart (FitzHugh) Knox (1751-1823). The mansion was lately the residence of Mr. and Mrs. Gari Melchers, both deceased, and was bequeathed by the latter to the State of Virginia as an art museum.

### BROMPTON

On Marye's Heights overlooking Fredericksburg is Brompton home of John Lawrence Marye, Esq: (1798-1868) and now the residence of the Chancellor of Mary Washington College.

## THE HOME OF COMMODORE MATTHEW FONTAINE MAURY

This brick residence at 214 Caroline Street was once the home of "The Pathfinder of the Seas," and is now the home of Mrs. Wister Wallace Braxton.

*Courtesy of Mrs. W. W. Braxton*

## THE HOME OF ROGER DIXON

At 216 Caroline Street stands the home of Roger Dixon, Gentleman, prominent pre-Revolutionary merchant of Fredericksburg, and now the residence of Mr. and Mrs. Kuszner Bauman.

### SAINT JAMES'

The quaint residence now standing at the corner of Charles and
Fauquier Streets was called Saint James' by its occupant, Judge James
Mercer (1737-1793) who was president of the Old Fredericksburg
Academy. It was lately the residence of the late Mr. and Mrs. Peter
Vivian Daniel and is now occupied by their daughter, Miss Vivian
Daniel.

### THE RUINS OF MANSFIELD

Just below Fredericksburg on the Tidewater Trail on the banks of
the Rappahannock River stood Mansfield, built in 1765 by Colonel
Mann Page (1719-1781) after the style of Mount Airy, the ancestral
home of his wife, Anne Corbin Tayloe. Destroyed during the War
Between the States, nothing now remains at Mansfield. This photo-
graph was taken in 1865. Courtesy of the National Park Museum.

## HOME OF DOCTOR CHARLES MORTIMER

This handsome brick residence at 213 Caroline Street was built in 1764
and was long the residence of Doctor Mortimer who attended Mrs.
Mary (Ball) Washington in her last illness. The property is now owned
and occupied by Miss Bessie Heflin.

### HOME OF
### PRESIDENT JAMES MONROE

The brick residence at 301 Caroline
Street was built by Judge Joseph
Jones (1727-1805) and occupied by
his nephew President James Monroe
during his residence in Fredericksburg. It is now owned by Mr. William Taylor Elmer of Front Royal,
Virginia.

### SCOTIA

Scotia was situated on Charles Street opposite the James Monroe Law Office and was demolished in the 1920s. It was the home of John Scott, Esq: (1773-1848), influential Scotch merchant of Fredericksburg, who married in 1799 Frances Susannah Stone Payne for whom he erected the residence shortly thereafter.

### CARLTON

Carlton overlooks the Town of Falmouth from a high eminence, having been built by John Short, Esq: (1763-1794), merchant. It was for many years afterwards the home of his widow Mrs. Judith (Ball) Short (*circa* 1770-1843). It was acquired by the late John M. O'Bannon in 1837 and occupied by his family for more than one hundred years. It is now the residence of Doctor and Mrs. E. Boyd Graves.

HOME OF DOCTOR JOHN TENNENT

The frame house now standing at 1106 Princess Anne Street was the residence of Doctor John Tennent who wrote an "Essay on Pleurisy" in 1735. It is now the home of Mrs. Marion Gordon Willis, Jr.

THE FALLS

Built by Colonel Francis Thornton (1711-1749) *circa* 1736, whose tombstone is in the cemetery nearby; The Falls was demolished when The Stratford Hotel (now The General Washington Inn) was constructed on its site in the early 1930s. Colonel Samuel Washington, brother of George Washington, once lived here and the tomb of his infant daughter is in the cemetery to the rear of the present Inn.

## FALL HILL

Built by Francis Thornton, Gentleman, (1737-1794), on the fall hill overlooking the Town of Fredericksburg and the Rappahannock Valley, this home is now owned and occupied by his lineal descendant, Mrs. Lynn W. Franklin.

## ELLERSLIE

A few miles above Falmouth in Stafford County stands Ellerslie the ancestral seat of the Wallace family. Here resided Colonel Gustavus Brown Wallace (1751-1802), distinguished Revolutionary officer.

*Courtesy of the owners, Messrs. W. D. and C. T. Purks*

HOME OF CAPTAIN CHARLES WASHINGTON

Formerly situated immediately on the northeast corner of Fauquier and Princess Anne Streets, this old house was moved a few yards some years ago to its present location at 209 Fauquier Street and is presently the home of Mr. and Mrs. William J. Wilmer.

THE SENTRY BOX

Located at 133 Caroline Street, this large frame house was built in 1784 by General George Weedon. He, dying childless, The Sentry Box became the home of his wife's nephew, Colonel Hugh Mercer (1776-1853). It is now owned and occupied by Mrs. George W. Heflin.

## HOME OF DOCTOR ROBERT WELLFORD

Doctor Wellford (1753-1823), a physician in the British Army, befriended American prisoners during the Revolutionary War and near the close of the war, at the insistance of General Washington, settled in Fredericksburg where he built the above house at 1501 Caroline Street which is now occupied by his lineal descendant Miss Eliza Alexander Roy.

## THE OLD FORBES HOME

Said to have been built by Robert Ellis, prominent Fredericksburg merchant, this house at the corner of Princess Anne and Hanover Streets was for many years the home of Miss Sallie Innis Forbes (1854-1952).

### HAZEL HILL

Situated near the Rappahannock River in the lower part of Fredericksburg, this old home is immediately opposite Ferry Farm. It was for many years the seat of General John Minor (1761-1816), and greatly altered about the turn of the century by Henry Warden, Esq: its owner.

*Courtesy Sidney L. Shannon, Jr., present owner.*

### SAINT GEORGE'S CHURCH

Situated on the corner of Princess Anne and George Streets, the present edifice was completed in 1849. The site was reserved by the Act creating the Town, 1727 and several churches have stood on the site, and the cemetery adjoining is the most ancient in Fredericksburg.

## BOND'S DRUG STORE

This old drug store situated at the corner of William and Caroline Streets is said to be one of the oldest drug stores in America in continuous operation.

## BAPTIST CHURCH

The present building was built in 1854 at the corner of Princess Anne and Amelia Streets. About 1767 a Baptist Meeting House was erected in Fredericksburg near the present R. F. & G. Railroad depot.

### CANAL BASIN

Near the intersection of Prince Edward Street, Canal Street, and Fall Hill Avenue was an artificial reservoir for canal and river transshipments.

### CITY HALL

The present building was erected in 1814 facing Princess Anne Street and adjoining the Old Market Square to the rear on which was the original Town Hall. Here in 1824 was held a very elaborate reception when General Lafayette paid an official visit to the town.

## THE GUNNERY SPRING

Long a land mark in the lower part of Fredericksburg, is old Gunnery Spring. Nearby stood the Public Revolutionary Manufactory of Arms which was managed by two active commissioners, Colonel Fielding Lewis and Mr. Charles Dick. This property was later converted to the Old Fredericksburg Academy.

## PORTION OF THE SITE OF THE HUNTER IRON WORKS

Situated in Stafford County, on the Rappahannock River, a short distance above Falmouth, the site of the iron works of James Hunter are yet visible. This operation was begun prior to the Revolutionary War and played a very prominent part in supplying the Continental Army.

### OLD TOWN HALL

On Market Square, back of the present City Hall, is the portion of an old building said to be a part of the Old Town Hall. This building was repaired in 1956 and is still in use.

### LEASELAND MARKER

A bronze tablet near Chatham Bridge marks the site of the grant of land to John Buckner and Thomas Royston, 1671, upon which the town of Fredericksburg was originally laid out, 1721 and authorized by legislative act, 1727.

## THE NATIONAL BANK

This old brick building at the corner of Princess Anne and George Streets formerly housed the Farmers Bank to which The National Bank was successor.

## THE SITE OF NEWPOST

In Spotsylvania County, about three miles below Fredericksburg on the Tidewater Trail, stands this marker on the banks of Massaponax Creek. Newpost was established by Governor Alexander Spotswood and upon his death passed to his eldest son Colonel John Spotswood (1725-1758).

## OLD STONE PRISON AND WAREHOUSE

This old building on Sophia Street near Chatham Bridge was used to confine shipments of slaves and for a debtors prison prior to the Revolution. It has for many years been used as a warehouse.

## ALUM SPRING
## ON HAZEL RUN

Near here was a Revolutionary Prison and Hospital. Hessians and Yorktown prisoners were confined here.

This chapter will list the literary, historical, philosophical, religious and scientific productions whose primary importance is determined mainly by their historical significance. They were written by men versed in the science of law, politics and statesmanship, by scholars, teachers, doctors, philosophers, travelers, historians and scientists—all of whom may be referred to as citizens or quasi citizens of this area.

Only a part of the literary genius of the Rappahannock region is included in this study. All persons or literary works treated here are those that have had the most significant influence on American history. These are not necessarily persons who belonged solely to this area. Each, however, was attached in some way to this region, either by birth, residence or other relationship.

The first of these writings is the *Journal* of John Lederer,[2] giving the earliest written account of the back parts of Virginia by this German scholar and traveler who discovered the sources of the James, York and Rappahannock rivers in 1669-70.

The William Fitzhugh *Letters*[3] were written between 1679 and 1699 by a lawyer, planter, merchant and shipper who lived at "Bedford" in Stafford County. His correspondence throws light on the course of trade between the Virginia colony and England in the latter part of the seventeenth century.

Serving as a Virginia Ranger on the frontier of the Virginia colony about 1670-1690, Cadwallader Jones in 1681/2 wrote an "Essay about the Indian Trade, with a MS map or plot of Louisiana."[4]

The "Official Letters of Alexander Spotswood"[5] show not only the state of affairs under this colonial governor but indicate the vision of Spotswood in regard to the future development of North American colonization. He pointed out in his official correspondence to the British officials in London (1) the danger of French expansion eastward; (2) a passage across the Blue Ridge Mountains for westward expansion of the English colonists; (3) the advisability of establishing an English colony on the Great Lakes to checkmate the French; (4) the need for friendly relations with the American Indians; (5) the opportunity for developing the iron industry which he started in the colony.

Robert Beverley, of "Beverley Park," near the head of the Mattaponi River near Fredericksburg, wrote the *History of the Present State of Virginia,* published in 1705. In 1722 he edited *The Abridgement of the Public Laws of Virginia.*

John Fontaine wrote the *Journal,* 1714-1715, describing the expedition across the Blue Ridge Mountains led by Governor Spotswood. The expedition, of which Fontaine was a member, is also described in his *Memoirs of a Huguenot Family.* The treatise also gives a vivid account of Germanna, Spotswood's home, and his frontier colonization project.

*The Papers of the Jones Family, 1649-1889,*—consisting of 35 bound volumes,[6] are a storehouse of information on every phase of colonial life for the entire period. They consist of letters, account books, invoices and other descriptive material on the trade and life of the Rappahannock country, the Atlantic Seaboard and the colony in general.

In 1736 John Tennent of Spotsylvania County, and later of Fredericksburg, wrote an *Essay on Pleurisy,* considered the first medical book to be published in Virginia. A voluminous writer on medical works, Tennent is the author of *Every Man his own Doctor; or the Poor Planter's Physician,* 1734; *An Epistle to Dr. Richard Mead, Concerning the Epidemical Diseases of Virginia, Particularly, Pleurisy and Peripneumony,* 1738; *A Reprieve from Death in Two Physical Chapters,* 1741; *Physical Enquiries,* 1742; *A Brief Account of the Case of John Tennent,* 1742; *Physical Disquisitions: demonstrating the real causes of the blood's morbid rarefaction and stagnation,* 1745.

A son of Robert (King) Carter of "Corotoman," Landon Carter, of "Sabine Hall," Richmond County, left his *Diary*[7] to posterity. He wrote numerous articles for the American Philosophical Society and is said to have drafted the historic remonstrances against the Stamp Act of 1765 while a member of the committee reporting on this matter.

Arthur Lee, of "Stratford Hall," was the author of numerous articles, including the famous *An Appeal to the English Nation.* He contributed articles to the American Philosophical Society, of which he was a member. He was also a member of the Royal Society of England and of the American Academy of Arts and Sciences.

Francis Lightfoot Lee assisted in preparing the "Articles of Confederation," and helped draft the "Westmoreland Declaration" against the Stamp Act, known as the Leedstown Resolution.

The Lees of "Stratford" were prolific writers. Among them are authors of more significant historical documents in early American history than can be found in any other colonial family. Richard Henry Lee wrote the Westmoreland or Leedstown Resolution against the Stamp Act, prepared the Remonstrances to the King of 1764, and formulated and introduced the famous resolution: "Resolved: That these United Colonies are and of a right ought to be free and independent." His *Memoirs* have been published by his grandson, Richard Henry Lee.

The famous expression "First in War, First in Peace, and First in the Hearts of his countrymen" was delivered by Henry Lee, who is also the author of a two-volume text: *War in the Southern United States.*

Thomas Ludwell Lee, of Stafford County, served on the Committee which drew up the Bill of Rights in the convention of 1776, and was on the committee with Thomas Jefferson, George Wythe, George Mason and Edmund Pendleton which met at Fredericksburg in 1777 to revise the laws for the State of Virginia and helped to draft the one hundred and twenty-six bills the committee formulated.

The outstanding contribution of George Mason is the authorship of the Virginia Bill of Rights, which is the basis for the Bill of Rights in the Constitution of the United States.

Mann Page, of "Mansfield Hall," contributed numerous articles to the American Philosophical Society of which he was a member, and carried on an extensive correspondence with individuals in all parts of the world.

Edmund Pendleton, of Caroline County, wrote the "Resolutions of Virginia favoring a Declaration of Independence," undoubtedly with the assistance of George Mason.

John Mercer, of "Marlborough," compiled Virginia laws into the well-known *Mercer's Abridgement.*

Charles Fenton Mercer, born in Fredericksburg but later removed to Kentucky, which he represented as a delegate in the Virginia Legislature, introduced to the Assembly in 1816-17 a "Bill for the promotion of public education," including a university, colleges, academies and primary schools. This preceded Thomas Jefferson's bill for the establishment of the University of Virginia. Earlier he sponsored the Bill for the Construction of the Chesapeake and Ohio Canal of which company he became the president.

William Allason, a Scotch merchant of Falmouth from 1757 to 1793, left the Allason Papers, containing valuable historical data pertaining to the extensive trade, correspondence, travel and business enterprises promoted by the firm of Allason & Company.[8]

*The Journal and Letters of Philip Vickers Fithian, 1767-1774,* give a vivid picture of the life in the Tidewater and the back country of Virginia prior to the Revolutionary War.[9]

John Harrower left his *Diary,* giving one of the best accounts of the life and times of the immediate vicinity of Fredericksburg between 1773 and 1776.[10]

*The Present State of Virginia,* written by Hugh Jones and published in 1724, ranks with Robert Beverley's *History of the Present State of Virginia.*

Dr. Thomas Walker and Christopher Gist left important historical journals, titled *First Explorations of Kentucky, Journals of Dr. Thomas Walker, 1750, and Christopher Gist, 1751.*[11] Dr. Walker was a Fredericksburg physician, while Gist had served as George Washington's personal guide on his trip to Ft. Duquesne in 1753. The two were employed by the Ohio and Loyal Companies. Dr. Walker's geographical and topographical data was the basis for John Mitchell Map of 1755 and served historians and map makers of later days. His exploration of Kentucky and Tennessee preceded Daniel Boone by twenty years. He gave the name of Cumberland to that southwest mountain, river and gap.

*The Letters of Lord Fairfax Relating to the Dispute over the Boundary of the Northern Neck, 1739-1745,*[12] are important historical data on the early settlements of the upper Rappahannock Valley.

Originally from Fredericksburg, Thomas Bullitt wrote "The Journal of Colonel Thomas Bullitt and Map of His Travels."[13] He was one of the early explorers and surveyors of the Ohio and Kentucky territories and his notes and maps are considered of great historical value.

Francis T. Brooke wrote *Narrative of My Life,* which gives interesting information on the early history of Fredericksburg, its neighborhood and the people.

Rev. William Douglas, headmaster of the Ducking Hole School, and teacher of Thomas Jefferson, wrote an *English Book of Common Prayer, Sacramental Dictionary* and a *Volume of Manuscript Sermons.*

There are "The Dixon Papers," the "Force Collection," the "Chatham Papers" and the "Letters of the Committees of Correspondence." Also "Letters of Robert Carter of 'Nomini Hall'"; "Papers of the James Ritchie & Co.," the "Hugh Mercer Papers," the "Vestry Books of St. George Church," "Minute Books of the Masonic Lodge of Fredericksburg" and numerous others showing the volume of literary materials produced by the men of the Rappahannock Valley.

The "Papers of George Rogers Clark" and the "Papers of the Meriwether Lewis and William Clark's Expedition" have a significant place in the American history. The Clark brothers were born in Caroline County while Lewis was a kinsman of Fielding Lewis and George Washington. All three played a major role in the opening of the West across the Rockies to the Pacific.

The greatest exponent of Jeffersonian philosophy was John Taylor, of "Hazelwood," Caroline County. His writings have influenced the political and social philosophy of later historians in greater degree than that of any other one writer. Historian Charles Beard observes that Taylor's *An Inquiry into the Principles and Policy of the Government of the United States* "deserves to rank among the two or three really great historic contributions to political science which have been produced in the United States."[14]

John Clayton and John Mitchell were two able scientists of world recognition. Their writings had a profound influence on the scientific and political thought of their day and later history.

Clayton was a botanist who came to Virginia in 1705 and settled in Gloucester County. He spent most of his time gathering and studying botanical specimens and working in his experimental botanical garden and herbarium. He corresponded extensively with Gronovius, Linnaeus, Alexander Coldren, Peter Kalm, Peter Collison, John Bartram, and others. His chief publications include *Observations on Virginia Flora, Flora Virginica,* and *A Collection of All the Acts of the Assembly of Virginia, 1661-1732.*

John Mitchell came to Virginia around 1721 or 1725 and settled in Middlesex County. He was a physician, botanist, traveler, author and map-maker. His writings contain observation and comments on botany, zoology, electricity, medicine, agriculture and cartography. He collected native plants. Some of his works are the Map of the British and French Dominions in North America, published in 1755, and considered the most important historic map in the American history; *The Contest in America between Great Britain and France; The Present State of Great Britain in North America* and *A New Complete History of America.* He achieved fame for treating yellow fever by a method which was followed by Dr. Benjamin Rush of Philadelphia, considered the most distinguished doctor in the colonies.

Other writings include Orderly Books and Military Records of men like George Washington, George Weedon, Gustavus B. Wallace, Thomas Posey, William Woodford, Oliver Towles, George Stubblefield, Hugh Mercer, George Baylor; and the naval records of John Paul Jones, Christopher Robinson, Captain Hudson Muse, George Brent and Charles Neilson.

There are voluminous collections of papers and writings of George Washington, James Madison, James Monroe, George Mason, John Marshall, and Thomas Jefferson. All these, but Jefferson, belonged to the Rappahannock Valley and were world personalities in their day. Washington alone belongs among the best journalists and men of letters of his day. His *State Papers, General Orders, Letters, Journals, Diaries* and other writings belong to the history of America.

Out of the seventy-five names listed in Tyler's *Cyclopedia of Virginia Biography*[15] under the heading "Fathers of the Revolution," a score were from the Rappahannock Valley. Of the eleven members from Virginia who were elected to the American Philosophical Society[16] between 1769 and 1785, ten were from the Rappahannock neighborhood. These ten included Dr. Arthur Lee, Col. Francis Lee, Dr. Hugh Mercer, Dr. Thomas Walker, Col. Landon Carter, Dr. Walter Jones, Dr. James McClury, Rev. James Madison, George Washington, Hon. James Madison and Hon. Mann Page, of "Mansfield Hall."

## NOTES

1. Moses Coit Tyler, *History of American Literature* (New York: Putnam, 1878).

2. Alvord & Bidgood, *op. cit.*, pp. 131-71.

3. Pub. in the *Virginia Magazine of History and Biography* I, 17-53, 105-26, 253-91, 391-410. Originals in the Virginia Historical Society, Richmond, Virginia.

4. Copy of the essay and map is in the Library of Congress, Manuscript Division, Public Records Office, British Transcripts, No. 1310.

5. *The Official Letters of Alexander Spotswood,* ed. by R. A. Brock (Richmond: The Society, 1882-85); the original Letters are in the Virginia Historical Society, Richmond, Virginia; the Sainsburg Abstracts of the Letters are in the Virginia State Library, Richmond, Virginia.

6. In the Manuscript Division of the Library of Congress, Washington, D. C.

7. The *Diary* has been published in the *William and Mary Quarterly,* Vol. XX.

8. The Allason Papers consisting of Letter Books, vols. I, II; Invoice Books. Order Books, Account Books, have not been edited. The originals are in the State Library, Richmond, Va.

9. *The Journal and Letters of Philip Vickers Fithian, 1767-1774,* edited by Hunter D. Farish, also by John R. Williams.

10. A copy of *Diary* is in the Library of Congress, Washington, D. C.; it has been reprinted in the *American Historical Review,* VI, No. 1, October, 1900.

11. *Filson Club Publications* (Louisville, Ky.: Morton, 1884-193-), No. 13.

12. In the Library of Congress, Washington, D. C.

13. Reproduced in the *Calendar of Virginia State Papers,* Vol. I.

14. *Dictionary of American Biography,* XVIII, 332.

15. Lyon A. Tyler, *Cyclopedia of Virginia Biography* (New York: Lewis, 1915), for much of the information given concerning persons listed.

16. Proceedings of the American Philosophical Society (Philadelphia: The Society, 1840-1911), I, p. XXII.

## 12

### DOCTORS IN COLONIAL FREDERICKSBURG

Biographies of the doctors listed here reveal not only that each was a scientist specializing in treating the ailing, but many were scholars, writers, statesmen, soldiers and participants in community and civic affairs. A number of them distinguished themselves in the field of medicine, pioneering in discovering ways of treating various maladies of the human body. Others distinguished themselves in helping to develop economically, socially, and politically Fredericksburg neighborhood and the western frontier.

There were at least thirty-seven practicing physicians in Fredericksburg between 1740 and 1785. Only Williamsburg had a comparable number, with about thirty-five during this period,[1] while Norfolk had twenty-seven, Alexandria twenty, Petersburg twenty-one and Richmond thirty. Half of Richmond's physicians came there after the end of the Revolutionary War.

The list of the distinguished physicians and scientists of colonial Fredericksburg includes Dr. Lawrence Brooke, Dr. Wm. Baynham, Dr. James Carmichael, Dr. Charles Landon Carter, Dr. Ewen Clements, Dr. Charles Dick, Dr. John Edwards, Dr. David Forbes, Dr. George French, Dr. Gills, Dr. Robert Halkerston, Dr. Elisha Hall, Dr. John Hall, Dr. Hand, Dr. Henry Heath, Dr. Hy Heath, Dr. Edward Jones, Dr. John Julian, Dr. David Corbin Ker, Dr. John Lewis, Dr. Wm. Lynn, Dr. Hugh Mercer, Dr. Paul Micou, Dr. George Mitchell, Dr. Charles Mortimer, Dr. Nordon, Dr. Wm. F. Patton, Dr. Thomas Powell, Dr. Lawrence Rose, Dr. James Henry Roy, Dr. Adam Stephens, Dr. John Sutherland, Dr. John Tennant,

Dr. Thomas Walker, Dr. Gustavus Brown Wallace, Dr. Wm. Waller, and Dr. Robert Wellford. All but one or two of these lived and/or practiced in this port on the Rappahannock prior to and during the Revolution.

The outstanding achievements of some of the physicians of this area are enumerated here to show that each was a leader in his profession and in the community.

Dr. Lawrence Brooke, of "Smithfield Hall," four miles below Fredericksburg, came from a distinguished family whose brother, Robert, was governor of Virginia, and Francis T. a prominent lawyer. Educated at the University of Edinburgh and the University of Paris, he served as surgeon on the *Ranger* and the *Bon Homme Richard,* commanded by John Paul Jones. He moved to Fredericksburg in 1783 and practiced there until his death in 1803. He was among the first physicians, if not the first, to perform trephine operations.

Dr. William Bynham attended the Thomas' Hospital in London, where he distinguished himself as an outstanding anatomist. Returning to Virginia, he settled in Essex County and later came to Fredericksburg. Credited with performing the first operation for extra-uterine pregnancy, Dr. Bynham won reputation in surgery, specializing in operations for stone, cataract and extra-uterine conception.

Dr. James Carmichael came to Fredericksburg from Scotland in the 1780's and was the first of a long line of physicians of his family in the Rappahannock Valley. He won reputation for his service in the treatment of yellow fever in the epidemic of 1803.

Dr. Charles Landon Carter, descendant of Robert ("King") Carter and son-in-law of Fielding Lewis, studied medicine at the College of Philadelphia. He served as mayor of Fredericksburg and rendered valuable service in the yellow fever epidemic of 1803.

Dr. Ewen Clements was a public-spirited citizen of Fredericksburg, in which he held many public offices. He was one of the Commissioners for the Manufactory of Arms established in 1775 to make arms for the Continental Army. He was also a trustee of the town.

Dr. David Forbes came to America in 1774, settling first at Dumfries and later removing to Fredericksburg, where he continued to practice medicine. His wife was the Lady Margaret Sterling, of Edinburgh, of the famous line of the Lords of Herbertshire, Scotland.

Dr. George French came from Scotland and settled in Fredericksburg, where he served as mayor of the town, rendered service in the yellow fever epidemic of 1803, and was in partnership with Wm. Drummond, a leading merchant and businessman of the town. He was a surgeon in the Revolutionary War.

Dr. Elisha Hall was one of Mary Washington's physicians, member of the Town Council and of the Masonic Lodge.

A brother of Dr. Elisha Hall, Dr. John Hall, was a surgeon on George Washington's staff, and was owner of considerable property in Fredericksburg.

Dr. John Julian, of Norfolk, settled in Fredericksburg in 1751 and became a partner of Hugh Mercer in the apothecary business from 1772 to 1776; he served as surgeon in the Continental Army, was director of the Public Hospital at Fredericksburg, and served as attendant surgeon with Dr. Charles Mortimer at the Alum Spring Hospital during the Revolution.

Dr. David Corbin Ker was a graduate of Edinburgh University; was attendant at Sligo Hospital in 1790; was mayor of Fredericksburg; and, with George Washington, James Mercer and others, a contributor to a fund started in 1759 to encourage wine and silk industries in the Rappahannock Valley.

Dr. John Lewis assisted with the Public Gunnery and rendered medical service during the war.

Dr. William Lynn came to Fredericksburg from Scotland in 1743 and was one of the early "doctors of physics" here. In 1746 he conducted an apothecary shop in the town; he served as captain and major of Spotsylvania County Independent Company of Foot, and dealt extensively in lands to the West.

Dr. Hugh Mercer was a distinguished physician and a general in the Revolutionary War who was killed in the battle of Princeton in 1777. He established an Apothecary Shop in Fredericksburg which is one of the oldest in America and is still standing. He was one of the physicians of the Washington family.

Serving as the first mayor of Fredericksburg after its incorporation in 1782, Dr. Charles Mortimer was a prominent doctor and a man of affairs in the town. He rendered valuable service during the Revolution and is said to have founded and conducted at his own expense a hospital for the sick and wounded soldiers quartered in Fredericksburg during the War. He was one of Mary Washington's physicians, was engaged in extensive trade, owned a fleet of ships, and became a wealthy man of the town. He was one of the signers of the Westmoreland Resolutions of 1766.

A descendant of Sir William Alexander, Earl of Stirling, who once held a grant to the whole of Canada, Dr. James Henry Roy was an outstanding doctor of Fredericksburg, where he owned a drug store.

Dr. John Tennant came to Virginia about 1725, first settling in Spotsylvania County and later removing to Fredericksburg. He wrote one of the earliest known treatises on pleurisy, published in 1735 and entitled, *Essay on Pleurisy*. After describing his experience in treating the disease with the use of rattlesnake root, a remedy which he learned from the Indians, Dr. Tennant was awarded 100 pounds by the House of Burgesses for his discovery. He wrote numerous broadsides on medical subjects.

Other doctors who served their community in Fredericksburg through practice of medicine and in civic affairs were John Edwards, Robert Halkerston, Hand, Henry Heath, Edward Jones, Thomas Powell, Adam Stephens, John Sutherland, William Waller, Gills, Hy Heath, George Mitchell, William Patton, Nordon and Lawrence Rose.

Dr. Thomas Walker was an outstanding physician, soldier, explorer and scientist who was a native of King and Queen County but established his home and practice in Fredericksburg. Credited with introducing the cultivation of the pippin variety of apples in Virginia, Dr. Walker was not only an eminent doctor and surgeon but owned and operated a store which conducted an extensive export-import trade, and took an active part in the exploring and acquiring lands in the West. He explored the vast grants of the Loyal Company and the Ohio Company in western parts of Virginia, Kentucky and Ohio in 1749. A year later he explored the wilderness of Kentucky and Tennessee, preceding Daniel Boone by nearly a score of years. He gave the name to Cumberland gap, river and mountains and made valuable observations on the animal and plant life and the mineral resources of the regions he explored. His recorded observations contained in the *Journals* were the principal source of information of Dr. John Mitchell's Map of 1755, which is considered the "most historic map of America."[2] His influence was great in the formulation of the western land policies of America.

Dr. Gustavus Brown Wallace was born at "Ellerslie" in Stafford County, and was a member of a prominent family whose descendants served the nation in numerous capacities. He was a general in the American Revolution.

Dr. Robert Wellford came from England in 1776 as a surgeon with the British forces under Gates in Philadelphia. He resigned as surgeon-in-charge of the American prisoners in Philadelphia in 1778 and established private practice in that city. In 1781 he came to Fredericksburg, where he practiced medicine and became one of its leading citizens.

## NOTES

1.  W. B. Blanton, *Medicine of Virginia in the 18th Century* (Richmond: Garrett & Massie, 1931), I, 339-67.
2.  *Dictionary of American Biography*, XIII, 51.
3.  Virginia Gazette, April 22, 1773.
4.  Wm. Terrell Lewis, Genealogy of the Lewis Family.
5.  Horace Edwin Hayden, Virginia Genealogies.

# ~∞ *13* ∞~

## The Role of The Fredericksburg Neighborhood in The Westward Movement

The second phase of the western migration of Germanic peoples began with the settlement of Jamestown and continued up the rivers along the Atlantic seaboard from Massachusetts to Georgia, between 1607 and 1733. The crossing of the Appalachian barrier from Virginia, particularly from the Rappahannock Valley in a northwesterly direction, started about 1716 with Spotswood's transmontane expedition which resulted in the discovery of the passes through "the Great Mountains."[1]

The vast hinterland and the great West played the most significant role in the life of Falmouth and Fredericksburg. From them these towns drew most of their sustenance and their prosperity. Not only did the West hold the key to their growth, but it largely determined their role in colonial history.

The westward movement attracted much of the thought and life of the inhabitants of the Fredericksburg region. In a very real sense it determined the course of action of individuals and community. This brief survey is an attempt to aid the reader in visualizing the concern and understanding of the part played by the citizens of Falmouth and Fredericksburg and adjacent neighborhood in initiating, promoting and culminating the work of the greatest force in American history: the Westward Movement.

Falmouth and Fredericksburg were among the principal colonial localities from which the first westward treks originated. They served as easy gateways through which the interior of the

# MILEAGE TABLE INSET ON THE JEFFERSON-FRY MAP OF 1751*

**From Williamsburg**

To: Delawar . . . . . . . . . 30 N.W.
Newcastle . . . . . . . . 50 N.W.
Hobs Hole . . . . . . . 67½ N.W.
Fredericksburg . . . . . 107½ N.W.
Lord Fairfax . . . . . . 186 N.W.
Winchester . . . . . . . 194 N.W.
Will's Creek . . . . . . 281 N.W.
Fort Necessity in the Great Meadow . . . . 346 N.W.
Fort du Quesne at the Conflux of the Monongahela and Ohio Rivers . . . . . . . . . 391 N.W.

**The Road from Fredericksburg**

To: Lord Fairfax . . . . . . . 76 N.W.
Winchester . . . . . . . 84 N.W.
Will's Creek . . . . . . 171 N.W.
Fort Necessity . . . . . 238 N.W.
Fort du Quesne on the Ohio . . . . . . . . 281 N.W.

**From Alexandria**

To: Lord Fairfax . . . . . . . 78 W.
Winchester . . . . . . . 86 W.
Will's Creek . . . . . . 175 N.W.
Fort Necessity in the Great Meadow . . . . 238 N.W.
Fort du Quesne at the Conflux of the Monongahela and Ohio Rivers . . . . . . . 285 N.W.

* It should be called to the attention of the reader that the map emphasizes the point that at that date "all roads [from Virginia] led to the West" via Fredericksburg, thence northwestward across the Blue Ridge to Winchester (where the supplementary road from Alexandria connects with the Road from Williamsburg.) there, also, the Road from Williamsburg intersects with the Great Wagon Road from Philadelphia down the Shenandoah Valley to Yadkin River in North Carolina; from Winchester the Williamsburg Road continues northwestward to Fort Necessity in the Great Meadow, thence to the Monongahela and down that river to Fort du Quesne (Pittsburgh) on the Ohio River.

country was reached from the Chesapeake Bay region. Most of the definitely organized early migrations to the West passed through these two towns.

The earliest legislative act regarding western exploration was enacted in 1642 "to encourage discoveries to the westward and southward."[2]

Sir William Berkeley took an active part in stimulating interest in the West. In 1669 he employed John Lederer, a German explorer and traveler, to discover a passage through the mountains. Lederer made three expeditions: the first was up the York River to the top of the Blue Ridge Mountains; the second was up the James River; and the third, begun in August, 1670, took him up the Rappahannock River to its source in the Blue Ridge Mountains. This third exploration took Lederer over the very sites now occupied by Falmouth and Fredericksburg. The account of his discoveries constitute the first scientific report made on the geology, botany, animals, trees and the native tribes of Indians of the region traversed.

Lederer's report, published as *The Discoveries of John Lederer,* had great influence on the thinking of leaders in the seventeenth century and exerted considerable weight on the efforts to explore and settle the territory beyond the great mountains of Virginia.

Upon reaching the summit of the Blue Ridge Mountains, Lederer conjectured concerning the land beyond the Appalachians:

> They are certainly in great error, who imagine the Continent of North America is but eight or ten days journey over from the Atlantic to the Indian Ocean . . . . . Yet I am far from believing with some, that such great and Navigable Rivers are to be found on the other side of the Apalataeans falling into the Indian Ocean, as those which run from them to the Eastward . . . . .[3]

Cadwallader Jones explored the upper regions of the Rappahannock near the close of the seventeenth century. His Essay and Map, which he addressed to the Lords of Trade in 1698/9, stimulated further interest in the West. Jones urged that adventurers be encouraged to trade with the Indians in the West. He declared that:

At the Westermost end . . . . are settled two great Nations [of Indians][2] and in between them is a narrow Straight, and a Passage from the upper Lake through which Every year passes 200 Canoes to Trade at Mount Reall, Quebec, and Issonnon-tavans that manage the trade which is conveyed to Ffourt Albay and Pennsylvania; there furrs so rich cannot be rationally val-ued less than one hundred pounds each Canoo amounts to ye Sum of twenty Thousand pounds Sterl.

There is computed in this country of Louisiana two hun-dred Nations which by the Conveyance from Lake to Lake down to Quebecke do yearly Trade though it is neare three thousand Miles . . . . .

In three yeares after the Trade is securely settled the value of furrs yearly frome hence return'd may be with much modesty Computed at one hundred Thousand pounds Sterl.

In five years according to the Law now Established as to ye. Indian Trade the Colledge would be Saluted w.th near the Sum of two thousand pounds Sterl. per year and all waies Increasing.

Moreover a Signall and prodigious advantage would appear to all this country for to Settle this Trade by a Company to Secure and propigate their Interest. It is manifestly requisite that they must Erect two fforts at Least one on this side the Mountaine Caucawsus, the other on Loussianna Side.[4]

Thus Cadwallader Jones anticipated the organization of the Ohio Company by more than fifty years. His writings and those of Lederer and Spotswood explain, in part, the reason for the Jefferson-Fry Map of 1751 containing a mileage chart of the dis-tances from Williamsburg to "Ft. du Quesne at the Conflux of the Monongahela and Ohio River."[5]

The road to the West described by Jefferson and Fry in their map of Virginia passed through Fredericksburg, thence through Ashby's Gap to Winchester, and thence to Fort Duquesne. No roads are shown leading west up the James or York Rivers and thence to the back country. The only road to the West is the northwest trail from Williamsburg through Fredericksburg, Winchester, thence to the Ohio.

This, then, was the main direction of the first great waves of westward migration, a fact evidenced further by the early patents to land in the Shenandoah Valley, Augusta County, the Western parts of Virginia, Kentucky, and the Ohio countries, obtained almost entirely by land speculators and home seekers from the Rappahannock Valley. It was the planters, merchants, lawyers, doctors and other groups residing in the Rappahannock and the South Potomac areas who organized and promoted the Western land schemes joined by a few promoters from the James and York river valleys.

The westward movement first took definite shape with Governor Alexander Spotswood, who established his home at Germanna after his retirement as Governor of Virginia. He settled a colony of Germans here in 1714, constituting a new frontier outpost which was the farther west than any yet established by the American colonists. Moving gradually westward this movement soon linked up with or intersected the great German wave of migration moving slowly down the Shenandoah Valley from Pennsylvania.

But with other early explorers, Spotswood labored under a misconception regarding the vastness of the western country. After his transmontane trip in 1716, he wrote to the English Board of Trade, on August 14, 1718, declaring:

The Chief Aim of my Expedition over the great Mountain in 1716, was to satisfy my Self Whether it was practicable to come at the Lakes. Having on that occasion found an easy passage over the great Ridge of Mountains w'ch before were judged unpassable, I also discivered, by the pass where I was it is but three Days' March to a great Nation of Indians living on a River w'ch discharges itself in the Lake Erie; That from ye Western side of one of the small Mountains, w'ch I saw, that Lake is very visible, and cannot, therefore, be above five days' March from the pass aforementioned, and that the way thither is also very practicable, the Mountains to the Westward of the Great Ridge being smaller than those on the Eastern Side, w'ch shows how easy a Matter it is to gain possession of those lakes.[6]

The erroneous geographical ideas entertained by these early explorers of the West may have been fortunate, for this belief encouraged further efforts to reach the Great Lakes by this passage and to tie the vast Ohio country with the Rappahannock Valley and the East. Spotswood had proposed just such a scheme in his letter of August 14, 1718. He urged that "Settlements [be made] on ye Lakes, and at the same time possess ourselves of those passes of the Great Mountains w'ch are necessary to preserve a Communication w'th such Settlements."[7]

Explaining his scheme for settling the west, he wrote again to the Board of Trade on September 27, 1718:

> Upon reviewing my Letter of the 14th of August, I begg leave to explain that part thereof wherein I say that ye Lake Erie can't be above five days' Journey from the passage over the great Mountains. My meaning is that the distance can't be further than a Man might Travel in five days, supposing that a good Road was made and no Interruption to the Passing the River; but it is probable that the difficultys may be such, in making roads, for a body of men to March in and contriving means for passing the River in the way w'ch running, through a vast Tract of Great Mountains, are lyable to be swell'd upon every Rain, that it may retard such March nearer two Months than five days, tho' the distance be so inconsiderable; but then the nearest way being found, and the Roads made practicable, all future difficultys of keeping a communication w'th the proposed settlement on the Lakes will be removed.[8]

Spotswood may be credited with a real share in initiating the westward migration policy of the nation. It started with his 1716 expedition, which was the first organized effort to extend the frontier line beyond the Appalachian Mountains. The objectives of his transmontane expedition were to check the French in the West; to discover the sources of Virginia rivers; and to establish friendly relations with the Indians to the Westward.

Soon after Spotswood's expedition, a great flood of grants to western lands began. Spotsylvania County was organized soon thereafter, having the Shenandoah River as its western boundary. Colonies of immigrants and parties of Rappahannock families began to push westward. By 1732 they began to move over the mountains into the Shenandoah. By 1734 so many settlers had crossed the Blue

Ridge and established homes west of that range that a new county of Augusta was erected in that year.

This, however, was but an acceleration of the westward movement that started at Jamestown in 1607. Even prior to Lederer's expedition many land patents had been issued to people who attempted settlements in the immediate vicinity of the Falls of the Rappahannock River. Maps[9] of the early colonial period show that the number of plantations established along the Rappahannock were far more numerous than those along either the James or the York rivers. By the time that Falmouth and Fredericksburg were erected in 1727, more than fifty plantations were located along the banks of the Rappahannock. Soon thereafter there began a major speculation in lands beyond the Blue Ridge which constituted the basis for the westward expansion in the upper Rappahannock Valley.

The earliest grant obtained to lands west of the Blue Ridge Mountains was that of Robert Green and William Duff, of Stafford County, and Joist Hite and Robert McKay, partners in business at Falmouth and Fredericksburg, who patented 120,000 acres in the Shenandoah Valley in 1732. The colonies of settlers from the Rappahannock established themselves near the present site of Winchester, Strasburg, Elkton and Staunton. The Germans from Pennsylvania began to enter the Valley after 1730.

The first grant to land in the Shenandoah was followed in rapid succession by numerous patents to western lands. Between 1733 and 1735 "grants were made . . . . of about 300,000 acres of land in that District"[10] (part of the Shenandoah Valley claimed by Lord Fairfax).

A steady stream of immigrants to the West, originating mainly in the Rappahannock Valley, moved into the back country between 1725 and 1740. Organized migration was a principal feature of the century that followed.

The dispute over the boundaries of the Lord Fairfax estate started in 1705, when the Crown disputed the boundaries upon the death of Lord Thomas Fairfax, the Fourth, the father of Lord Thomas Fairfax, the Fifth, of "Greenway Court," who had inherited the 5,282,000-acre estate through his mother, Catherine, the daughter of Lord Culpeper. In 1706 a commission was appointed to determine the boundaries of the estate. The commission, however, reported that it was unable to determine the boundaries. The dispute dragged on until 1733, when Lord Fairfax obtained a restraining order forbidding grants from being made to land in the territory until the matter was settled.

The controversy came to a head in 1735, when grants were being made by the colonial legislature to territory supposed to be parts of the lands belonging to the Fairfax estate, in defiance of orders to the contrary. The decision rendered on the matter in 1745, declared this estate included most of the lower part of the Shenandoah Valley and extended westward to the crest of the Alleghany Mountains—embracing nearly one-fourth of Virginia.

Scores of grants continued to be made by the colonial legislature to lands in the West, regardless whether they involved the western extremities of the Fairfax estate. Most of these patents were obtained by individuals from the Rappahannock Valley. In 1745, John Robinson, of King and Queen County, received a grant of 100,000 acres. Thomas Lee and others were granted 200,000 acres in 1749. In the same year John Lewis and others were granted 800,000 acres. Thomas Lewis, James Maury, Thomas Walker, Nicholas Meriwether, John Willis, and others, received large grants in 1752.[11]

In 1727 Robert Lewis, William Lynn, Robert Brooke, Jr., James Mills, William Lewis and Beverley Robinson petitioned the Virginia Legislature for 50,000 acres of land on Cow Pasture and the James River, now Bath County.[12] Mann Page, of "Rosewell," owned a tract of 8,007 acres near Staunton.[13] William Beverley received a grant of 118,000 acres in 1736 and tried to induce immigrants from Ireland and Scotland and Pennsylvania to settle in the Valley.[14]

Edmund Pendleton was granted in 1756 a tract of land of 3,000 acres in what is now Sullivan County, Tennessee, near Kingsport.[15]

In 1748 the first of the great western land schemes came into existence when the Loyal Company was organized with a grant of 800,000 acres. The Ohio Company was organized in the same year with a grant of 500,000 acres. These lands were in the Ohio and Kentucky regions.

These two companies, and the Mississippi Company, were organized almost exclusively by men of the Rappahannock Valley: George Washington; Lawrence Washington; Augustine Washington; George Mason; John Mercer, of "Marlborough," and his three sons, George, James, and John Francis Mercer; Thomas Lee and Richard Lee, of "Stratford"; Thomas Ludwell Lee; Philip Ludwell Lee; Robert Carter, of "Nomini Hall"; John Tayloe of "Mt. Airy"; Col. William Thornton; Lord Fairfax; Gawin Corbin; Dr. Thomas Walker; John Lewis, and others. To name all the members of the companies is to call the roll, for men of the Rappahannock Valley not only comprised most of the membership but held by far the greater portion of stock, filled all the executive positions and directed the affairs of the schemes.

Dr. Thomas Walker, of Fredericksburg, was delegated by the Loyal Company to explore its 800,000-acre grant. George Rogers Clark was sent as a special agent of the Ohio Company to explore and survey its grant in Ohio. The meetings of the latter company were held at "Marlborough," home of the Mercers.[16]

The Mississippi Company was organized at a meeting held in the Stafford Courthouse in 1763. Its organizers were Francis Lightfoot Lee, Richard Henry Lee, Arthur Lee, and the Washingtons. Its purpose was to occupy southern Illinois, Indiana and western Kentucky. The petitioners asked for a grant of 2,500,000 acres. This project was never consumated, but the effort indicates the extent of interest in the West shown by the planters and merchants of the Fredericksburg area.

In addition to the above schemes, the following proposals for colonizing the West were promoted or shared in by the leaders from the Fredericksburg neighborhood:

Westsylvania, soon after 1750.

Franklin's Plan and Pownall's Proposition, 1754.

Hazard's Plan, 1755.

Charlotiana Scheme and the New Wales Colony, 1763.

Phineas Lyman Plan and the Illinois Scheme, 1766.

Ampherst-Detroit Plan, 1767.

Indiana Company, 1768.

Vandalia Scheme, 1769.

Transylvania Scheme, 1775.

Soon after the end of the Revolutionary War, several other projects involving western lands were promulgated. These were the Georgia Company, the Georgia-Mississippi Company, the Tennessee Company, the Upper Mississippi Company, and others.

While all these schemes were not started by Virginians, men of the Rappahannock Valley did take a lead in organizing the first companies promoting westward movement of colonists.

When the tide of the westward movement began, thousands of settlers did not wait for patents to be granted them. It is estimated that 100,000 squatters settled on western lands by 1726, and "of the 670,000 acres occupied between 1732 and 1740, it is estimated that 400,000 acres were settled without grants."[17]

During this period many large tracts were granted to speculators like the Beverleys, the Carters, Lord Fairfax, the Lees, the Lewises, Washingtons, and others, whose holdings stimulated greatly the movement of peoples to these western regions from the Rappahannock. The large speculators encouraged people to emigrate from Europe and settle on these lands. They also urged Rappahannock Valley citizens to go west to establish homes.

The trek from the Fredericksburg area was in full swing by 1750. At about this time the first large wave of people from Pennsylvania began entering the Shenandoah Valley. This became especially heavy in the periods 1769-1773, 1778-1779, and 1780-1781. These two waves met, crossed, or merged in the Shenandoah, continuing to move ever westward. The vanguards of these streams of pioneers were men and women who braved the wilderness as explorers, traders, speculators and homemakers. They poured into the new territory between 1716 and 1750. Most of these people had either debarked at Fredericksburg or Falmouth, or had removed from this section to seek fortunes beyond the mountains.

The size of these migrating groups grew tremendously large during the two decades before and after the Revolutionary War. While visiting the colonies in 1796, one European observer noted that "In the course of last year upwards of 4,000 persons passed through the place Winchester going to Tennessee and Kentucky."[18]

This is an average of nearly one hundred persons a week or more than 300 a month passing through a single town. Other contemporary sources mentioned "companies of 500 persons," or "1500 persons" moving in a unit going west. Records in the numerous offices of the Rappahannock area show comparable statistics. People were migrating west by whole families, by groups of kindred families, and by colonies.

The impact of these great masses upon the westward movement, upon the history of the West, and upon the particular sections of country to which they migrated can only be surmised. The people from the Rappahannock Valley comprised a large element in the population of the Northwest Territory and of the states which were carved out of it; of Kentucky and Tennessee; and of the states west of the Mississippi. Many of the governors, members of the state legislature, congressmen and senators, judges, ministers, educators, lawyers and other professional men and tradesmen who became prominent in these localities were originally from the Fredericksburg area or were descendants of families of this section of Virginia. Since most of the Kentucky and Ohio country remained a segment and an integral part of Virginia until after 1787, it was logical that the representatives from these areas in colonial legislatures and governors of new states formed should be either Virginians or their descendants.

Dr. Thomas Walker and George Rogers Clark exerted powerful influence on the early policies of Virginia concerning the West. George Washington, George Mason, the Lees, Thomas Jefferson, Patrick Henry, James Madison—all were moving spirits in determining the final policies toward the western territories. Joseph Jones perhaps exerted the greatest single influence in the Virginia legislature in securing the state's relinquishments to her western land claims, an act which determined the first territorial policy of the United States.[19]

It was perhaps Captain John Smith who first pierced the primordial wilderness surrounding the falls of the Rappahannock River; Governor Spotswood was the first to open the way across the Appalachians; George Rogers Clark was the first to extend the frontier to the Mississippi and the Great Lakes; and William Clark and Meriwether Lewis were the first to cross the Rockies and the Sierras and end the trail at the Pacific, thus ending the story of the second phase of the western migration of Germanic peoples started at Jamestown in the seventeenth century.

Over these routes the pioneers from the Rappahannock went West. Many immigrants whose port of debarkation or whose early American home was in or near Fredericksburg formed, initiated and/or joined in some of these treks.

These pioneers moved from the Fredericksburg area along the three trails which crossed the Blue Ridge Mountains at Ashby's Gap, Swift Run Gap, and Rock Creek Gap, the most direct and convenient passes across the mountains into the Shenandoah Valley and beyond. Thence continuing their course westward, they again divided into three great streams: one going northwestward toward the Monongahela and the Ohio; a second going down the Kanawha or New River to the Ohio; and a third moving southwesterly down the Clinch and Holston Rivers into Tennessee and through the Cumberland Gap into the Kentucky and Ohio countries. Pushing on in successive waves they crossed the Allegheny, the Blue Ridge, and the Cumberland mountains. These pioneers penetrated the Ohio's forests on foot or floated down the beautiful river on rafts or flat boats. They crossed the Scioto, the Wabash, and continued their course down the Ohio, the Cumberland, and the Tennessee rivers to the Mississippi. Up the Red River, the Arkansas, the White, the Missouri, and the Mississippi rivers the procession advanced across the plains of Texas on to the far southwest, Arizona, New Mexico, and California; or through Arkansas swamps and forests out on to the Oklahoma prairies; or up the Missouri or Mississippi through the bottom lands, the rolling country, or the wide plains of Missouri, Kansas, Nebraska, Minnesota, the Dakotas, thence across the Rockies into Utah, Nevada, Montana, Oregon, and Washington to the Pacific.

Descendants of the early families or immigrants to the Rappahannock Valley have gone into every state of the Union over some of these exact paths and have helped to build the state and the nation of which they became a part. They invested toil, hope and blood in conquering the wilderness, the prairie, the valley, the mountain and the plain. They formed the woof and warp of a garment of many colors, races, nationalities, and strains. Explorers, surveyors, travelers, hunters, traders, trappers, fishermen, woodsmen, wagoners, boatmen, sawmillmen, loggers, raftsmen, axmen, soldiers, scouts, interpreters, guides, speculators, agents, settlers, cattlemen, herdsmen, home-builders, housewives, domestics, servants, slaves, doctors and ministers composed the migrants. These constituted the pioneers of the new world. They became the nation's farmers, ranchmen, doctors, preachers, lawyers, teachers, fishermen, merchants, manufacturers, artisans, miners, grocers, bankers, factory workers, producers, processers, distributors, railroadmen, shippers, seamen, soldiers, painters, artists, authors, poets, musicians, journalists, statesmen, scientists, students, actors, and homemakers.

## NOTES

1. Spotswood, *op. cit.*, II, 304.
2. Hening, *op. cit.*, I, 262.
3. Lederer, *op. cit.*, p. 170.
4. Cadwallader Jones, "Essay about the Indian Trade with a MS Map of plot of Louisiana," copy in MS Div., Lib. of Congress, Pub. Record Office, Colonial Office, British Transcripts, No. 1310.
5. *Ibid.*
6. Spotswood, *op. cit.*, III, 731; Transcripts in the Va. State Library, Richmond, Sainsburg Abstracts; Also in R. A. Brock, *Official Letters of Alexander Spotswood* (Richmond: Va. Hist. Soc., 1882-5), II, 286-98.
7. *Ibid.*, also Brock, *op. cit.*
8. Spotswood, *op. cit.*, II, 304.
9. Augustine Herman Map of Va. and Md., 1673; the Herman Moll Map of Va. and Md., 1729; the John Warner Map of the Northern Neck, 1737; Peter Jefferson and Robert Brooks Map of the Northern Neck, 1747; Mayo Map of 1737; Map of Thornton May, Alias Rappidan, 1742; all are in the Map Division, Library of Congress.
10. Lord Fairfax, Letters, Fairfax vs Hite, Papers Relating to the Report of the Board of Trade.
11. Thomas P. Abernethy, *Western Lands and the American Revolution* (New York & London: D. Appleton-Cen., 1937), p. 7.
12. *Calendar of Va. State Papers* and Other Manuscripts (Richmond: State Printing, 1875-1885), I, 214.
13. Hening, *op. cit.*, V, 277-84.
14. *William and Mary Quarterly*, III, 226.

15.   James Getty McConnell Ramsey, *The Annals of Tennessee* (Philadelphia: Lippincott, 1853), p. 66.

16.   *Maryland Gazette*, May 19, 1763.

17.   Turner, *op. cit.*, p. 101.

18.   The Duke of La Rochefoucauld-Liancourt, *Travels through the U. S. of North America, 1795-7* (London, 1800), p. 117.

19.   Abernethy, *op. cit.*, pp. 243-44, 272; *Letters of Joseph Jones*, ed. by Worthington C. Ford (Washington: Dept. of State, 1889), pp. 15-16; Jefferson MSS. in Lib. of Cong., Letter of John Walker to Jefferson, July 11, 1780; W. C. Rives, *James Madison* (Boston: Little, Brown, 1859-68), I, 261-62.

## FREDERICKSBURG NEIGHBORHOOD IN THE REVOLUTION

Perhaps the greatest contribution which the Fredericksburg neighborhood made to American history and to posterity may be told by describing the role the people of this vicinity played in creating and formulating the ideals and philosophies which produced the American Revolution; by telling something of the part the community played in that struggle; and by indicating the importance of its leaders in winning independence and in establishing the Republic.

The Fredericksburg neighborhood was the moving spirit or mainspring of the Revolution. The leaders of this district took a major part in initiating the movement for independence. They were in the forefront of that movement. John Fiske in *The American Revolution* says that "Formal defiance came first from Virginia."[1] The statement is made in reference to the Parson's Case of 1763, in which Patrick Henry and Rev. James Maury were prosecutor and defendant, and both were prominently connected with Fredericksburg. Outside Williamsburg, and in several respects not excepting Williamsburg, the Fredericksburg neighborhood served as the hub of the Revolution in Virginia.

The leaders of this section drew up the famous Leedstown or Westmoreland Resolutions in protest to the Stamp Act of 1765. The drafting of the Resolutions took place at Leedstown in Westmoreland County, a few miles below Fredericksburg, February 27, 1766. They were perhaps written by Richard Henry Lee. "They assert in bold language the rights essential to CIVIL LIBERTY

and constitute the first formal defiance subsequently maintained
by the Revolution."[2]

The Westmoreland Resolutions were signed by one hundred
and fourteen Northern Neck Virginians, at least ten or twelve of
whom were from the town of Fredericksburg proper, namely, Lewis
Willis, Charles Washington, Samuel Washington, Rev. Rodman
Kenner, Samuel Selden, Francis Thornton, Jr., Dr. Charles Mortimer, Richard Mitchell, William Garrison, John Richards and
Thomas Ludwell Lee.

George Washington and George Mason took the lead in oppos-
ing British trade restrictions and in favoring the non-importation
agreement.[3] The agreement received the support of Richard Henry
Lee, Patrick Henry, and Thomas Jefferson in the House of Burgesses. The plan, proposed at a private body of members of the
House of Burgesses, was presented by George Washington, and
embodied the essentials of a draft made by George Mason, May 18,
1769.[4]

The merchants and planters of the Fredericksburg vicinity gave
generous support to the Continental Association formed in 1774
and ratified in 1775, despite the opposition and unsympathetic attitude of a few Scotch merchants within the section.

Efforts of this vicinity to raise funds for Boston after the famous
"Tea Party" resulted in most favorable returns from public sale
of cargoes of goods in their behalf. The Andrew Woodrow Cargo
in King George County, for example, netted a profit of £ 19.11s.[5]

Resolutions protesting the tea tax and other restrictions, were
drawn up by various bodies in the town, and in the counties and
towns adjacent to Fredericksburg. Spotsylvania County drew up
such resolutions at a meeting held June 24, 1774.[6] Prince William
County had formulated resolutions to this effect at a meeting held
at Dumfries on June 6, 1774; Westmoreland on June 22; and Stafford County held a meeting for this purpose in the early part of July;
and Caroline on July 14, 1774.[7] Other counties and towns did likewise.

Fredericksburg had initiated this movement. For on Wednesday,
June 1, 1774, "At a Meeting of the Inhabitants of Fredericksburg
. . . . at the Town House,"[8] resolutions were drafted expressing

sympathy for the people of Boston "in the Hostile Invasion of the rights and liberties of the town of Boston."[9] The Association appointed a Committee of Correspondence consisting of:

> Fielding Lewis, Charles Dick, Charles Mortimer, James Mercer, Charles Washington, William Woodford, James Duncanson, William Porter, George Thornton, and Charles Yates to constitute a Committee to correspond with the neighboring towns and counties for the purpose of communicating to each other in the most speedy manner, their sentiments on this present interesting, alarming situation of America.[10]

This was nearly a week earlier than the first of the meetings cited above and shows the effectiveness of the work of the Fredericksburg Committee.

The meetings had been called and resolutions drafted in response to requests of the Fredericksburg Committee. The other towns and counties besides those named drew up similar protests at the suggestion of the Fredericksburg Committee of Correspondence.

The Virginia protest against the Boston Tea Act, made May 27, 1774, contains a most significant statement which reads as follows:

> It is further our opinion, that as Tea on its importation into America, is charged with a duty, imposed by parliament for the purpose of raising a revenue, without the consent of the people . . . . we are further clearly of opinion that an attack, made on one of our sister colonies . . . . is an attack made on all British America.[11]

The expression used in these Resolutions to the effect that "Tea . . . . is charged with a duty, imposed by parliament . . . . without the consent of the people," became the basis for the popular slogan and war-cry of the Revolution: TAXATION WITHOUT REPRESENTATION. This may well identify the origin of the slogan, therefore, with Virginia and with the Fredericksburg neighborhood. That part of the Resolution which says that "an attack made on one of our sister colonies, is an attack on all British

America," is one of the earliest openly avowed statements to that effect, a significant fact clearly recognized by the Virginia leaders of the Fredericksburg area.

Protest Resolutions were signed by eighty-nine members of the late House of Burgesses. Among them were Edmund Pendleton, Richard Henry Lee, George Washington, Robert Carter, Thomas Jefferson, Mann Page, Jr., Patrick Henry, Henry Lee, Rodman Kenner, Charles Carter, Richard Lee, James Taylor, Henry Taylor, Francis Lightfoot Lee, to name only a few of those from the Fredericksburg neighborhood.

The foregoing resolutions and protest illustrate the work of the Virginia Committees of Correspondence, especially of the Fredericksburg Committee. These resolutions themselves indicate the gradual development of the scheme of National Independence, which inspired the minds and hearts of the Fathers of the Republic, and they also show something of the importance of the men of the Fredericksburg neighborhood during the preliminary stage of the American Revolution.

Another part of the picture is revealed by the following points:

J. F. D. Smyth, who visited America in 1774, makes the following comments about the Weedon Tavern in Fredericksburg in his *A Tour of the United States:*

> After passing through a small town named Falmouth . . . . we crossed that river [Rappahannock] in a ferryboat, and arrived at Fredericksburg, putting up at an inn or public house kept by one Weedon, who is now a general in the American Army, and was then very active and zealous in blowing the flames of sedition.[12]

The Weedon Tavern was the popular gathering place of the patriots of the Fredericksburg neighborhood.

> Here . . . . the Lees, George Mason, Pendleton, Wythe, George Washington and his brothers, Fielding Lewis, Charles Dick, and other leading men met at the tavern where Weedon was 'zealous in blowing the flames of sedition'; and after the

Revolution it was a further gathering place for such men as James Monroe, and Thomas Jefferson.[13]

This fact then would partly explain why Fredericksburg was taking the initiative in the Revolutionary movement, and why she continued to play the leading role in that historic movement.

The representatives from the Fredericksburg neighborhood also had a singular share in the genesis and work of the Continental Congress, as well as in the work of the House of Burgesses, the Executive Council of Virginia, the Committees of Safety and Correspondence, as members of various Conventions and in many other responsible capacities. A few of these may be commented on briefly.

In the Continental Congress, we find that of the three delegates from Virginia who served as Presidents of the Congress two of them were from the Rappahannock Valley, namely Richard Henry Lee and Cyrus Griffin, the former from Westmoreland and the latter from Richmond County.[14]

Of the thirty-nine delegates from Virginia to the Continental Congress, half of them were from the Rappahannock Valley and adjacent counties, and they were among the most able and influential members of the Congress:

*Col. Carter Braxton*, of King and Queen County;

*Hon. John Dawson,* of Spotsylvania County and Fredericksburg, graduate Harvard University, member with James Monroe of the Virginia Convention on the Ratification of the Constitution where he opposed its ratification;

*Mr. William Fitzhugh,* of King George County;

*Mr. John Harvie,* of Albemarle County, friend and associate of Thomas Jefferson and Dr. Thomas Walker;

*Mr. James Henry,* of Hanover County (?);

*Gov. Patrick Henry,* of Hanover County, prominent in Fredericksburg affairs; called the meeting at Fredericksburg in 1775 in protest to Dunmore's Plot to remove the powder from the magazine at Williamsburg; the meeting was attended by over six hundred representatives from the various surrounding counties;

*Pres. Thomas Jefferson,* of Albemarle County;

*Judge Joseph Jones,* of King George County, one of the ablest and most influential men of Virginia;

*Dr. Arthur Lee, Francis Lightfoot Lee, Richard Henry Lee,* of "Stratford Hall," Westmoreland County, brothers of William Lee, "the most talented group of brothers in Virginia history";

*Mr. Henry Lee,* of "Leesylvania," near Dumfries, Prince William County; he is better known as "Light-Horse Harry Lee"; he was brother of Richard Bland Lee and Charles Lee;

*Pres. James Madison,* of Port Conway, King George County, and of Montpelier, Orange County;

*Mr. James Mercer,* son of John Mercer of "Marlborough," Stafford County, and Fredericksburg;

*Mr. John Francis Mercer,* of "Marlborough," brother of James Mercer;

*Pres. James Monroe,* of Fredericksburg;

*Hon. Mann Page,* of Gloucester County and of "Mansfield Hall," Spotsylvania County;

*Judge Edmund Pendleton,* of Caroline County;

*Mr. Meriwether Smith,* of Essex County; and

*Gen. George Washington,* of Westmoreland, King George, near Fredericksburg, and Fairfax Counties.[15]

Most of these men had served as members of the House of Burgesses, of the Virginia Committee of Safety, of Committees of Correspondence, of Revolutionary and Constitutional Conventions, etc.

The Virginia Committee of Safety consisted of nine members. Six of whom were from the Fredericksburg area: *Edmund Pendle-*

*ton,* President, of Caroline County, *George Mason,* of Stafford County, *Thomas Ludwell Lee,* of Stafford, *James Mercer,* of Spotsylvania County, *Carter Braxton,* of King William County, *John Page,* of Gloucester County. The other three members were Richard Bland, Paul Carrington, and Dudley Digges, from outside the Rappahannock area. Two-thirds of the Committee members, therefore, were from the Rappahannock section of Virginia.

At the first meeting of the Continental Congress on September 5, 1774, there were present from Virginia the following delegates:

Hon. Peyton Randolph,
George Washington,
Richard Bland,
Edmund Pendleton,
Richard Henry Lee,
Patrick Henry, Jr., and
Benjamin Harrison, Esqrs.[16]

At a "Convention of Delegates for the Counties and Corporations in the Colony, held at Richmond town . . . . 20th of March, 1775," the following delegates attended:

Judge Edmund Pendleton, and
James Taylor, Esqrs., for Caroline;
Benjamin Harrison, and
William Acrill, Esqrs., for Charles City;
George Washington, and
Charles Broadwater, Esqrs., for Fairfax;
Thomas Marshall, and
James Scott, Esqrs., for Fauquier;
Joseph Jones, and
William Fitzhugh, Esqrs., for King George;
Henry Lee, and
Thomas Blackburn, Esqrs., for Prince William;
George Stubblefield, and
Mann Page, Esqrs., for Spotsylvania;
John Alexander, and
Charles Carter, Esqrs., for Stafford; and
Richard Henry Lee, and
Richard Lee, Esqrs., for Westmoreland.[17]

It will be observed from the foregoing list that delegates who composed the historic convention at Richmond were all from counties and towns of the Rappahannock District, except the two delegates from Charles City. This was typical of almost all the Virginia Conventions. The representatives from the Rappahannock area nearly always formed the majority, which shows the initiative and leadership being taken by the men from this part of Virginia.

It will be remembered that Richard Henry Lee was one of the Presidents of the Continental Congress, and it was he who introduced the famous "Richard Henry Lee Resolution—Resolved: That these United Colonies are, and of a right ought to be, free and independent States, that they are absolved from all allegiance to the British Crown, and that all political connections between them and the State of Great Britain is, and ought to be, totally dissolved."[18]

At a "Convention of Delegates Held at Williamsburg, May 6, 1776,"[9] Edmund Pendleton was elected President, and the Convention adopted the famous "Declaration of Rights," containing sixteen articles or principles, known as the "Edmund Pendleton Resolutions," since he presented them to the Convention and championed their adoption. Pendleton wrote the "Resolutions favoring a Declaration of Independence." The articles which they contained were, however, largely based on the work of George Mason. The George Mason Bill of Rights was later adopted as the Virginia Bill of Rights, and they formed the essence of the Bill of Rights of the United States.

This Convention formulated, resolved upon, and agreed to the principles later embodied in the Constitution and Government of the State of Virginia and of the United Colonies. Again the men from the Rappahannock Valley were playing the significant role.

The General Assembly of Virginia, on May 5, 1776, appointed a Committee consisting of Thomas Jefferson, George Wythe, George Mason, Edmund Pendleton, and Thomas Ludwell Lee, to revise the Colonial laws of Virginia.[20] The Committee met in Fredericksburg, on January 13, 1777. George Mason, however, declined to accept, and Thomas Ludwell Lee died before the Committee made its final report on June 18, 1779.

The Final Report consisted of 126 bills which the Committee recommended. The Report was given under Chapter Headings, numbered from I-CXXVI. Among the most important of these bills were: Chapter LXXXII, entitled "A Bill establishing religious freedom," and Chapter LXXIX, called "A Bill for the more general diffusion of Knowledge." Two others of almost equal importance were the Bill for the repeal of the laws of entail, and the Bill to abolish the law of primogeniture.

These four laws became the basic principles of every State Constitution, and of the Constitution of the United States. The first meant to achieve that goal toward which man has aspired for ages, namely, religious freedom; the second laid the foundations for a free system of public education; the third was a significant step toward preventing the accumulation and perpetuation of wealth in the hands of a few select families; and the fourth ended the discrimination in favor of the oldest son against the other children.

We should remember that these great principles are just as basic and fundamental to democracy today as they were in 1776. How faithfully are we adhering to the principles embodied in the George Mason Bill of Rights which declared that "All men are equally entitled to the free exercise of religion, according to the dictates of conscience," and which principle was made a part of Jefferson's Bill for Religious Freedom? How nearly are we approaching the ideals expressed in the Jefferson "Bill for the more general diffusion of Knowledge"? Or how nearly are we coming to achieving the objective set forth in the "Bill for the repeal of entail," which seeks to prevent the accumulation and perpetuation of wealth in the hands of a few select families? Or how nearly have we fulfilled the promise entertained in the "Bill to abolish primogeniture," which strives for equality before the law of all children?

In summarizing this aspect of the Revolution, reference may be made to Tyler's *Encyclopedia of Virginia Biography*. Of the seventy-five names which he lists under "Fathers of the Revolution,"[21] about sixty of them were from the counties of the Rappahannock Valley or adjoining counties.

With respect to the military aspects of the Revolution, the first important action on the part of the colonists took place at Fredericksburg.

The following resolutions were drawn up at a meeting held at Fredericksburg on April 25, 1775, in protest against Governor Dunmore's removal of the powder from the Magazine at Williamsburg. The men who gathered at Fredericksburg styled themselves the "Friends of Constitutional Liberty and America," as will be observed in the Resolutions. Over seven hundred men from all parts of Northern Virginia had gathered at Fredericksburg at the call of Patrick Henry.[22]

The meeting formed itself into a:

Council of one hundred and two Members, Delegates of the Provincial Convention, Officers, and special Deputies of fourteen Companies of Light-Horse, consisting of upward of six hundred men, friends of Constitutional Liberty and America, now rendez-voused here in consequence of an alarm occasioned by the Powder being removed from the County Magazine, in the City of Williamsburg, on the night of Thursday the 21st instant, and deposited on board an armed Schooner, by order of his Excellency the Governor:

The Council having before them the several matters of intelligence respecting this transaction, and particularly a Letter from the Honourable Peyten Randolph, Esquire, Speaker of the late House of Burgesses of Virginia, received here last night by an express despatched to Williamsburg for the purpose of gaining intelligence, informing the gentlemen of the City of Williamsburg and neighborhood have had full assurance from his Excellency this affair will be accommodated, and advising that the gentlemen assembled here should proceed no further at this time. This Council came to the following determination, and offer the same as their advice to those public spirited Gentlemen, friends to British liberty and America, who have honoured them by this appointment: Highly condemning the conduct of the Governour on this occasion, as impolitic, and justly alarming to the good people of this Colony, tending to destroy all confidence in Government, and to widen the unhappy breach between Great Britain and her colonies, ill-timed and totally unnecessary, consider this instance as a full proof, that no opinion which may be formed of the good intensions of the Governour in private life, can afford security to our injured and oppressed Country; but that obedience to arbitrary, ministerial mandate, and the most tyrannical system of Government, must be the fatal line of conduct of all his Majesty's present servants in America; at the same time justly dreading the horrors of civil war, influenced by motives of the strongest affection to our fellow subjects of Great Britain, most ardently wishing to heal our mutual wounds, and therefore prefering peaceable measures whilst the least hope of reconcilliation remains, do advise that the several companies now rendez-voused here do return to their respective homes. But considering the just rights and Liberty of America to be greatly endangered by the violent and hostile proceedings of an arbitrary Ministry, and being firmly resolved to resist such attempts at the utmost hazard of our lives and fortunes, do now pledge ourselves to each other to be in readiness, at a moment's warning, to reassemble, and by force of arms to defend the laws, the liberty, and rights of this, or any sister colony, from unjust and wicked invasion. Ordered that express be despatched to the troops assembled at the Bowling Green, and also to the companies from Frederick, Berkeley, Dunmore, and such other counties as are now on their march to return to them thanks for their cheerful offers of service, and to acquaint them with the determination now taken. God Save The Liberties of America.

The foregoing determination of Council having been read at the head of each company, was cordially and unanimously approved.[23]

The above draft is known as the Fredericksburg Resolutions. They were drafted by the Fredericksburg Committee enlarged temporarily. *The Virginia Gazette* of May 13, 1775, gave prominence to the Meeting and published the Resolutions, so important were they considered for the whole Colony.

This act on the part of the citizens of the Fredericksburg area established the Fredericksburg Minute Men, perhaps the first group of its kind to be organized in the Colonies. The Resolutions were formulated and announced four weeks before the famous Mecklenburg Resolutions of May 31, 1775, and hardly more than a week after the battle of Lexington, April 19, 1775.

At this mass meeting of citizens and militiamen at Fredericksburg, a Committee representing the Companies and Citizens, composed of Hugh Mercer, George Weedon, Alexander Spotswood, and John Willis, all of Fredericksburg, on April 25 addressed a fiery letter to Col. George Washington, offering to march to Williamsburg in protest against Lord Dunmore's removal of the powder from the Magazine at Williamsburg.[24]

The same quick response by other places which had followed the initiative of Fredericksburg in drafting Resolutions protesting the Boston Tea Act, now followed her more drastic action regarding Lord Dunmore's removal of the gun powder. On receipt of a letter from Hugh Mercer signed by the other members of the Fredericksburg Committee, Capt. William Grayson and Francis Lee of Dumfries addressed a communication to Col. Washington expressing readiness of the Dumfries Company to march to Williamsburg in protest to the act of Gov. Dunmore.[25] Four days after the Mass Meeting at Fredericksburg, the leaders of Charlottesville sent a letter to Col. Washington, stating that "We should have attended at Fredericksburg, in order to have proceeded to Williamsburg to demand a return of the powder."[26]

The Charlottesville letter is cited here for an additional purpose. It illustrates the fact that the people of practically the whole of northern Virginia geographically gravitated to or felt that they belonged with Fredericksburg. They looked upon it not only as their entrepot but as their headquarters, their rendezvous, their principal political, historical, cultural, and social center.

The *Virginia Gazette* for March 7, 1777, has the following announcement:

> The Continental Officers of the new raised troops of the following counties: Augusta, Amherst, Fairfax, Culpeper, Orange, Spotsylvania, Caroline, Stafford, Fauquier, and King George are desired to take notice that by a Resolution of the Hon. the Governor and Council, they are formed into Batallion, to be under my command and as soon as any of them

complete their quota of men they are hereby desired to march immediately to Fredericksburg where they will receive further instructions . . . . .

> Edwards Stevens,
> Col. 10th Bat.[27]

A notice similar to that above had appeared in an earlier issue of the *Gazette*, No. 8, 1776, and read:

> The Officers of the 2nd. regiment who are now recruiting will please inform me immediately of their success, and as soon as their companies are formed . . . . to be directed to me near Fredericksburg . . . . .
>
> > Alex. Spotswood,
> > L. C 2 d. regiment.[28]

Immediately after the overt act had been committed on April 19, 1775, at Concord and Lexington, the citizens of the Fredericksburg area quickly joined the fight. They had led in the war of ideas, and now they were ready and among the first to enter the military arena of that struggle.

They were not long in raising and organizing troops. The Courthouse Green in Fredericksburg became the training ground for the various companies made up of volunteers from Spotsylvania and the other counties of the Rappahannock area. A Revolutionary Army Camp was established at "Nottingham" near Fredericksburg, and the Weedon Military Camp on the hills above Falmouth was prepared to guard the Hunter Iron Works. The strong defense afforded this town no doubt kept Tarleton from approaching nearer than Bowling Green in his raid of 1781.

It is interesting to note the military line-up which was organized at the opening of the War, particularly as it related to the Fredericksburg neighborhood. There were nine Regiments formed, with the following officers in charge:

1st Regiment—*Patrick Henry* of Hanover County;

2nd Regiment—*Wm. Woodford* of Caroline;

3rd Regiment—*Hugh Mercer* of Fredericksburg, Spotsylvania County;

4th  Regiment—*Adam Stephens* of Fredericksburg, Spotsylvania;

5th  Regiment—*Wm. Peachy* of Richmond County;

6th  Regiment—*Mordecai Buckner* of Gloucester County;

7th  Regiment—*Wm. Dangerfield* of "Belvidere," Spotsylvania County;

8th  Regiment—*Peter Muhlenberg* of Woodstock, Shenandoah Valley;

9th  Regiment—*Thomas Fleming* of Goochland County.[29]

Thus it will be seen that with two exceptions, that of the Peter Muhlenberg Regiment, and the 9th Regiment commanded by Thomas Fleming, the whole command of Virginia troops was under leaders of the Rappahannock Valley and the adjoining county of Hanover.

Besides these it must be remembered that *George Washington* was Commander-in-Chief of the combined Continental Armies, and *John Paul Jones* was Commander-in-Chief of the Colonial Navies. Both of them had lived in Fredericksburg.

A further fact to be noted is that Fredericksburg supplied six generals besides the foregoing Commanders-in-Chief, namely, Generals *Hugh Mercer, Thomas Posey, Oliver Towles, Gustavus B. Wallace, George Weedon,* and *William Woodford,* besides *George Rogers Clark,* Conqueror of the Northwest Territory, *Adam Stephens, Alexander Spotswood,* and *William Dangerfield,* men of extraordinary military abilities. In addition there were several lower-ranking officers from the Fredericksburg vicinity who performed meritorious service in the Revolution, such as *Lawrence Brooke,* Surgeon on the Bon Homme Richard; *Col. George Baylor; Lt. Francis T. Brooke; Capt. Eliezer Callender,* in the Virginia State Navy; *Major James Monroe; Capt. Beverley Stubblefield; Lawrence Lewis,* son of Fielding Lewis, and favorite nephew of George Washington, and others.

Shortly after the beginning of the Revolution, in July 1775, the Virginia Assembly established a Manufactory of Small Arms at Fredericksburg, with Fielding Lewis, Charles Dick, Mann Page, William Fitzhugh, and Samuel Seldon the Commissioners.

A few extracts from the contemporary references to Fredericks-

burg as Arsenal and Supply Depot of the Revolution will be sufficient to indicate its particular importance.

On March 28, 1776, the Council of the State of Virginia ordered
the establishment of "many public stores . . . . in the Town of
Fredericksburg under the care of . . . . James Hunter, gent [and]
appointed [him] to that trust . . . . ."[30] For a detailed account of
the Public Stores at Fredericksburg, the reader is referred to Books
II, IX, in the State Library.

May 4, 1776, the Council "Ord: That 1200 lbs. powder remain
at Fredericksburg for use of the Vessells in Rappahannock river and
100 lbs. for proving arms at the Manufactory & at Mr. Hunter's."[31]

On July 12, 1776, the Council "Ordered that fifty two Musquets & Bayonets be delivered to Capt. Wm. Mitchell from Mr.
Hunter's Manufactory at Fredericksburg."[32]

Again on July 29 the Council "Ordered that the Muskets in
the Magazine which are not fit for use, and cannot be immediately
repaired in this City [Williamsburg], be sent up to the Manufactory
at Fredericksburg to be put into the best order with all possible
dispatch . . . . ."[33]

August 10, 1776, the Council "Ordered that General George
Weedon . . . . be permitted to apply to the Commissioners of
the Gun Manufactory at Fredericksburg or to Mr. James Hunter
for such Arms as they may have already finished for the Publick . . . . ."[34]

Besides the Manufactories of Arms, there were Salt Works,
Lead Mines, Powder Factory and Powder Magazine at Fredericksburg. The Public Salt Works at Fredericksburg are referred to in
the Council's order of August 8, 1776: "Ordered that a Warrant
issue to Mr. James Hunter, for £360.5S. for sixty Muskets, 2 pair
Bullet Moulds & three pounds five shillings for Iron supplied Anderson the public Armorer, and for Waggonage of the Iron and the
Musquets, and for £253.11S. for spades and shovels furnished for
the use of the Publick Salt Works."[35]

Another reference is made to salt purchased at Fredericksburg
in an order of December 18, 1776: "Ordered that a Warrant issue
to James Hunter for the use of Captain Elwood Ross for £956.5S.

being the amount of 1500 Bushells of Salt purchased by the Governor and Council."[36]

On November 11, 1776, the Council "Ordered that a Warrant issue to James Hunter for £1340.12S 1½d. being the amount of his account for Arms, Camp Utensels, Waggonage and other necessaries . . . . ."[37]

The Council seemed to reckon the productive capacity of the Iron Works at Fredericksburg to be very high, for on February 7, 1777, they "Resolved therefore that a Letter be addressed to Mr. James Hunter desiring him immediately to fabricate so many Arms requisite for Cavalry as may be sufficient to arm a Regiment compleat."[38]

The Letter of the Governor of March 20, 1777, gives instructions to erect Lead Mines at Fredericksburg. The order reads: "Ordered that Mr. Beverley [of the Fredericksburg Iron Works] be directed to prepare in the most expeditious manner the proper Clay for erecting the necessary works at the Lead Mines, and have the same conveyed there as soon as possible."[39]

In a letter of Gov. Patrick Henry of May 31, 1777, he gives his opinion of the importance of the Hunter Iron Works at Fredericksburg. He says, "As there was no Manufactory of Iron in this State which was carried on to such an Extent, and to Purpose of such vast Importance as Mr. Hunter's near Fredericksburg, I took the Liberty of promising him the Assistance of the Public in the Prosecution of his Works on a more enlarged Plan. In consequence of this Mr. Hunter laid my Letter before Mr. John Strode, his Manager . . . . ."[40]

Mr. Strode submitted a detailed plan as requested for enlarging the Iron Works at Fredericksburg.[41]

On January 10, 1781, when Tarleton was making his raid into the interior of Virginia, Jefferson as the successor of Patrick Henry to the Governorship of Virginia, wrote to Hunter urging him to take all precautions to guard the Iron Works at Fredericksburg against destruction by the enemy. He indicates his opinion of the worth of these works to the patriots' cause by saying, "The importance of your Works to the operations of War will doubtless point them out as a proper object of destruction to the desolating Enemy

now in our Country . . . . . I write to Genl. Weedon to take measures for protecting them . . . . "⁴²

In reply to Jefferson's warning, Hunter states in his letter of
January 25, 1781, that he had taken steps to protect the works and
town against any enemy attack. He asks that he be paid the amount
of a warrant for £50,000 in tobacco, and also for certificates from
General Gates for sundries from his Works, for the army under
his command, to the amount of £130,000. These figures alone
would indicate that he had furnished the Continental Armies with
over a million dollars worth of equipment, supplies, etc. This would
no doubt be a small fraction of the total value of supplies and
equipment furnished the Colonial Armies by the Hunter Iron
Works and other manufactories of arms in Fredericksburg.

In this connection the reader is referred to the huge claims of
Fielding Lewis against the State for money which he had supplied
out of his own personal funds to keep the armies in the field
equipped with armaments and munitions. The practically worthless
warrants which were finally issued to him tell something of the
large quantities of arms and munitions which were produced by
the manufactory of which he was the director. It is said that he
went bankrupt by sacrificing his large fortune in the cause for
which the patriots fought.

James Mercer in his letter to Jefferson of April 14, 1781, summarizes the value and contribution of the two iron works of Fredericksburg. He writes:

> There is not in this State a place more deserving of public
> mention than this Town and its appendage, Mr. Hunter's Iron
> Works. I am sure I need not tell you that it is from Mr. Hunter's
> Works that every Camp Kettle has been supplied for the Con-
> tinental and all other Troops employed in this State or to the
> Southward this year . . . . .
> As to the Town itself, I need not inform you that the
> public Manufactory of Arms is here—To this however, I may
> add that there is not one spot in the State so generally useful
> in our military operations—full one-third of all new Levies
> rendezvous here; all the Troops from the North must pass
> through this Town, where wagons are repaired, horses shoed

and many other and as which they could not proceed without. The Troops get provisions here to the next Stage, and no place is so convenient to a very extensive and productive Country for the reception of Grain and other Articles of Provision . . . . .[43]

Finally we should mention the fact that there were at least three and perhaps four Revolutionary Hospitals in Fredericksburg: one at the southeast corner of Caroline and William Streets, another at Alum Springs, a third at Sligo.

Fredericksburg was the principal "Arsenal," "Public Store-house," "Military Headquarters and Training Grounds," "Rendez-vous," "Revolutionary Hospital Center," and the "Fountain-head of the Revolution," particularly in Virginia. The Fredericksburg neighborhood spearheaded the Revolution intellectually and militarily.

### NOTES

1. John Fiske, *The American Revolution* (New York: Houghton, 1891), p. 18.
2. Alvin T. Embrey, *History of Fredericksburg, Virginia* (Richmond: Old Dominion, 1937), p. 94.
3. W. C. Ford, *Writings of George Washington* (New York & London: Putnam, 1889-93), II, 263-67.
4. *Ibid.,* II, 268-69.
5. *Va. Gazette,* Jan. 28, 1775.
6. *American Archives* (Washington: U. S. Dept. of State, 1837-53), I, 448.
7. *Ibid.,* I, 338, 1034; 539, 618.
8. *American Archives,* I, 373.
9. *Ibid.*
10. *W. &M. Quart.,* (1), p. 73f; the *Am. Archives,* 4th Series, I, Column 373-74; also the *Calendar of Virginia State Papers.*
11. *American Archives,* I, 448-49.
12. Smyth, *op. cit.,* II, 151.
13. Goolrick, *op. cit.,* p. 37.
14. *Biographical Directory of the American Congress, 1774-1927* (Washington: Printing Office, 1928), p. 31.
15. *Ibid.,* p. 36.
16. Journal of the Congress held at Philadelphia, Misc. Pamphlets, Sept. 5th, 1774, Rare Book Collections, Lib. of Cong., p. 3.
17. *Ibid.,* p. 4.

18. *Journals of the Cont. Cong., 1774-1789* (Washington: Govt. Printing, 1904-37), V, 1776, 425.

19. *Journals or Proceedings of the Convention of Delegates Held at Williamsburg, May 6, 1776* (Richmond: Nicolson & Prentis, 1785), pp. 3-6, in the State Library, Richmond.

20. Report of the Committee of Revisors Appointed by the General Assembly of Virginia, Final Report, June 18, 1779, in State Lib., Richmond.

21. Tyler, *op. cit.,* II, 3-41.

22. Jared Sparks, *Writings of George Washington* (New York: Harpers, 1847), II, 508; also Wm. Wirt, *Life of Patrick Henry* (Philadelphia: Webster, 1817), p. 135.

23. American Archives, *op. cit.,* Fourth Series, II, 443.

24. *Ibid.,* II, 287.

25. *Ibid.,* II, 395.

26. *Ibid.,* II, p. 387.

27. *Virginia Gazette,* March 7, 1777.

28. *Ibid.,* November 8, 1776.

29. Tyler, *op. cit.,* pp. 3-41.

30. *Journals of the Council of the State of Virginia* (Richmond: Div. of Printing, 1931), I, 474.

31. *Ibid.,* II, 496.

32. *Official Letters of Governors of Virginia* (Richmond: Pub. Printing, 1926-), Letters of Patrick Henry, I, July 12, 1776, 5.

33. *Ibid.,* I, 19.

34. *Ibid.,* I, 30.

35. *Journals of the Council, op. cit.,* I, 113.

36. *Ibid.,* 235.

37. *Ibid.*

38. *Official Letters of the Governors of Virginia,* I, 100.

39. *Ibid.,* I, 126.

40. *Ibid.,* I, 156.

41. Executive Communications, Memorial of John Strode, Oct. 20, 1777, to Jan. 24, 1778, in Va. State Library.

42. *Official Letters of the Governors of Virginia,* II, 269.

43. *Calendar of State Papers, op. cit.,* II, 39-40.

# 15

## THE IMPACT OF THE FREDERICKSBURG NEIGHBORHOOD ON AMERICAN HISTORY

Forces and events that shape the nature of human civilization are first conceived in the minds of men. Given suitable circumstances, ideas and ideals can transform a primitive frontier territory into a neighborly community where men may ply their trades and develop their talents and abilities to benefit not only themselves but other men at home and abroad.

Colonial Fredericksburg was a community harboring many men of noble ideas and broad vision. Here were born and lived authors whose ideals and ideas produced some of the most significant documents in American history. Their works were instrumental in shaping the development of the new republic and its democratic form of government. Here also were men of action.

Men of Fredericksburg area produced two of the three greatest documents contributed by Virginians to the ideas which helped found the American nation. The third document was written by Thomas Jefferson, who lived in the nearby Albemarle County.

Edmund Pendleton, of Caroline County, presented his Declaration of Rights to the Virginia Convention on May 6, 1776. The document's greatness lies in the fact that this was the "first declaration" produced in America, stating that the colonies are "free and independent States."[1] This declaration contained 16 principles which became the pattern of government, not only for Virginia, but for each of the other States and for the United States.

The second historically unprecedented document produced by

a Virginian residing in the Rappahannock Valley is the Bill of Rights, originally known as the Declaration of Rights, drawn up by George Mason.

This document, drafted on May 15 and adopted on May 29, 1776, formed Virginia's first constitution, served as a model for the other states, and was embodied almost in toto as the Bill of Rights of the Constitution of the United States. One of its principles declared all men "by nature equally free and independent."[2] Jefferson in his Declaration of Independence modified the phrase to read "all men are created free and equal." The Mason Declaration contained the principles set forth in the "English Convention Parliament of 1689 . . . . and is a statement of the rights of individual liberty dear to the Anglo-Saxon."[3]

The Declaration of Independence, written by Jefferson, and signed by the members of the Continental Congress, July 4, 1776, is considered one of the greatest documents "ever struck off by the hand of man." It embodied in essence the principles expressed in George Mason's Declaration of Rights.

Formulated by Jefferson in Fredericksburg, January 13, 1777, his Statute of Religious Freedom belongs with the immortal documents of America's political heritage.[4]

Many other great men of ideas and events were born, lived or were associated with the Fredericksburg neighborhood. Their impression on the local, state and national development is American history today. There were George Washington, James Madison, James Monroe, John Marshall, John Paul Jones, the Lees, Matthew Fontaine Maury, Alexander Spotswood, John Taylor, Dr. Thomas Walker, the Mercers, John Sevier, Nathaniel Gist, Robert Beverley, Fielding Lewis, George Rogers Clark and William Clark.

Perhaps one of the best standards of judging the greatness of historical persons from the American point of view is the recognition given by the Hall of Fame of New York University, New York City. By this criterion, seven persons from the Rappahannock area have been admitted into this Hall of Fame. Selected for this signal honor are five men whose birthplace, home or residence was the Fredericksburg neighborhood. These are Washington, Madison, Monroe, Marshall and John Paul Jones. The sixth person is Jefferson, who received his preparatory schooling in this area, and was intimately associated with Fredericksburg in many personal and official ways. Patrick Henry is the seventh person, and he was perhaps even more intimately connected with Fredericksburg than Jefferson. He was a familiar figure in the court life of the town, and led some of the political actions taken by the citizens of the area.

Besides these men of colonial times who have been adjudged worthy of inclusion in the American Hall of Fame are a number of individuals who lived here at later periods. These would include Robert E. Lee, Matthew Fontaine Maury and others.

The significance of the distinction accorded Fredericksburg men by the Hall of Fame becomes even more impressive when the total picture is revealed. Only 73 persons in all American history down to 1945 have been honored in this manner. The Fredericksburg neighborhood has furnished nearly 10 per cent of the total receiving this distinction. This percentage would run even higher if colonial figures alone were counted, for only 15 of the 73 names included in the gallery of fame belonged to the colonial period.

How great has been the impact of the Fredericksburg area on the state and national history is further suggested by the town's importance as a cosmopolitan trading center, its place in the Revolutionary War, its influence on the settlement of the western territories, and by the manifold contributions of its doctors, lawyers, planters, merchants, teachers, ministers, and literary men.

Another interesting criterion for judging the significant contribution Fredericksburg made to the development of the western hemisphere is indicated by the American Historical Prints of the Phelps Stokes and Other Collections. The collection includes a "list of the one hundred and sixty towns and cities in the United States and forty outside the United States selected as having individually made the greatest contributions to the development of the western hemisphere as being the most characteristic of important phases of that development."[5]

Only three Virginia towns are named in this list for the colonial period, to wit: Fredericksburg (c.1775-1783); Williamsburg (c.1740-); and Yorktown (1781).

To get a better perspective of this significance, colonial towns in other American colonies for this period cited for their "contribution to the development of the western hemisphere" are listed below:

Connecticut:  Hartford and New Haven
Delaware:  Wilmington
Georgia:  Atlanta and Savannah
Maryland:  Annapolis and Baltimore
Massachusetts:  Boston, Lexington, Plymouth and Salem
New Hampshire:  Portsmouth
New Jersey:  Princeton and Trenton
New York:  Albany and New York City
North Carolina:  Charlotte, New Bern, Salsbury and Wilmington
Pennsylvania:  Philadelphia, Pittsburgh, Lancaster and York
Rhode Island:  Newport and Providence
South Carolina:  Charleston and Port Royal

How far-reaching were the influence and reputation of Fredericksburg in the colonial era is also indicated by paintings of Joseph Vernet, whose prints are in the Stokes Collection. This French artist of the eighteenth century was concerned with portraying the leading American ports enjoying international trade and reputation. His list of the American ports includes these three: Fredericksburg, Virginia, Port Royal, South Carolina, and Savannah, Georgia.

To appraise adequately the impact of the Fredericksburg neighborhood on American history is a difficult task, for in truth, it cannot be measured. Only its relation to other schemes in the affairs of men of the world can be pointed out in this bird's eye view of the Rappahannock Valley.

Since men make events, reference must be made to the original inhabitants of the Fredericksburg area. The native tribes of Indians who lived here before the coming of the white man made their contributions. Their civilization had its bearing and influence on succeeding generations of men. The extent of this, however, remains a closed chapter. This is also true of the first white settlers who braved the wilds to found forts and homes on the frontier.

The continuity that follows here is an attempt to sketch a broad outline centering attention on a few individuals whose activities in some way affected the course of American history. These men and women were born, lived or owned property in the Fredericksburg area. Each contributed toward the genesis of some great force or movement which has played a significant role in the history of this nation.

The first names on this historical roster are those of John Buckner and Thomas Royston, who patented "Leaseland" and became "fathers" of Fredericksburg. Buckner is also remembered for his part in establishing the first printing press in Virginia and publishing the laws of the colony as early as 1680. Major Lawrence Smith was the commander of the first garrison at the falls of the Rappahannock River, erected in 1676. Descendants of these "first" men played their parts in the history of the town and its vicinity.

But the first major event occurring in this neighborhood that shed its influence on the development of the United States was the transmontane expedition led by Governor Alexander Spotswood in 1716. When Spotswood and his Knights of the Golden Horseshoe crossed the Blue Ridge Mountains and looked into the fertile Shenandoah Valley and beyond, the vast territorial expansion of the nation westward was assured. With Spotswood and this famous trip began the westward movement which has been the greatest force in American history.

Before the official erection of Fredericksburg in 1727, Spotswood built his "castle" at Germanna, where he had previously settled a colony of immigrants from the Palatinate mining regions of Germany. Here he started the development of the iron industry at four separate furnaces: the Tubal Works, near Germanna; the Catherine Furnace just west of Fredericksburg; the Fredericksville Furnace in the southwestern part of Spotsylvania county; and his finest one at Massaponax, just outside Fredericksburg. This was the beginning of a permanent iron industry in Virginia[6] and the forerunner of the great steel industry of the United States.

He advocated an enlightened Indian policy whose wisdom has been proved by time. Equally significant was his land policy, which advocated actual settler occupancy as opposed to mere speculation by absentee landowners. Showing statesmanlike vision for his day, Spotswood advocated a policy to contain or expel the French in the Ohio territory by settling English colonies there and about the Great Lakes.

In 1730, Spotswood became the deputy postmaster general of the British Dominions of North America and the West Indies with headquarters at Newpost, below Fredericksburg. His efforts extended the postal service throughout the colonies and his influence was instrumental in the appointment of Benjamin Franklin as postmaster for the northern colonies and William Hunter for the southern region. His grandson, General Alexander Spotswood, was an outstanding Revolutionary military leader who continued the land and mining interests developed by Governor Spotswood.

Captain Augustine Washington, who in 1738 moved to "Ferry Farm," across the river from Fredericksburg, was not only the father of the first President of the United States, but a historic personage in his own right. He was a trustee of the town and a stock-holder, owning one-twelfth interest, of the Principio Company, of Maryland, which was the largest American exporter of pig iron in the colonial period. He also managed the company's iron mines located in the Fredericksburg vicinity.

It was, of course, at Fredericksburg that George Washington received his formal schooling, attended church, became a Mason, acquired a host of friends and participated in some of the town's most stirring events.

There were other historic personalities belonging to this area whose contributions to the nation's development are familiar. The list includes James Madison, James Monroe, George Mason, John Marshall, John Paul Jones, George Rogers Clark, William Clark, John Sevier, Fielding Lewis, Francis Thornton, and others.

Once a resident of Fredericksburg, Dr. Thomas Walker was an outstanding physician, soldier, explorer and author. He was the first white man to make a recorded exploration into Kentucky. His trip in 1749 preceded Daniel Boone's expedition by twenty years. His influence was great in the establishment of western land policies of the United States.

Members of the Mercer family wielded considerable influence in the Fredericksburg community and their contributions are many in the affairs of the state and the nation. James Mercer was a member of the early (1774 and 1776) Revolutionary Conventions of Virginia; a delegate to the Continental Congress; a member of the first Virginia Committee of Safety. An able lawyer, he was a member of the General Court of Appeals of Virginia, and president of the old Fredericksburg Academy.

His brother, John Francis Mercer, was a member of the Virginia Assembly and of the Congress of the United States. Later he removed to Maryland which he represented at the Constitutional Convention of 1787. He opposed centralization of government and the ratification of the Constitution. Later he was governor of his adopted state, Maryland.

Their father, John Mercer, who had come to Virginia from Ireland in 1726, was an able lawyer and owned one of the largest private libraries in the Virginia colony, author of *Abridgement of Virginia Laws, 1737*.

Charles Fenton Mercer, the son of James Mercer, is remembered for introducing a bill for the promotion of public education while a member of the Virginia House of Delegates in 1816-17. This bill, calling for the establishment of a university, college, academies and primary schools, preceded the one later introduced by Jefferson.

Besides being a brother-in-law of Washington, Fielding Lewis was a wealthy planter and business man of Fredericksburg; a burgess from Spotsylvania county; and chief commissioner of the public Manufactory of Arms at Fredericksburg during the Revolution. In this latter capacity, Lewis gave of his means, sacrificing his personal fortune in the cause of American independence.

The Marshall family was another influential group of this area. Thomas Marshall was the father of John, the chief justice of the Supreme Court; of James Markham, who went to Kentucky, where he fought for the retention of the western territory as part of the United States rather than allowing secession to Spanish dominion of the Mississippi Valley; and of Louis, who was a physician and teacher. The family lived near Germantown in Fauquier County, but traded in and commuted with Fredericksburg.

The Waller family of "Newport" was also prominent. John Waller belongs to a group of leading Americans because of his fight for religious freedom and his influence in spreading the Baptist faith.

The Beverley family of Middlesex County produced a number of influential members. Robert Beverley wrote the *Present State of Virginia*. William Beverley, his son, was instrumental in settling Scotch-Irish immigrants in the Shenandoah Valley.

Representatives of the Brooke family deserve special mention also. Dr. Lawrence Brooke was an eminent physician. He was surgeon on the *Bon Homme Richard*, commanded by John Paul Jones, and is credited with performing the first trephine operations in history. Robert Brooke was a leading lawyer in the colony who later became governor of Virginia and a justice of the Supreme Court of the United States. Francis T. Brooke was also a lawyer and an eminent judge.

John Minor is remembered for introducing into the Virginia General Assembly a bill for the emancipation of slavery, 1784.

The Carters were another prominent family who were among the first Virginia colonists. Robert ("King") Carter was agent for Lord Fairfax and was second to his employer as the largest landowner in the colony. Landon Carter migrated to the western country in 1770's, settling near the present town of Kingsport, Tennessee. He, John Sevier, another native of Fredericksburg, and James Robertson founded the State of Franklin, which is now the State of Tennessee.

The Brents of Northern Neck made contributions to the state and the nation. Col. Giles and Margaret Brent, of "Peace," helped found the first Catholic colony in Virginia at Aquia. Col. Giles Brent was a commissioned officer under Nathaniel Bacon in 1676. Margaret Brent championed the rights of women.

Colonel Joseph Jones, of King George County, uncle of James Monroe, was a burgess; member of the Committee of Safety; a delegate to the Continental Congress and to the Convention of 1788; and a member of the United States Congress. His special con-

tribution was his fight to have Virginia relinquish her Northwestern
Territorial claims to the United States. This helped to establish the
territorial policy of the nation. His influence was significant in
such matters as the nation's internal questions, the grant of impost,
the payment of British debts, the foreign commercial policy of the
Union, and the formation of today's Democratic Party.

To enumerate the contributions and influence of the individual
members of the Lee family is to repeat well-known facts of Virginia
and American history. Suffice it to mention that Richard Lee of
"Cobbs Hill" in Northumberland County was the immigrant ancestor of this noted family which produced Richard Bland Lee, 1761-
1827, a member of the first Congress of the United States; Richard
Henry Lee, 1732-1794, who authored the war cry of the Revolution:
"Taxation without Representation," which was originally "taxation
without consent"; Arthur Lee, 1740-1792, who served with Franklin
and Silas Deane on the Commission of 1776 sent to France to negoti-
ate a treaty; Francis Lightfoot Lee, 1734-1797, who signed the Declaration of Independence with his brother Richard Henry Lee;
Henry Lee, 1756-1818, better known as "Light Horse Harry," the
father of Confederate General Robert E. Lee, and the man who
spoke the famous words: "First in war, first in peace, first in the
hearts of his countrymen"; William Lee, 1739-1795, is credited with
being the first American to express the opinion that the colonies
should separate from England; and a host of other Lees.

Robert Green, and his uncle, William Duff, who came to Virginia about 1717 and settled in Stafford County, are remembered
for their efforts in encouraging settlers in the Shenandoah Valley
and the Northwest. These two obtained the earliest grant of land
west of the Blue Ridge Mountains, and they encouraged people
from the Rappahannock Valley to settle in this frontier country.
Green may be called the father of textile industry in America, for
his cotton and textile manufactures at Falmouth were perhaps the
first of their kind in America, antedating those of New England
by many years.

The Fredericksburg area gave six military generals to the Revolutionary War. They are William Woodford, of Caroline County;
Hugh Mercer, Gustavus B. Wallace; Thomas Posey; George Weedon

and Oliver Towles, besides Gen. George Washington, Adm. John Paul Jones, and other prominent military leaders.

Numerous other individuals and families could be named who belonged to this area and contributed much to the development of the state and the nation. All these have had an influence upon American thought and life and upon the course of events since colonial times.

Historian Charles Beard summarized this impact of personalities associated with Fredericksburg in a letter to this author:

> What a list! All superlatives pale in any attempt at a brief estimate. Whole volumes are needed to tell the truth about them (if "the" truth is not beyond human minds).
>
> As to John Taylor . . . . it [referring to Taylor's *An Inquiry into the Principles & Policy of the Government of the United States*] deserves to rank among the two or three really historic contributions to political science which have been produced in the United States.
>
> As I search my mind, I am inclined to the opinion that Madison exerted more influence on my studies of American history when I began. I am inclined to place John Adams second, and John Taylor third. Yet such assigning of weights is dubious. Nor must I leave out Jefferson. At all events, apart from John Adams, it has been four or five Virginia men whom mentioned, to whom I am most indebted for guidance in my studies of American history during 'the heroic age' of our national life. With them, however, I must associate Jefferson. Moreover, as I continue my studies of American institutions, I am constantly recurring to Washington, Madison, Taylor, Mason, and other great Virginians and wondering how they would view the personalities and tendencies of these times.[7]

All these, except Adams, belong to the Fredericksburg neighborhood.

## NOTES

1.  Proceedings of the Convention of Delegates Held at Williamsburg, May 6, 1776, pp. 3-6, in the State Library, Richmond, Va.

2.  George Mason Declaration of Rights, State Library, Richmond.

3.  Pease, *op. cit.*, p. 201.

4.  Report of the Committee of Revisors Appointed by the General Assembly of Virginia, Final Report, June 18, 1779, in the State Library, Richmond.

5.  Daniel C. Haskell, *American Historical Prints, Early Views of American Cities* (New York: The New York Public Library, 1932), pp. xxxiii-xxxiv.

6.  Adam Anderson, *History of Commerce* (London, 1789), III, 63.

7.  Charles A. Beard, Letter dated December 22, 1946, to Oscar H. Darter. Letter in possession of the present author.

# ⋰ *16* ⋰

## CONCLUSION

American colonial towns are generally described or thought of as self-sufficient, provincial communities. They are pictured as localities whose contacts, interests and life in general extended hardly beyond the immediate environs of their geographic boundaries.

This is an erroneous concept of life in colonial towns. In many respects they were cosmopolitan. Certainly they were in trade, culture, race and nationality of the residents, and to a degree, in social and political life.

This study has supported the thesis that colonial towns were predominantly cosmopolitan and has presented detailed evidence on the following points:

First: the population of Falmouth and Fredericksburg was heterogeneous. It was composed primarily of English, but had a fairly large number of Germans, French, Scotch, Irish and Welsh immigrants. There were also a number of Hebrews, a few Dutch, Poles and Swedes. Italians, Spaniards, Swiss and other nationalities were also either as settlers, temporary travelers or visitors, or itinerant tradesmen. Negroes and American Indians completed the population.

Although English was the language used throughout the thirteen colonies, German, Gaelic, Dutch, French, Spanish, Portuguese, African and Indian dialects were constantly heard in all the colonial seacoast towns. Bancroft says that in 1775 one-fifth of the American people had for their mother tongue some language other than the English.

Second:   the cultural, social and political life of these towns was the sum total of the traditions, education, customs, manners, and political ideologies of the countries represented by the people residing in the community. All social classes were also represented by the settlers and their descendants. There were members of the English gentry, the French nobility, the Prussian junkers, the bourgeoisie, the artisans and the lowly peasant. The amalgamation and assimilation of all these factors went into the composition of the social, economic and political life of the towns and villages. Its pattern became the warp and woof of the history of Virginia and the United States.

Intellectual interests of the colonials were varied and extensive. Invoices of the merchants show that although books of religious themes predominated, many other types of reading were represented in the book orders and hence in the private libraries. There were texts on art, natural sciences, education, adventure, music, biography, travel, history, philosophy, literature, poetry, fiction, grammar, law and philology. A cross-sampling of reading matter shows such volumes as *Beauties of Nature and Art; Buckaneers of America; Campbells' Trials; Christian Education; Cyrus' Expedition; Dacier's Plato;* Aesop's *Fables; Free Thinker; Gentleman's Library;* Hume's *History of England; History of China; Goody Two Shoes; Horn Books;* Johnson's *Dictionary; Newtonian Systems of Philosophy; Pilgrim's Progress;* Haddington's *Poems;* Pope's *Essay on Man;* Homer's *Iliad and Odyssey; Robinson Crusoe; Scotch Magazines;* Seneca's *Works;* Shakespeare's *Works; The Spectator;* Voltaire's *Force of Education.*

The size and frequency of book orders disclosed by merchants' invoices and the types of reading matter found in many of the large and small private libraries of citizens reflect a broad rather than a provincial interest and outlook.

Many leaders of the colonies were educated in Europe. The composition of faculties in the colonial colleges shows that they included representatives from Scotland, Ireland, England and continental Europe. The curricula in these institutions of higher learning were based on that of the Old World. Many of the colleges and universities were located in towns and smaller population centers of colonial America.

Besides libraries, the colonials had access to magazines and periodicals published in the colonies and abroad. Learned societies, the theater and other cultural interests also were contributing factors in the creation of worldmindedness and an international outlook.

Religion was another force working for cosmopolitanism and international goodwill despite the various degrees of religious intolerance that prevailed throughout the colonies. Protestants, Catholics and Jews lived as neighbors in these smaller urban communities. The Society for the Propagation of the Gospel in Foreign Parts not only sought to evangelize the natives, but furthered educational interests through the establishment of colleges, educational societies and libraries.

The development of means of communication such as improved roads and highways, the stagecoach and stageboat travel, the establishment of a postal system, the beginning of journalism, fraternal organizations such as Free Masonry, and learned societies constituted vital forces in the development of cosmopolitanism.

Towns were the principal residences of most of the colonial leaders of the professions, such as the clergy, doctors, journalists, educators, scientists and lawyers. Public meetings, fairs and other gatherings drew outsiders into the towns. All these made for wider interests and common destinies of the people.

Travelers from all parts of the civilized world frequented colonial ports and towns. Many Americans visited Europe, the West Indies and other parts for study, health, recreation and business.

Third: The extensive trade contacts of the merchants of the towns indicate the interdependence of the peoples of the world, including the colonials in American towns. Trade was conducted on an international scale.

Goods which made up the stock-in-trade of the merchants of Falmouth and Fredericksburg came from sixty-five foreign towns and ports. In addition to trading regularly with these towns, the merchants also bought and sold in forty different foreign countries.

Besides this foreign trade, the merchants conducted an extensive business with at least forty-three towns scattered throughout the American colonies and the Atlantic seaboard, extending from Quebec to Mobile, New Orleans and the West Indies.

Not all this trade was direct, but a vast part of it was conducted by local merchants directly with those in other towns and ports.

Many businessmen and members of the upper class in the towns had regular connections with the Old World and frequented these countries. Business carried the planters, clergy, state officials and others to all parts of the world. Constant intercourse and economic interests contributed immeasurably toward the cosmopolitan attitude of the colonials. Such interests brought them into contact with the main currents of European thought and progress.

Because trade, particularly on an international scale, supplies the mutual wants of men regardless of locality, race, creed or nationality, it tends to erase petty prejudices harbored by man against man when he remains isolated from those who differ from him in language, customs, politics or religion. Merchants supplied colonials of Virginia and other American settlements with such daily necessities as Aberdeen yarn stockings, Bristol nails, Florence oil, China silk, Brazil wood, Damask, Dresden porcelain, Dutch blankets, French rum, German serge, Geneva gin, Bordeaux wine, Barcelona silk handkerchiefs, Castile soap, Guinea slaves, Jamaica gin, Persian nets, Russian sheeting, Torrington rugs, mohair, Nankeen, Malaga wines, Mantua silk, Liverpool nails, pimento, Leghorn hats, gum seneca. These originated in the one hundred or more countries and towns with which Falmouth and Fredericksburg merchants traded.

To identify these items which comprised a large share of the colonists' daily needs was to know something about the people and the country which produced them. Names of countries and towns where such merchandise was produced were household words. This familiarized the colonists with other peoples and nations of the world. It extended the geographic knowledge of the old and the young. Moreover, because these peoples and nations supplied some item of food, shelter or clothing needed in the daily existence of the colonists, the men and women from afar were not regarded as total foreigners or enemies. It was logical that a cosmopolitan attitude should result from this interdependence of man for sustenance of life.

The favorite son of the Fredericksburg area, George Washington, typifies this cosmopolitanism engendered by international trade. In 1786 he wrote to Lafayette: "I cannot avoid reflecting with pleasure on the probable influence that commerce may hereafter have on human manners and society in general. On these occasions I consider how mankind may be connected like one great family in fraternal ties."[1]

And in the final analysis, simple logic demanded that residents of colonial towns assume and nurture a broad and an international outlook rather than a provincial attitude in matters pertaining to everyday living. The very nature of the people who became colonists and frontiersmen in America defied the acceptance of a provincial approach to life. Settlers, explorers, adventurers and homemakers in a new land constantly met new problems which orthodox and tried methods could not always solve.

Venturing forth into a new land, the colonists used their means and minds to found homes and fortunes. No barrier, human or physical, was regarded as sacred. No fear appeared unsurmountable. The philosophy of conquering new lands presupposed that man and nature in the virgin country were enemies but could become allies of the intruders.

Thus it was that the early colonists assumed that the whole world and its inhabitants constituted a stage where every pioneer played his part. To create a more complete drama, the colonist found it necessary and profitable to borrow many properties for this presentation. He made business and social friends among all manner of men in his own town and those scattered throughout the world. Interchange of manners, customs, ideas, and tangible needs helped the colonist to achieve his ambitions.

Cosmopolitanism, rather than provincialism, was a natural development of man's life on a new frontier represented by the colonial towns of America in the eighteenth century.

---

1. *Letter* of George Washington to Lafayette, 1786, George Washington Bicentennial Commission, *Washington as President,* Pamphlet No. 8, pp. 32-33.

# APPENDIX A

## SEPARATE BUSINESS CONCERNS IN OR NEAR COLONIAL FREDERICKSBURG[1]

(Figures in parenthesis indicate the estimated number of businesses of that particular kind). This is not a complete registry of businesses.

Academy, Fredericksburg (1)
American Ink Powder Concern (1)
Apothecaries (15)
Bakeries (5)
Barber Shops (5)
Blacksmith Shops (15)
Building and Construction Concerns (10)
Churches (6)
Cooperage Shops (10)
Customs and Clearing Houses (4)
Dairies (indefinite)
Factories (6)
Ferries (4)
Flour and Grist Mills (35)
Foreign Establishments (7)
Founderies (5)
Fredericksburg Company (1)—Probably a mercantile establishment
Gardenry (a part of each colonial estate or large residential home)
Goldsmith Shops (3)
Horse Racing (5 courses and one or more jockey clubs)
Iron Furnaces (9)
Iron Mines (6)
Law Firms (many lawyers with law offices)
Livery Stables (10)

---

1. Spotsylvania County Records, 1721-1798; the *Virginia Gazette*, 1735-1775.

Lumber Yards  (many)
McDettrick Company  (1)—Probably a mercantile establishment
Merchant Stores  (at least 50)
Millinery Shops  (3)
Powder Factory  (1)
Printing Establishments  (4)
Public Stores  (3)
Quarries  (6)
Saddlery Businesses  (10)
Salt Works  (2)
Saw Mills  (many)
Schools  (30 or more)
Shipping Companies  (12)
Ship-building Concerns  (4)
Slave Dealers  (several)
Tailor Shops  (5)
Tanneries  (a score or more)
Taverns or Ordinaries  (30 or more in town, 1727-1780)
Warehouses  (11 or more)

Estimated number of separate concerns:  350. This compares
with 583 separate concerns in Fredericksburg today.

# APPENDIX B

## Activities and Interests Detailed, 1571-1787[2]

(Given alphabetically with approximate date of existence with examples). This is not a complete registry of activities and interests.

ACADEMY, FREDERICKSBURG (1783-1801)—Fredericksburg Academy, James Mercer, first President.

AGENTS (1650-on)—Factors, Commissioned Merchants for various foreign and domestic concerns, the Ohio and Loyal Companies.

APOTHECARY SHOPS (1738-on)—There were at least thirty-seven doctors in Fredericksburg between 1750 and 1780.

ARMY AND NAVAL INTERESTS (1671-on)—Military post established in 1676; Spotswood Iron Co., 1714; Principio Co., c.1737; the Bloomery or Foundry, c.1765; Hunter Iron Works, the Gunnery, James Mercer and John Semple Iron Interests, flourishing during the Revolution; Recruiting, Rendez-vous, Drilling Camp and Barracks, Ship-building, Rev. Hospitals.

BAKERIES (1750-on)—Jacob Whilly, Hugh Mercer's, Roger Dixon's, John Allen's, and scores of others.

BREWERIES (1764-on)—The Old Fredericksburg Brewery of Roger Dixon, and many others.

BRICK YARDS—BRICK-MAKING (c.1750-on)—Edward Vass, and many others.

BUILDING TRADES (from first settlements)—Carpenters, brick masons, stone masons, etc.

CABINET MAKING (?)—Many.

CEMETERIES (1730-or earlier)—*St. George's* where Wm. Paul, the brother of John Paul Jones is buried, also Fielding Lewis, John Dandridge, father of Martha Dandridge Washington, and over fifty others, nine of whom were foreign born, nine born in other counties of Virginia and outside the Colony.

*Old Masonic Cemetery* where are buried Lewis Littlepage,

---

2. Spotsylvania County Records, 1721-1798; *Virginia Gazette*, 1735-1775.

## THE TAILOR SHOP OF WILLIAM PAUL

Situated at the corner of Caroline and Prussia Streets, this property was acquired by William Paul in 1770 and he operated a tailor shop here until his death in 1774. He is buried in St. George's Churchyard. Here he was visited by his brother later Admiral John Paul Jones.

## ROCKY LANE

In the 200 block of Caroline Street is an original and unique Rocky Lane leading down a steep hill to Sophia Street on the river side where was situated the Lower Ferry, over which colonial travellers passed to Ferry Farm, the boyhood home of Washington.

### SLAVE BLOCK

Symbolic of the heavy slave traffic of colonial Fredericksburg this old slave auction block stands at the corner of William and Charles Streets. In the picture, standing, is Albert Crutchfield, ex-slave, and long a unique character in Fredericksburg.

### TENTEMENT QUARTERS

On lower Sophia Street are several such buildings which are said to have been used for workers in the Old Bloomery Iron Works. Several of these ancient houses have recently been demolished.

## OLD HOUSE AT SOPHIA AND WOLFE STREETS

Near here were Thornton's Tavern and a Ferry Landing. These were much accustomed places in colonial times.

## OLD TAVERN IN WAGONERS TOWN

Now standing on Liberty Street between William and George Streets is this quaint old building which is said to have been used as a tavern for wagoners coming to Fredericksburg in early times. Demolished, May, 1957.

## MEDITATION ROCK

Tradition says that Mary Washington frequently resorted to this place
on the plantation of her son-in-law Colonel Fielding Lewis for meditation and the reading of her Bible. It was her request that she be
buried near to this natural beauty, which was done.

## MARY WASHINGTON
## MONUMENT

This handsome granite monument
on the north end of Washington
Avenue was erected in 1894 over
the remains of Mrs. Mary Ball
Washington who died in 1789. It
replaced another monument which
was begun in 1833 but never completed.

## McPHERSON CHARITY SCHOOL

Archibald McPherson (1705-1754), Scotch merchant of Fredericksburg, by will established a trust fund for a charity school in Fredericksburg. The school was incorporated in 1796 and in 1801 the old Fredericksburg Academy was sold and the funds transferred to the McPherson Charity School. This building was demolished a few years ago to make way for the new Masonic Lodge Building.

## MASONIC CEMETERY

James Somerville (1742-1798), wealthy Scotch merchant of Fredericksburg, gave one quarter block at the intersection of Charles and George Streets to the Masonic Lodge in 1784 to be used as a burial ground for their members and their families. Many distinguished Fredericksburgers rest here.

RAPPAHANNOCK RIVER AT THE FALLS

The remains of Indian fish traps at the falls of the river are perhaps
the oldest landmarks of the Fredericksburg vicinity.

REMAINS OF OLD CANAL

This pre-Revolutionary canal ran from Falmouth to Hunter's Iron
Works which was for many years one of the principal manufacturing
businesses in this vicinity.

## INDIAN PUNCH BOWL

On the south side of the Rappahannock River not far above Falmouth Bridge is a unique landmark. Said to have been used by the Indians during hunting festivals as a punch bowl, it was found by Major Francis Thornton (1682-1758) upon his land and by him engraved "1720."

## GRAVE OF JAMES HUNTER
### (1721-1784)

James Hunter came to Virginia, 1746, from Scotland and soon was a leading merchant at Falmouth where he later established his noted Iron Works. On this iron fence which surrounds his grave in Falmouth Cemetery were ornate iron letters, JAMES HUNTER, all of which have now disappeared.

## GENERAL GEORGE ROGERS CLARK MEMORIAL

On Washington Avenue stands a small monument to General George Rogers Clark (1752-1818) who grew to manhood near Fredericksburg. The inscription reads in part: "In general acknowledgement of the valor and strategic victories of General George Rogers Clark . . . The old Northwest owes its freedom from the British tyranny to this distinguished patriot and soldier."

## MONUMENT TO RELIGIOUS LIBERTY

On the grounds of Maury School stands this monument recalling that a committee of which Thomas Jefferson was a member framed a Bill for Religious Liberty in Virginia on January 13, 1777 in Fredericksburg.

GARDEN OF THE MERCER APOTHECARY SHOP
1936

MARY (BALL) WASHINGTON
(*circa* 1708-1789)

This traditional portrait of Mary
the Mother of Washington now
hangs in The Mary Washington
House.

## SCHOOL HOUSE ATTENDED BY GEORGE WASHINGTON

Traditionally John Hobby, school master and sexton at nearby Falmouth Church, taught George Washington in this little building which was restored in 1930.

### GENERAL LAFAYETTE
### (1757-1834)

The Marquis de Lafayette played an important role in American Independence, was a life time friend of Washington, and visited his mother here. In 1824 he revisited Fredericksburg and was given an elegant reception at the Town Hall.

COURTHOUSE OF FREDERICKSBURG

The present building was erected in 1852 and has undergone extensive interior alterations. The original courthouse of Spotsylvania County was built on this site about 1739.

COLONEL
GEORGE WASHINGTON
(1732-1799)

### SLIGO

The present residence is on the site of the home of John Ferneyhough, Sr. which is said to have been used as a Revolutionary hospital.

### GOVERNOR JOHN FORSYTH
(1780-1841)

Born in Fredericksburg, his family moved to Georgia shortly after the Revolutionary War. He was elected to the U. S. Senate, served his adopted state as governor, and was Secretary of State under Presidents Van Buren and Tyler.

DOCTOR GEORGE FRENCH
(1751-1824)

Dr. French came to Fredericksburg from his native Scotland and became a prominent physician and business man. Between 1789 and 1813 he served eight terms as Mayor of Fredericksburg. He married in 1780 Anne Brayne Benger, a great niece of Mrs. Alxander Spotswood.

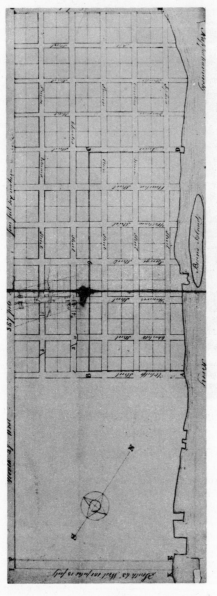

## MAP OF FREDERICKSBURG

Taken from Map in "Land Causes and Appeals, 1808-1821,"

Page 51, Clerk's Office, Courthouse, Fredericksburg, Virginia.

EXPLANATION: "The Figures ABCDA–Represent The Outer Boundary Of the Town As Established in 1742 (Same as in 1727). The Figures KIGHK–Represent The Outer Boundary Of The Town As It Now Stands Agreeable To The Directions Of Two Acts Of Assembly Passed In the Years 1759 And 1769."

[Signed]

"C. Smith, Surveyor King George County."

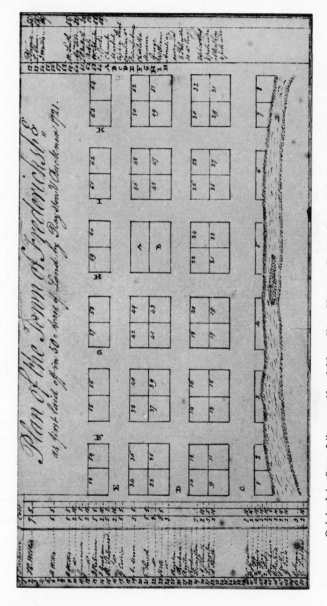

Original in State Library, gift of Mary Kate Hunter, Descendant of Robert Taliaferro (1661),
Major Lawrence Smith (1666), John Taliaferro (1680), and Wm. Hunter (1744),
Trustees of Colonial Fredericksburg.

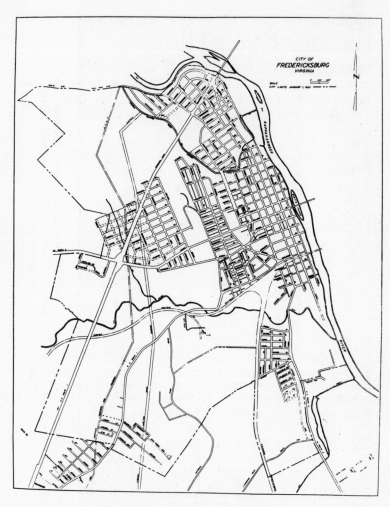

Map of Fredericksburg Today (1955)

Basil Gordon, Dr. James Carmichael, Benj. Day, Charles Yates, John Scott, Robert Lewis, nephew of George Washington, and more than 90 others, of whom 23 were natives of foreign countries, many were from other counties of Virginia and from other colonies.

CHURCHES (1570-and later)—*Father Segura Mission,* 1570; *Episcopal Church* at Germanna c.1720; *St. George's,* c.1726 (Rev. Patrick Henry, uncle of the Orator, was rector of St. George's, also Rev. James Marye and son);

*Quakers,* probably in the vicinity by 1650;

*Jews-Judaism,* perhaps in the vicinity by 1650;

*Presbyterians,* here by 1730 or earlier;

*Baptists,* present in the region by 1714;

*Methodists,* here as early as 1740.

COACH-MAKING (1730-on)—Many shops.

COBBLERY (from the first)—

COLLIERY (1714-on)—From the Palatinate Mines of German and others had undoubtedly been established earlier.

COOPERAGE (1715-on)—Fredericksburg was a great center for making barrels, kegs, hoops, etc.

COUNTING OR CLEARING OR CUSTOM HOUSES (1731-or earlier)—Michael Gratz had a Counting House in Fredericksburg by 1776, Eliezer Callender, Port Master.

COURT-HOUSE (1731-or earlier)—*Famous Trial of Baptist Dissenters* 1768;

*Famous Judges who presided over the Court:* James Monroe, James Mercer, Francis T. Brooke;

*Notables who were licensed to practice law here*: James Monroe, John Marshall, John F. Mercer, Bushrod Washington, Wm. Waller Hening, John Taylor, John T. Brooke, Robert Brooke, Andrew Buchanan, Oliver Towles, etc.

DISCOVERY— (Given under Exploration)

DOCTORS— (Given in the chapter on Doctors in Colonial Fredericksburg)

ENGINEERING— (Given under Surveying)

EXPLORATION (1521, 1525, 1570, 1608, 1643, 1653, 1670, 1673)—The first two dates in parenthesis represent the Spanish explorations in the region of the Chesapeake—Gordillo, Quexos, Ayllon, Gomez; 1570, Father Segura established the Catholic Mission on the Rappahannock near the Falls; 1608, Captain John

Smith voyaged to the Falls of the Rappahannock; 1643, Walter
Ashton's Expedition; 1653, Wm. Clairborne's Expedition; 1670,
John Lederer explored the Rappahannock to its source; 1673,
Augustine Herman produced his map of Virginia and Mary-
land. Dr. Thomas Walker's expedition into Kentucky and
Tennessee was made in 1749; George Rogers Clark explored
the Ohio Valley in 1772. Both of these men had lived in Fred-
ericksburg.

EXTRACTIVE INDUSTRIES (?)—Turpentine, tar, pitch, sumac, ginseng,
linseed oil, flax, hop extracts, etc.

FACTORS (?)— (See Agents)

FAIRS (1738-on)—Held twice a year at the Market Place, Kenmore,
etc.

FERRIES (1730-on)—There were four ferries across the Rappahannock.

FISHING (?)—Fishing, pickling, drying of fish, and catching of oysters
were important interests of the area.

FOREIGN ESTABLISHMENTS (1750-on)—George Mitchell, principal of
Robert Jardine of London; James Maury, principal for James
Maury and Co., of Liverpool; William Reid, principal for
Messrs. Cunningham & Co., of Glasgow; and a number of others.

FOUNDRIES (c.1714-on)—Alexander Spotswood's foundry at Germa-
na, 1714; Principio Co. of Maryland, established interests near
the Falls of the Rappahannock about 1737; Hunter Iron Works,
the Bloomery or Foundry, the Gunnery Manufactory, etc.

FRATERNAL AND LEARNED SOCIETIES— (Listed under Societies)

GARDENRY (?)—Every large planter and owner of large homes cultivated beautiful gardens.

GENERAL MERCHANDISE STORES (1738-on)—There were at least fifty
general merchant stores in the town at the peak of its prosperity, 1780; Dixon's, Mitchell's, Hunter & Taliaferro's, Hall
& Co., Lenox, Scott & Co., Maury's, Kuhn's, Somerville's, Yates's,
Glassell's, Ritchie & Co., etc.

GOLDSMITH SHOPS (1750-on)—James Hamilton, and several others.

HOMES, FAMOUS COLONIAL—Fifty homes have been definitely located
in Spotsylvania County, many of which are still standing; half
that number in the town proper or immediately adjoining it,
many of the latter are still in existence: Beverley's, Brooke's,
Dr. Carmichael's, Dr. Carter's, Dangerfield's, Daniel's, Dick's,
Fitzhugh's, Forbes', Glassell's, Herndon's, Lewis's, Marye's,

Maury's, Mercer's, Minor's, Monroe's, Dr. Mortimer's, Posey's, Page's, Maj. Smith's, Spotswood's, Stanard's, Strother's, Talia-ferro's, Thornton's, Wallace's, Washington's, Dr. Woodford's, etc.

HORSE-RACING (1750-on)—Jockey Clubs, Race Track at "Chatham," famous horses run—"Kitty Fisher," "Fearnaught," etc.

HOSPITALS (1750-on)—At Alum Springs, the Gunnery, Sligo, and another located at the corner of Caroline and William Street; prisoners from Yorktown brought to Fredericksburg, also Hessian prisoners.

INNS OR TAVERNS (1730-on)—Thornton's, probably first, Gordon's, Indian Queen, Rising Sun, Weedon's and over forty others between 1750 and 1780.

INSURANCE AND INSURERS (as early as 1769)—Bennett & Browne, and several others.

IRON INDUSTRY— (Given under Foundries)

JEWELRY SHOPS (1750-on)—John Lampe, and several others.

JOCKEY CLUBS (1750-on)— (Listed under Horse-racing)

KILNS (?)—Many lime kilns, brick, pottery, drying of malt and hops, fruits, etc.

LAND COMPANIES (1748, 1749, 1754-66, 1763, 1766, 1768, 1769, 1775) —Dates in the parentheses represent the Ohio Company, the Loyal Company, the Franklin Plan, Mississippi Company, Illinois Scheme, Indiana Company, Vandalia, Transylvania; the Ohio, Loyal, and Mississippi Companies were organized and managed almost entirely by citizens of the Fredericksburg area; citizens of this section were interested in all the other western schemes.

LAW PROFESSION (1670-on)—Wm. Fitzhugh of "Bedford," Richard Lee of "Stratford," James, John, and John Francis Mercer of "Marlborough," Mann Page of "Mansfield," Patrick Henry of "Hanover," Francis T. Brooke of "Smithfield," Robert Danger-field of "Belvidere"; James Monroe, John Marshall, John Taylor, John T. Brooke, Robert Brooke, John Minor, Andrew Buchanan, Oliver Towles, John F. Mercer, Bushrod Washington, Richard Brent, Wm. W. Hening, etc., were licensed to practice by the Court at Fredericksburg.

MANUFACTURING (1750-on)—Somerville & Muir Stocking Factory, Allan's Stocking Factory, Mitchell's American Ink Powder Co., John Pride, et al, Tobacco & Snuff Manufactory, Potash Plant.

Weaving Factory, Cotton & Textile Mills, Salt Works, Tanneries, etc.

MAP-MAKERS (1673-on)—Augustine Herman's Map of Virginia and Maryland, 1673; John Mitchell Map, 1751; Fry-Jefferson Map, 1751; Jones's Map of "Louisiana," 1698; Henry Map of Virginia, 1771; Dr. Walker's maps and sketches of his journeys to Kentucky and Tennessee; Clarke's surveys for the Ohio Co.; Gist's surveys for the same Co.; Lewis's surveys for Lord Fairfax; George Washington's surveys and maps; Jefferson's maps, etc.

MARINERS (?)—The city was constantly filled with sailors and shipmasters.

MARKET-HOUSE (c.1730)—Provided for in the original Plat of the Town, 1727; meeting place of the Masonic Lodge, banquets, concerts, etc.

MASONIC LODGE (c.1752-on)—Mother Lodge of George Washington; Jacob Von Braam, Washington's interpreter on his trip to Ft. Duquesne, 1754; other prominent members include Lewis Burwell, Charles Carter, Wm. Dangerfield, Rev. James Maury, Fielding Lewis, Rev. james Marye, Hugh Mercer, James Mercer, Mann Page, Sr. and Jr., Thomas Posey, Jno. & Robt. Spotswood, the Thorntons, Oliver Towles, Gustavus B. Wallace, Dr. Thomas Walker, George Weedon, Henry Willis, William Woodford, etc. The Lodge furnished seven generals to the Revolution: Washington, Mercer, Posey, Towles, Wallace, Weedon, and Woodford.

MEETING HOUSES (c.1570)—Probably the first church or mission was that of Father Segura, 1570; first Episcopal Church was at Germanna, c.1720; the "Lower Church on the Rappahannock," c.1726; the Quakers were in the vicinity perhaps as early as 1700; the Catholics established a church at Aquia, about 1686-7; Jews were in the vicinity at a very early date; Presbyterians came to the region as early as 1737; the Baptists were here by 1714 or earlier; the Methodists had entered the area around 1740.

MILLERS AND STONE MASONS (1754 or earlier)—Cuthbert Sandys, and many others.

MILLINERIES (1750-on)—Catherine Rathall, 1766, and others.

MILLING (1750-on)—There were all sorts of mills in and around Fredericksburg, flour, grist, bake-shops, brewing, carding, cider, flax, hemp, linseed, pewter, potash, potter, saw-mills, soap, sorghum, stone tanning, tread, besides the iron and other types of mills. There were 35 flour and grist mills within and in the immediate vicinity of Fredericksburg. Dixon's and Hunter's works were the most famous.

MINING AND QUARRYING (1740-on)—Spotswood's iron interests, Augustine Washington and the Principio Co., Hunter's Iron Works, the Gunnery, Semple and Mercer's iron interests; quarries along the banks of the Rappahannock, above the town, etc.; clays for brick-making; sulphur mines at Mineral near Fredericksburg; mica deposits; Indian stone quarries at Embrey Creek; gold found in the area in the Eighteenth Century but not developed until the turn of the century; lead.

MINISTRY (17th. Century or earlier)— (See Church and Meeting-houses)

MISSIONARIES (1570-on)—Father Segura's Mission to the Indians in 1570; Protestant efforts to Christianize the Indians; Society for the Propagation of the Gospel in Foreign Parts; expansion of the Dissenting groups into the West, etc.

MUSIC ACADEMIES (1750-on)—Traveling Troupes as early as 1752; John Victor's Music School before the close of the Revolution, and other music schools.

NAVAL AND MILITARY (1676-on)—Virginia Rangers under Cadwallader Jones, and others; military fort at the Falls in 1676; recruits for the French and Indian War; headquarters of the military forces of Northern Virginia during the Revolution; rendezvous; training camps; armies stationed here under Gen. Weedon, and others; several ships built here for the Virginia and Continental navies; several Hospitals were located here during the Revolution.

ORDINARIES (1730-on)— (Listed under Inns)

PAINTING (?)—Family portraits, notables, and miniatures; portraits of members of families painted while in Europe and by artists from Europe.

PAINTING, HOUSE-PAINTING (?)—Many of this trade besides the slaves and indentured servants.

PIONEERS (1570-on)—Father Segura (1570), Capt. John Smith (1608), Walter Ashton (1643), William Clairborne (1653), Margaret Brent (1659), John Lederer (1670), Cadwallader Jones (c.1681), Robert Taliaferro (prior to 1670), Alexander Spotswood (1716), Dr. Thomas Walker (1749), George Rogers Clark (c.1750),

Christopher Gist (prior to 1754), John Sevier (c.1775), and scores of others.

PLANTERS AND PLANTATIONS (1671-or before)—William Fitzhugh of "Bedford," 1670; William Brent of "Woodstock," c.1686; Giles Brent of "Peace," 1646; Robert Taliaferro of "Taliaferro's Mount," prior to 1670; Francis Thornton of "Fall Hill," c.1720; Zachary Lewis of "Belair," c.1730; the Wallers of "Newport," c.1730; Alexander Spotswood of Germanna and "Newpost," c.1720 and 1730; Spotswood of "Nottingham," c.1750; Richard Brooks of "Smithfield," before 1716; Mann Page of "Mansfield," c.1760; Stanards, Woodfords, Baylors, Strothers, Fielding Lewis, Mercers, and hosts of others.

PLAY-HOUSE (perhaps as early as 1750)—Market House, 1730; Player Troupes, 1750; at Fairs, Concerts, c.1750; Theater, before 1798, etc.

POLITICS (?)—Parishes as political units, King's Councillors, Court Officials, Burgesses, etc.

POST-OFFICE—POSTAL SERVICE (?)—Planters were responsible at first; Post Riders; "Newpost" as headquarters of British Dominions in North America and the West Indies, first post-office in the colonies; Alexander Spotswood as Deputy-Postmaster General who influenced the appointment of Benjamin Franklin, postmaster of Philadelphia, thus paving the way for his appointment with William Hunter of Williamsburg as joint postmasters for all the colonies.

POTASH PLANT (c.1750)—Large exporter of soap, also important in the Revolution.

POTTERY SHOPS (by 1750)—Many such shops found in the town.

PRINTING ESTABLISHMENTS (by 1778-or before)—John Buckner of Gloucester County and connected with the founding of "Lease-land" which became Fredericksburg was the first printer in Virginia, 1682; William Hunter of Williamsburg may have had printing interests in Fredericksburg, 1750; Roger Dixon and Thomas Nicolson had printing establishment in the town by 1780; Robert Scott was engaged in book-binding and plate engraving here by 1778.

PUBLIC OFFICIALS (?)—Vestrymen as public officials of the parish; King's Agents; Court Judges; Court Clerks; Burgesses; Port Masters; Customs Officers; Town Trustees, etc.

PUBLIC STORES (1750-or earlier)—At least four public tobacco ware-houses; public warehouses for wheat and hemp; public supply stores.

QUARRYING (by 1730-or before)— (Given under Mining and Quarry-ing)

RACING (1750-on)— (See Horse-racing)

REAL ESTATE DEALERS (?)—Many of the large planters, merchants, and doctors engaged in land speculation.

ROPE MAKING (?)—Great demand for cordage, twine, and rope of all kinds.

SADDLERIES (1750-on)—Richard Lewis, John Green, William Hous-ton, and many others.

SAILORS (?)— (See Marines)

SALT WORKS (Indians worked salt beds here)—Salt works at Fred-ericksburg supplied the Continental forces during the Revolu-tion.

SCHOLARS (?)—Noted ministers and tutors as well as statesmen, doctors, jurists, lawyers, etc., such as Rev. Marye, Rev. Archi-bald Campbell, Rev. Archibald Alexander, Rev. Philip Fithian, John Harrower, Walker Maury, John Marshall, James Madison, James Monroe, James and John Francis Mercer, Arthur Lee, Joseph Jones, Dr. Lawrence Brooke, ad finitum.

SCHOOLS (1735-on)— (Treated under chapter on Schools)

SCIENTISTS (?)—John Clayton of Urbanna, John Mitchell of Glou-cester County, Dr. Arthur Lee, and several others.

SHIP-BUILDING—SHIP DEALERS (1716-on)—Spotswood, Principio Co., Hunter, Fielding Lewis, Roger Dixon, John Allan, James Maury, John Glassell, James Ritchie & Co., William Allason, Michael Gratz, Mitchell & Co., Dekar-Thompson & Co., Fitz-hugh, Brent, Joist Hite Co., Basil Gordon, and many others.

SLAVE TRADE—DEALERS (?)—Fredericksburg was a considerable slave market, ships often brought as many as four hundred at a time; sixty, fifty, thirty lots often advertised for sale at a time.

SOCIETIES—Fraternal, Learned, Scientific (1750-on)
  *The Masonic Lodge*: Washington's Mother Lodge; Lafayette an Honorary member; practically all the leaders of Fred-ericksburg were members; the Lodge furnished seven gen-erals to the Revolution, including the Commander-in-Chief and Admiral of the Navy.

*Va. Chapter of the Soc. of Cincinnati*: The Virginia Chapter
was organized in Fredericksburg, 1783; the generals, colo-
nels, majors, captains, and subalterns, including the most
of those from this area who had fought in the Revolution
to the total number of 99 officers; Col. Oliver Towles was
made Secretary and General George Weedon was appointed
delegate to the General Meeting; the total membership was
264.

*Am. Phil. Soc*: The Virginia members in 1769 were Dr. Arthur
Lee, Colonel Francis Lee, Dr. Hugh Mercer, John Walker,
Colonel Landon Carter, all from the Rappahannock area;
those who were admitted from Virginia in 1774 were Dr.
Walter Jones and Dr. McClurg, Jones was from the Valley;
in 1780, Rev. James Madison and George Washington were
admitted; and in 1785 James Madison, Mann Page of
"Mansfield," were made members—of these members all
but two were from the Rappahannock Valley.

In 1771 the Society had 255 members, distributed as follows:

|      |     |                              |
|------|-----|------------------------------|
| (1)  | 157 | were inhabitants of Pennsylvania |
| (2)  | 10  | were from Massachusetts      |
| (3)  | 2   | were from Rhode Island       |
| (4)  | 4   | were from Connecticut        |
| (5)  | 11  | from New York                |
| (6)  | 11  | from New Jersey              |
| (7)  | 3   | from Delaware                |
| (8)  | 5   | from Maryland                |
| (9)  | 5   | from Virginia                |
| (10) | 5   | from South Carolina          |
| (11) | 1   | from Georgia                 |
| (12) | 10  | from the West Indies         |
| (13) | 25  | from Europe                  |

The states and countries represented by the membership of the
Society in 1798 included:

| 11 American colonies | India            | Poland     |
|----------------------|------------------|------------|
| Antigua              | Ireland          | Portugal   |
| Austria              | Italy            | Prussia    |
| Barbados             | Jamaica          | Russia     |
| Belgium              | Kgd. of Sicilies | St. Croix  |
| Bohemia              | Latvia           | Santa Dom. |
| Denmark              | Lithuania        | Scotland   |

| England | Majorca | Spain |
| France | Netherlands | Sweden |
| German States | Nova Scotia | Venetian R. |
| Iceland | Papal States | West Fla. |

SOLDIERNG (?)—Commander of the Fort at the Falls built in 1676 was Major Lawrence Smith;

Prominent Virginia Rangers included Cadwallader Jones, Zachary Lewis, and many others;

Many of the officers of the French and Indian War were from Fredericksburg and vicinity;

Fredericksburg was the rendez-vous, recruiting, and training center during the Revolution;

Revolutionary training fields were at the Courthouse Green and at "Nottingham";

The Commander-in-Chief of the Continental Armies and the Commander of the American Navy were from Fredericksburg;

Fredericksburg furnished six generals—Mercer, Posey, Towles, Wallace, Weedon, and Woodford—, and many other able officers of the armies and the navy;

George Washington and Nathaniel Green received the felicitations of the City of Fredericksburg upon the successful conclusion of the War—their replies are in the Minutes of the Council of the City.

SPRINGS (?)—Alum Springs, Steel Water Spring, Sulphur Springs of Fauquier County, the Gunnery Spring, Sweet Water Spring of Indian lore, and many others in the vicinity.

STAGE-COACH AND WAGON MAKING (?)—Large demand for these commodities.

STATESMEN (?)—George Washington, Thomas Jefferson, James Madison, James Monroe, Joseph Jones, Mann Page, Benjamin Grymes, William Fitzhugh, John Taylor, Edmund Pendleton, the Lees of "Stratford," Mercers of "Marlborough," George Mason, Fielding Lewis, ad finitum.

STORES (1730-or earlier)— (Given under Merchants, Mercantile, Public)

STUDENTS (?)— (See Chapter on American and Foreign Colleges— Education)

SURVEYING (from the very first)—George Washington was the most noted surveyor of the neighborhood.

TAILORS (1750-or earlier)—William Paul, brother of John Paul Jones, had a tailor shop in Fredericksburg; dozens of other shops.

TANNERIES (1750-or earlier)—There were many tanning mills in the vicinity.

TAVERNS (c.1720)— (See Inns or Ordinaries)

TEACHERS-TUTORS (?)— (See Chapter on Tutors)

TRADE AND TRAPPING (?)—Thriving business throughout the period.

TRAVELERS (1608-on)— (See Chapter on Travelers of the 18th Century)

TUTORING (?)— (See Chapter on Tutors)

VINEYARDS (?)—Nearly every planter and large estate owner cultivated vineyards and engaged in making cider.

WARE-HOUSING (1730-on)—There were at least eleven tobacco warehouses in Fredericksburg; also several wheat and hemp warehouses.

WHEELWRIGHTS (1750-on)—Many.

WRITERS (1671-on)— (See Chapter on Literary Production)

## APPENDIX C
## STATISTICAL TABLES OF TRADE

(The following statistical tables furnish a detailed[3] picture of the importance and character of the trade and trade contacts of the Rappahannock area; they also give the total volume of trade of other ports and areas of North America).

Port Rappahannock Imports from Mar. 11, 1727 to Oct. 4, 1727

| Commodity | Quantity | British Isles | British Continental Colonies | British Caribbean Area | Foreign Caribbean Area | Other Areas & Ports |
|---|---|---|---|---|---|---|
| *Ballast* | 80 tons | | Patuxent | | | |
| *Goods, Eu.—* | 1 Shipment<br>1 Shipment<br>1 Shipment | British<br>Exeter<br>James R. | | | | |
| *Passengers* | 101<br>89 | Ireland | | | | |
| *Cider—* | 20 bbls. | | James River | | | |
| *Fish—* | 10 Quintals | | New England | | | |
| *Ginger—* | 70 lbs. | | | Bermuda | | |
| *for Ship's Provisions, Store* | 1 Shipment | | | | | |

[3] Customs House, Series 16, I, Transcripts in Div. of MSS., Library of Congress; Naval Office Lists of Imports and Exports, Public Records Office, London, in Univ. of Calif.

Port Rappahannock Imports from Mar. 11, 1727 to Oct. 4, 1727
—Continued—

| Commodity | Quantity | British Isles | British Continental Colonies | British Caribbean Area | Foreign Caribbean Area | Other Areas & Ports |
|---|---|---|---|---|---|---|
| Salt | 1600 bu. 10 hhds. 700 bu. | | James River New England | Bermuda | | |
| Sugar | 1 Cask 19 Tierces | | James River New England | | | |
| Straw Ware— | 1 Shipment | | | | | |
| Rum— | 2 bbls. 4 bbls. | | James River New England | | | |
| Lumber— | 1 Shipment | | New England | | | |
| Household & Husbandry Goods— | | | | | | |
| Furniture— | 1 Shipment | | N. Carolina | | | |
| Household Goods— | 1 Shipment | | N. Carolina | | | |
| Miscella- neous: | | | | | | |

Port Rappahannock Imports from Mar. 11, 1727 to Oct. 4, 1727
—Continued—

| Commodity | Quantity | British Isles | British Continental Colonies | British Caribbean Area | Foreign Caribbean Area | Other Areas & Ports |
|---|---|---|---|---|---|---|
| *Goods, Eu.—* | 3 Shipments | Bristol | | | | |
| | 1 Shipment | Dunbar | | | | |
| | 1 Shipment | Exeter | | | | |
| | 4 Shipments | Glasgow | | | | |
| | 1 Shipment | Irvine | | | | |
| | 2 Shipments | Liverpool | | | | |
| | 2 Shipments | London | | | | |
| | 1 Shipment | Topsham | | | | |
| | 1 Shipment | | Accomac | | | |
| | 1 Shipment | | Maryland | | | |
| | 1 Shipment | | Philadelphia | | | |
| *Teeth* | 10 lbs. | Bristol | | | | |
| | 50 lbs. | Liverpool | | | | |
| | 10 lbs. | | | Barbados | | |
| *Negroes, Servants, & Passengers:* | | | | | | |
| *Negroes—* | 108 | | | Barbados | | |
| *Provisions & Food Stuffs:* | | | | | | |

Port Rappahannock Imports from Mar. 11, 1727 to Oct. 4, 1727
—Continued—

| Commodity | Quantity | British Isles | British Continental Colonies | British Caribbean Area | Foreign Caribbean Area | Other Areas & Ports |
|---|---|---|---|---|---|---|
| *Hops—* | 5 Bags | | Boston | | | |
| *Salt—* | 472 bu. | | Boston | | | |
| *Salt—* | 1500 bu. | | | Bermuda | | |
| *Madeira—* | 10 Casks | | | Barbados | | |
| *Sugar & Molasses:* | | | | | | |
| *Molasses—* | 5 hhds. | | Boston | | | |
| *Sugar—* | 18 Casks | | Boston | | | |
| *Sugar—* | 11 Casks | | | Barbados | | |
| *Textile & Fiber Products:* | | | | | | |
| *Calico—* | 3 Pieces | | Boston | | | |
| *Linen—* | 16 Pieces | Bristol | | | | |
| *Ozenbrig* | 3 Pieces | | Boston | | | |
| *Silk Mfg.—* | 2 Cases | | Boston | | | |
| *Wines & Spirits:* | | | | | | |

Port Rappahannock Imports from Mar. 11, 1727 to Oct. 4, 1727
—Continued—

| Commodity | Quantity | British Isles | British Continental Colonies | British Caribbean Area | Foreign Caribbean Area | Other Areas & Ports |
|---|---|---|---|---|---|---|
| Rum— | 17 Casks | Bristol | | | | |
| Rum— | 37 Casks | | Boston | | | |
| Rum— | 6 Casks | | New England | Barbados | | |
| Rum— | 22 Casks | | | Bermuda | | |
| Rum— | 7 Casks | | | | | |
| Wine— | 3 Pipes | Glasgow | | | | |
| Wine— | 7 Pipes | Leven | | | | |
| Wine— | 6 Pipes | Liverpool | | | | |
| Wine— | 2 Pipes | | Boston | Barbados | | |
| Wine— | 1 Pipe | | | | | |
| Madeira— | 4 Pipes | | New England | | | |
| Port— | 3 Pipes | | New England | | | |
| Wood Products: | | | | | | |
| Staves— | 6,000 | Bristol | | | | |
| Woodenware— | 1 Crate | | Boston | | | |

*Other Listings*:

*Dry Goods—Clothing—*
  Calico
  Linen
  Ozenbrig
  Silk

*Furs, Leather, Skins*:

*Household & Husbandry Goods*:

*Straw Ware*:

*Wooden Ware*:

*Miscellaneous*:
  Family
  Passengers
  Teeth
  Negroes
  Servants

*Provisions—Food Stuffs*:
  Cider
  Ginger
  Fish
  Hops

*Provisions—for Ship*:
  Salt
  Ship Supplies
  Ballast

*Wines & Spirits*:
  Rum

*Sugar & Sugar Products*:
  Molasses
  Sugar
  Wines

*Wood & Wood Products*:
  Lumber
  Staves

Rappahannock—1765—Imports

| PORT OF ORIGIN | COMMODITY | QUANTITY |
|---|---|---|
| Glasgow | Goods, Euro.— | 1 Shipment |
| Greenock | Goods, Euro.— | 3 Shipments |
| Halifax | Ballast | 190 tons |
| Liverpool | Goods, Euro.— | 3 Shipments |
| London | Goods, Euro.—<br>Ballast | 3 Shipments<br>140 tons |
| Port Glasgow | Goods, Euro.— | 6 Shipments |
| Scarborough | Ballast | 200 tons |
| Southampton | Goods, Euro.— | 1 Shipment |
| Whitehaven | Goods, Euro.— | 1 Shipment |
| Boston | Rum | 7 hhds.<br>8 tierces<br>10 bbls. |
|  | Molasses | 1 hhd.<br>5 tierces<br>3 hhds. |

Rappahannock—1765—Imports
—Continued—

| PORT OF ORIGIN | COMMODITY | QUANTITY |
| --- | --- | --- |
| Boston, *Cont.* | Handkerchiefs | 1 Parcel |
| | Cheese | 500 lbs. |
| | Salt | 10 hhds. |
| | Earthenware | 1 Shipment |
| | Romales | 1 Shipment |
| | Iron Ware | 1 Shipment |
| | Blubber | 1 bbl. |
| | Fish | 12 Quintals |
| | | 3 bbls. |
| | Chocolate | 50 lbs. |
| | | 2 Boxes |
| | Wooden Ware | 1 Shipment |
| | Brimstone | 74 cwt. |
| | Goods, Euro.— | 3 Bales |
| | | 1 Bag |
| | Pepper | 12 lbs. |
| Maryland | Ballast | 40 tons |
| Nantucket | Rum | 5 hhds. |
| | Sugar, Brown | 3 bbls. |
| | Mollases | 12 hhds. |
| | Cheese | 1000 lbs. |
| | Sugar, Loaf | 500 lbs. |
| New York | Ballast | 25 tons |
| | Sugar, Refined | 2000 lbs. |
| | Apples | 200 bu. |
| | Chocolate | 200 lbs. |
| | Cordage | 1 Parcel |
| Philadelphia | Ballast | 25 tons |
| | Rum | 1 hhds. |
| | | 14 hhds. |
| | | 36 hhds. |
| | | 2 hhds. |
| | | 53 hhds. |
| | | 1 tierce |
| | Mollasses | 5 hhds. (?) |
| | | 26 hhds. (?) |
| | | 3 hhds. (?) |
| | Sugar, Loaf | 256 lbs. (?) |
| | | 2000 lbs. (?) |
| | | 6000 lbs. (?) |
| | Wine, Madeira & Fayal | 5 Qtr. Casks |
| | | 18 Qtr. Casks |

Rappahannock—1765—Imports
—Continued—

| PORT OF ORIGIN | COMMODITY | QUANTITY |
|---|---|---|
| Philadelphia, *Cont.* | Cotton | 1 Bag |
| | Soap | 1 Box |
| | Limes | 10 bbls. |
| | | 15 bbls. |
| | | 8 bbls. |
| | | 33 bbls. |
| | Chocolate | 1 Box |
| | Rice | 1 Cask |
| | Indigo | 25 lbs. |
| | Leather | 1 Bundle |
| | Pimento | 8 Bags |
| | Coffee | 1 Bag |
| | | 1 bbl. |
| | Raisins | 1 Cask |
| | Candles | 1 Box |
| | Bread | 4 kegs |
| | Ginger | 1 Bag |
| | | 1 Bag |
| Port Hampton | Goods, Euro.— | 4 Shipments |
| | Coal | 300 bu. |
| | Ballast | 90 tons |
| | Goods, Sundry | 1 Shipment |
| Port Lewis | Salt | 120 tons |
| Port York | Goods, Euro.— | 1 Shipment |
| | Tobacco | 70 hhds. |
| | Iron, Pig | 22 tons |
| | Staves | 10 M |
| | Logs, Walnut | 10 |
| Rhode Island | Dollars, Cash | 120 |
| | Rum | 5 bbls. |
| | | 37 hhds. |
| | Molasses | 14 hhds. |
| | Sugar, Loaf | 875 lbs.  (?) |
| | Sugar, Brown | 1 bbl. |
| | Coffee | 1 bag |
| | | 2 bbls. |
| | Desks | 3 |
| | Chocolate | 3 boxes |
| | | 20 lbs. |
| | Rice | 1 Cask |
| | Tea | 1 Canister |
| | Cheese | 87 lbs. |
| | | 1300 cwt. |
| | Dish | 1 |

Rappahannock—1765—Imports
—Continued—

| PORT OF ORIGIN | COMMODITY | QUANTITY |
| --- | --- | --- |
| Salem | Rum | 3 hhds. |
| | | 15 bbls. |
| | Sugar, Brown | 10 bbls. |
| | Sugar, Loaf | 290 |
| | Cheese | 1950 |
| | Salt | 18 hhds. |
| | Fish | 4 bbls. |
| | | 2 Quintals |
| | Chocolate | 130 lbs. |
| | Aniseed, Water | 2 Casks |
| | Earthen-ware | 1 Shipment |
| | Molasses | 10 hhds. |
| | Goods, Sundry— | |
| | Euro. | 1 Shipment |
| | Goods, Euro.— | 1 trunk |
| | | 38 prs. Shoes |
| | Tinware | 1 Shipment |
| | Iron Ware | 2 Shipments |
| | Woodware | 2 Shipments |
| Anguilla (Anguila) | Salt | 1200 bu. |
| Antigua | Ballast | 35 tons |
| | Rum | 116 hhds. |
| | | 7 bbls. |
| | | 16 bbls. & |
| | | tierce |
| | Sugar, Brown | 10 bbls. |
| | Coffee | 13 Bags |
| | Molasses | 2 Tierces |
| | | 1 bbl. |
| | Sugar, Muscovy | 35 bbls. |
| Barbados | Rum | 158 hhds. |
| | Molasses | 2 hhds. |
| | Sugar, Muscovy | 1 hhds. |
| | | 3 bbls. |
| | Sugar, Brown | 100 |
| Bermuda | Ballast | 40 tons |
| Greenock | Rum | 1 bbl. |
| | | 21 hhds. |
| Cette | Ballast | 430 tons |
| Quebec | Ballast | 180 tons |
| Rotterdam | Ballast | 140 tons |

## EXPORTS AND IMPORTS, 1768-1769
## VESSELS

| PORTS | TOTALS EXTRA CONTINENTAL | | | TOTALS WITHIN THE CONTINENT | | | GRAND TOTALS | | |
|---|---|---|---|---|---|---|---|---|---|
| | Topsails | Sloops, etc. | Tonnage | Topsails | Sloops, etc. | Tonnage | Topsails | Sloops, etc. | Tonnage |
| *South Potomac* | 26 | 7 | 4469 | 1 | 7 | 420 | 27 | 14 | 4889 |
| *Rappahannock* | 31 | 13 | 4731 | — | 22 | 724 | 31 | 35 | 5455 |
| (Lower Part)) | 119 | 79 | 16628 | 8 | 48 | 1645 | 127 | 127 | 18273 |
| James (Upper Part) | 50 | 12 | 6660 | 12 | 19 | 2010 | 62 | 31 | 8670 |
| Charles Town | 214 | 83 | 29396 | 28 | 123 | 5053 | 242 | 206 | 34449 |
| Patuxent | 78 | 25 | 11792 | 12 | 64 | 3165 | 90 | 89 | 14957 |
| Philadelphia | 261 | 16 | 25071 | 26 | 225 | 9898 | 287 | 321 | 34970 |
| New York | 167 | 118 | 16476 | 22 | 155 | 5371 | 189 | 273 | 21847 |
| Boston | 145 | 89 | 19848 | 14 | 281 | 12135 | 159 | 370 | 31983 |
| York River | 20 | 16 | 2175 | 2 | 18 | 912 | 22 | 34 | 4482 |
| Salem-Marblehead | 57 | 152 | 13248 | 5 | 77 | 3398 | 62 | 229 | 16646 |
| Piscataqua | 67 | 105 | 10979 | 3 | 46 | 1965 | 70 | 151 | 12944 |
| Rhode Island | 74 | 120 | 7262 | 9 | 200 | 4329 | 83 | 325 | 11591 |
| Newfoundland | 92 | 22 | 7865 | 20 | 30 | 2969 | 112 | 52 | 10834 |
| Falmouth (Mass.) | 26 | 35 | 5916 | 2 | 25 | 1080 | 28 | 60 | 6996 |
| New London | 28 | 16 | 5181 | 30 | 51 | 2156 | 58 | 67 | 7337 |
| North Potomac | 34 | 4 | 4620 | 6 | 36 | 2306 | 40 | 40 | 6926 |
| Roanoke River | 23 | 25 | 3256 | 6 | 99 | 4048 | 29 | 124 | 7304 |
| Brunswick | 41 | 30 | 6073 | 10 | 24 | 1265 | 51 | 54 | 7338 |
| Savannah | 50 | 35 | 6082 | 7 | 56 | 1774 | 57 | 91 | 7856 |
| Halifax | | | | | | | | | 7006 |
| Quebec | | | | | | | | | 7687 |

Rank:   Philadelphia (1), Charleston (2), Boston (3), James (4), New York (5), Salem (6), Patuxent (7), Piscataqua (8), Rhode Island (9), Newfoundland (10), *South Potomac and Rappahannock* (11).

## IMPORTS, 1770-1771
## VESSELS

| PORTS | TOTALS EXTRA CONTINENTAL | | | TOTALS WITHIN THE CONTINENT | | | GRAND TOTALS | | |
|---|---|---|---|---|---|---|---|---|---|
| | Topsails | Sloops, etc. | Tonnage | Topsails | Sloops, etc. | Tonnage | Topsails | Sloops, etc. | Tonnage |
| *South Potomac* | 34 | 2 | 4046 | 11 | 20 | 2221 | 45 | 22 | 6267 |
| *Rappahannock* | 28 | 10 | 4204 | 3 | 26 | 1134 | 31 | 36 | 5428 |
| (Lower Part) James | 124 | 80 | 15996 | 8 | 70 | 2919 | 132 | 150 | 18915 |
| (Upper Part) | 54 | 3 | 6502 | 6 | 29 | 1472 | 60 | 32 | 7974 |
| Charles Town | 145 | 125 | 21412 | 30 | 155 | 6142 | 175 | 280 | 27554 |
| Patuxent | 133 | 34 | 16328 | 15 | 66 | 3915 | 148 | 100 | 20243 |
| Philadelphia | 342 | 101 | 35538 | 27 | 280 | 11951 | 369 | 38 | 47489 |
| New York | 148 | 184 | 17771 | 21 | 247 | 7768 | 169 | 431 | 25539 |
| Boston | 141 | 144 | 19558 | 33 | 501 | 18802 | 174 | 648 | 38360 |
| York River | 25 | 7 | 3671 | 2 | 22 | 1046 | 27 | 29 | 4717 |
| Salem-Marblehead | 55 | 126 | 11302 | 2 | 108 | 4420 | 57 | 234 | 15722 |
| New London | 29 | 113 | 5521 | 7 | 282 | 7078 | 36 | 395 | 12599 |
| Rhode Island | 79 | 127 | 7622 | 16 | 394 | 11045 | 95 | 521 | 18667 |
| Falmouth (Mass.) | 41 | 47 | 9186 | 2 | 47 | 2003 | 43 | 94 | 11199 |
| Brunswick | 50 | 24 | 6931 | 6 | 43 | 1691 | 56 | 67 | 8622 |
| Savannah | 45 | 45 | 6258 | 8 | 52 | 1921 | 53 | 97 | 8179 |
| North Potomac | 34 | 6 | 4818 | 5 | 34 | 1947 | 39 | 40 | 6765 |
| New Haven | 12 | 68 | 3345 | 3 | 133 | 3279 | 15 | 201 | 6624 |
| Roanoke | 24 | 41 | 3572 | 5 | 67 | 2525 | 29 | 108 | 6097 |
| Beaufort | 8 | 30 | 1474 | — | 91 | 2338 | 8 | 121 | 3812 |
| Newfoundland | | | | | | | | | 13337 |
| Quebec | | | | | | | | | 4120 |
| Nova Scotia | | | | | | | | | 8363 |
| New Hampshire | | | | | | | | | 15312 |

Rank:  Philadelphia (1), Boston (2), Charleston (3), James (4), New York (5), Patuxent (6), Rhode Island (7), Salem (8), New Hampshire (9), Newfoundland (10), New London (11), *South Potomac and Rappahannock* (12).

## EXPORTS, 1771-1772
## VESSELS

| PORTS | TOTALS EXTRA CONTINENTAL | | | TOTALS WITHIN THE CONTINENT | | | GRAND TOTALS | | |
|---|---|---|---|---|---|---|---|---|---|
| | Topsails | Sloops, etc. | Tonnage | Topsails | Sloops, etc. | Tonnage | Topsails | Sloops, etc. | Tonnage |
| *South Potomac* | 44 | 3 | 5600 | 4 | 20 | 1385 | 48 | 23 | 6986 |
| *Rappahannock* | 39 | 21 | 6201 | 4 | 22 | 1135 | 45 | 43 | 7336 |
| York | 31 | 11 | 4925 | 1 | 25 | 953 | 32 | 36 | 5878 |
| (Lower Part) | 123 | 114 | 16130 | 7 | 58 | 2463 | 130 | 172 | 18593 |
| James (Upper Part) | 76 | 9 | 10600 | 3 | 40 | 1563 | 79 | 49 | 12163 |
| Charles Town | 182 | 127 | 24835 | 33 | 145 | 6196 | 215 | 272 | 31031 |
| Patuxent | 136 | 28 | 17052 | 10 | 75 | 3514 | 146 | 103 | 20566 |
| Philadelphia | 274 | 90 | 27341 | 86 | 291 | 15688 | 360 | 381 | 43029 |
| New York | 138 | 172 | 17258 | 46 | 168 | 8275 | 184 | 340 | 25533 |
| Boston | 123 | 94 | 16301 | 55 | 522 | 22694 | 176 | 616 | 38995 |
| Newfoundland | 241 | 42 | 20828 | 15 | 21 | 1781 | 256 | 63 | 22609 |
| Piscataqua | 118 | 86 | 15315 | 10 | 127 | 4950 | 128 | 213 | 20256 |
| Salem-Marblehead | 52 | 169 | 14051 | 11 | 122 | 5578 | 63 | 291 | 19629 |
| Rhode Island | 76 | 163 | 8800 | 27 | 387 | 11609 | 103 | 550 | 20409 |
| Falmouth (Mass.) | | | | | | | | | 9041 |
| Halifax | | | | | | | | | 7378 |
| Quebec | | | | | | | | | 7064 |
| North Potomac | | | | | | | | | 7659 |
| Savannah | | | | | | | | | 7823 |
| Brunswick | | | | | | | | | 9928 |

Rank:   Philadelphia (1), Boston (2), Charleston (3), New York (4),
Newfoundland (5), Patuxent (6), Rhode Island (7), Pisca-
taqua (8), Salem (9), Lower James (10), Upper James (11),
Brunswick (12), Falmouth (Mass.) (13), Savannah (14),
North Potomac (15), Halifax (16), *Rappahannock* (17),
Quebec (18), South Potomac (19), York (20).

## IMPORTS, 1771-1772
## VESSELS

| PORTS | TOTALS EXTRA CONTINENTAL | | | TOTALS WITHIN THE CONTINENT | | | GRAND TOTALS | | |
|---|---|---|---|---|---|---|---|---|---|
| | Topsails | Sloops, etc. | Tonnage | Topsails | Sloops, etc. | Tonnage | Topsails | Sloops, etc. | Tonnage |
| *South Potomac* | 38 | 5 | 5105 | 8 | 21 | 1775 | 46 | 26 | 6880 |
| *Rappahannock* | 32 | 17 | 4955 | 3 | 22 | 1006 | 35 | 39 | 5961 |
| York | 25 | 11 | 4200 | 4 | 18 | 992 | 29 | 29 | 5192 |
| (Lower Part) | 140 | 89 | 17756 | 20 | 68 | 4101 | 160 | 157 | 21857 |
| James (Upper Part) | 51 | 8 | 6820 | 10 | 33 | 2401 | 61 | 41 | 9221 |
| Charles Town | 165 | 112 | 23750 | 52 | 160 | 7842 | 217 | 272 | 31592 |
| Patuxent | 128 | 32 | 16871 | 14 | 60 | 3348 | 142 | 92 | 20219 |
| Philadelphia | 293 | 95 | 29444 | 39 | 292 | 12296 | 352 | 387 | 41740 |
| New York | 145 | 178 | 17796 | 29 | 205 | 7247 | 174 | 383 | 25043 |
| Boston | 148 | 137 | 20712 | 22 | 514 | 18708 | 170 | 651 | 39440 |
| New Hampshire | 76 | 72 | 9732 | 16 | 122 | 5857 | 92 | 194 | 15569 |
| Salem-Marblehead | 59 | 135 | 12537 | 1 | 127 | 5040 | 60 | 262 | 17577 |
| Rhode Island | 80 | 153 | 8555 | 14 | 377 | 10832 | 94 | 530 | 19387 |
| Newfoundland | | | | | | | | | 17876 |

Rank: Philadelphia (1), Boston (2), Charleston (3), New York (4), Lower James (5), Patuxent (6), Rhode Island (7), Newfoundland (8), Salem (9), New Hampshire (10), Upper James (11), South Potomac (12), *Rappahannock* (13), York (14).

## EXPORTS, 1772-1773
## VESSELS

| PORTS | TOTALS EXTRA CONTINENTAL | | | TOTALS WITHIN THE CONTINENT | | | GRAND TOTALS | | |
|---|---|---|---|---|---|---|---|---|---|
| | Topsails | Sloops, etc. | Tonnage | Topsails | Sloops, etc. | Tonnage | Topsails | Sloops, etc. | Tonnage |
| *South Potomac* | 43 | 1 | 6157 | 7 | 23 | 1680 | 50 | 24 | 7837 |
| *Rappahannock* | 39 | 12 | 6022 | 2 | 22 | 836 | 41 | 34 | 6858 |
| York | 41 | 8 | 4510 | 3 | 25 | 1080 | 44 | 33 | 5590 |
| (Lower Part) | 146 | 109 | 18539 | 12 | 89 | 3754 | 158 | 198 | 22293 |
| James (Upper Part) | 79 | 4 | 10891 | 2 | 18 | 792 | 81 | 22 | 11683 |
| Charles Town | 178 | 84 | 23423 | 54 | 169 | 8125 | 232 | 253 | 31548 |
| Patuxent | 131 | 32 | 16669 | 4 | 90 | 3597 | 135 | 122 | 20266 |
| Philadelphia | 291 | 113 | 29723 | 62 | 293 | 15099 | 353 | 406 | 45822 |
| New York | 138 | 176 | 16675 | 50 | 336 | 11899 | 188 | 512 | 28574 |
| Boston | 142 | 110 | 18026 | 62 | 531 | 24480 | 204 | 641 | 42506 |
| Newfoundland | 152 | 29 | 13015 | 15 | 15 | 2375 | 167 | 44 | 15390 |
| Piscataqua (N.H.) | 125 | 88 | 15075 | 16 | 86 | 4275 | 141 | 174 | 19350 |
| Salem-Marblehead | 59 | 185 | 13488 | 10 | 112 | 5339 | 69 | 297 | 18827 |
| Rhode Island | 92 | 165 | 9651 | 17 | 423 | 12229 | 109 | 588 | 21880 |
| New London | 38 | 144 | 7443 | 5 | 234 | 5449 | 43 | 378 | 12892 |
| Quebec | | | | | | | | | 7106 |
| Halifax | | | | | | | | | 7577 |
| Falmouth (Mass.) | | | | | | | | | 10007 |
| New Haven | | | | | | | | | 6936 |
| North Potomac | | | | | | | | | 9088 |
| Brunswick | | | | | | | | | 8736 |
| Savannah | | | | | | | | | 9124 |

Rank:   Philadelphia (1), Boston (2), Charleston (3), New York (4), Lower James (5), Rhode Island (6), Patuxent (7), Piscataqua (8), Salem (9), Newfoundland (10), New London (11), Upper James (12), Falmouth (Mass.) (13), Savannah (14), North Potomac (15), Brunswick (16), South Potomac (17), Halifax (18), Quebec (19), New Haven (20), *Rappahannock* (21), York (22).

## IMPORTS, 1772-1773
## VESSELS

| PORTS | TOTALS EXTRA CONTINENTAL | | | TOTALS WITHIN THE CONTINENT | | | GRAND TOTALS | | |
|---|---|---|---|---|---|---|---|---|---|
| | Topsails | Sloops, etc. | Tonnage | Topsails | Sloops, etc. | Tonnage | Topsails | Sloops, etc. | Tonnage |
| *South Potomac* | 45 | 2 | 6262 | 4 | 21 | 1365 | 49 | 23 | 7627 |
| *Rappahannock* | 38 | 13 | 5895 | 2 | 19 | 815 | 40 | 32 | 6710 |
| York | 24 | 9 | 4255 | 3 | 31 | 958 | 27 | 40 | 5213 |
| James (Lower Part) | 147 | 85 | 19591 | 18 | 82 | 4375 | 165 | 167 | 23966 |
| (Upper Part) | 52 | 7 | 6768 | 11 | 22 | 2322 | 63 | 29 | 9090 |
| Charles Town | 181 | 78 | 22899 | 40 | 157 | 7034 | 221 | 235 | 29933 |
| Patuxent | 116 | 30 | 14139 | 11 | 87 | 4182 | 127 | 117 | 18321 |
| Philadelphia | 298 | 112 | 29949 | 41 | 279 | 12351 | 339 | 391 | 42300 |
| New York | 141 | 177 | 17682 | 35 | 357 | 11179 | 176 | 534 | 28861 |
| Boston | 171 | 146 | 23137 | 26 | 509 | 20496 | 197 | 655 | 43633 |
| Newfoundland | 171 | 25 | 15733 | 35 | 49 | 4752 | 206 | 74 | 20485 |
| New Hampshire | 75 | 80 | 11179 | 12 | 92 | 3864 | 87 | 172 | 15043 |
| Salem-Marblehead | 47 | 122 | 10595 | 1 | 120 | 4687 | 48 | 242 | 15280 |
| Rhode Island | 75 | 127 | 7757 | 10 | 394 | 11076 | 85 | 521 | 18833 |
| New London | 22 | 110 | 5391 | 8 | 264 | 6692 | 30 | 374 | 12085 |
| Quebec | | | | | | | | | 7065 |
| Falmouth (Mass.) | | | | | | | | | 7861 |
| New Haven | | | | | | | | | 6801 |
| North Potomac | | | | | | | | | 8379 |
| Roanoke | | | | | | | | | 6858 |
| Brunswick | | | | | | | | | 9775 |
| Savannah | | | | | | | | | 7650 |

Rank: Boston (1), Philadelphia (2), Charleston (3), New York (4), Lower James (5), Newfoundland (6), Rhode Island (7), Patuxent (8), Salem (9), New Hampshire (10), New London (11), Brunswick (12), Upper James (13), North Potomac (14), Falmouth (Mass.), (15), Savannah (16), South Potomac (17), Quebec (18), Roanoke (19), New Haven (20), *Rappahannock* (21), York (22).

# APPENDIX D

The most common items imported were:

Allspice
Almonds
Artificial Flowers
Ballast
Basins (Wash)
Beams (Scales)
Bedcord
Beds
Bedticking
Bellows
Bells
Blankets
Bonnets
Boots
Brandy
Brass (Candlesticks, Pans, etc.)
Bricks
Broadcloth
Brushes (Clothing, Paint, etc.)
Buckles (Breeches, Shoe, etc.)
Bushel Measures
Buttons (All Kinds-Brass, Pearl, etc.)
Calicoes
Cambric
Candle Moulds
Candle Sticks (Brass, Iron, etc.)
Canisters
Capes
Caps
Cards (Playing, cotton, flax wool)
Carpenter's Tools
Carpets
Castile Soap
Chairs
Chamber Pots
China (Bowls, cups, saucers, etc.)
Chintz
Chocolate
Cinnamon
Cloaks
Clocks
Clothing
Cobbler's Tools
Cocoa
Coffee
Coffee Mills (Pots)
Combs
Copper (Pots, Pans, Kettles, Stills)
Copperas
Cork
Cotton (Laces, Handkerchiefs, Gowns, Towels, etc.)
Counterpanes
Cranberries

---

4. Customs House, Series 16, I, Transcripts in Div. of MSS. Library of Congress; Naval Office Lists of Imports and Exports, Public Records Office, London, in Univ. of Cal.

Crochet Needles
Cups and Saucers
Cutlery (All Kinds)
Damask
Delftware (All Kinds)
Diapers (Table Clothes)
Dishes
Dowlas
Drugs and Medicines, etc.
Duffle
Dutch Ovens
Dutch Quills
Dye Stuffs (All Kinds)
Earthenware (All Kinds)
Elastic
Embroidery Needles
Ermine
Everlasting
Feather Beds
Fiddles
Fish Hooks
Flannels
Flax Hackles
Florence Oil
Frying Pans
Funnels
Fustian
Pimento
Pins
Pipes (Tobacco)
Plates
Playing Cards
Ploughs
Pocket Books
Pot Hooks
Pots and Pans
Pounce (Boxes and Stands)
Powder
Pulleys
Raisins
Razors

Razor (Strops, Hones)
Reap Hooks
Ribbon
Rice
Rings
Romals
Rope
Rubbers
Rugs
Rulers (Foot, Yard, etc.)
Rum
Russia Sheeting
Saddlery (All Kinds)
Sail Canvas
Salt
Salt Petre
Satins
Saucers and Cups
Scales
Scissors
Scythes
Seed (Field, Garden)
Seines
Serge
Sewing Thread
Shirts
Shalloons
Shears (Sheep, Tailor)
Sheeting
Shoe Buckles
Shoes
Shovels
Sickles
Sieves
Sifters
Silk (All Kinds of Articles)
Silk Gloves
Silk Handkerchiefs
Silk Laces
Snuff
Snuff Boxes

Spectacles
Spices
Spoons
Stationery
Stays
Steelyards
Stockings
Stoneware (All Kinds)
Sugar
Surgical Instruments
Surveying Instruments
Sweet Meats
Table Clothes
Tables (All Kinds)
Tankards
Tapers
Tartar
Tea
Thread
Thimbles
Tinware (All Kinds)

Toasters
Tongs
Toys
Traps
Trunks
Turpentine
Twist
Two-foot Rules
Umbrellas
Velvet
Vises (Hand)
Violins
Watch Chains
Watches
Whips
Whiskeys
Wigs
Wines (Bordeaux, Lisbon, Geneva, Oporto, Madeira, etc.)
Woolens
Writing Paper

# APPENDIX E

## Items Exported[5]

The largest portion of the shipping interests of both Falmouth and Fredericksburg were with the West Indies. Barbados, Caracoa, Surinam, Cayenne, St. Croix, the Leeward Islands, Jamaica, etc., are most frequently mentioned in the Order Books and Invoice Books of the merchants of Falmouth and Fredericksburg.

A list showing the items exported from Falmouth and Fredericksburg is given below, taken from the Allason Papers, papers of other merchants, and the Naval Lists of "Exports":

Apparel
Apple Brandy
Bar Iron
Barley
Bass
Beans
Beaver Skins
Beef
Bees Wax
Billets
Boards
Brandy { Apple / Peach
Brass Products
Buck Skins
Butter
Candles
Casks
Cast Iron
Cattle
Chemicals
Cherry Rum

Cheese
Cider
Clapboard
Coal
Corn
Deals
Deer Skins
Dried Fish
Doe Skins
Drugs
Ducks
Dye Stuffs
Feathers
Fish { Bass / Dried / Herring / Pickled / Shad / Sturgeon
Flax Seed

5. Customs House, Series 16, I, Transcripts in Div. of MSS. Library of Congress; Naval Office Lists of Imports and Exports, Public Records Office, London, in Univ. of Cal.

269

Flour
Food Stuffs
Furs: Beaver, Bear, Fox,
   Deer, Otter
Geese
Ginseng
Gold Ore
Headings
Hemp
Herring
Hides
Hogs
Hominy
Honey
Hoops
Hops
Horses
Indian Corn
Indigo
Ipecacuanha

Iron {
   Bar
   Cast
   Ore
   Pig
   Sow

Iron Products
Lard
Leather (tanned)
Livestock
Logwood
Lumber
Mast Planks
Masts
Malt Liquors
Maple Sugar
Meal
Metal and Mineral Products
   (Brass, Cast Iron, Bar Iron,
   Pewter)

Military Stores
Minerals
Molasses
Muskrat Skins
Naval Stores
Negroes
Oak Planks
Oats
Ore
Otter Skins
Peach Brandy
Peas

Peltry {
   Beaver Skins
   Deer Skins
   Muskrat Skins
   Otter Skins

Pewter Products
Pickled Fish
Pig Iron
Pine Planks
Pipe Staves
Pitch
Potatoes
Provisions: beans, corn, peas,
   pork, tallow, wheat
Raisins
Redwood
Rice
Rum (cherry)
Rye
Sassafras
Scantlings
Seed
Servants
Sheep
Shingles

Skins {
  Beaver
  Buck
  Deer
  Doe
  Muskrat
  Otter
}

Slaves
Snake Root
Soap
Spars
Staves  (Barrel, Hogshead, Pipe)
Stone
Sturgeons
Sugar (Maple)
Sumac
Tallow
Tanner Leather
Tar

Teeth
Timber
Tobacco
Turpentine
Walnut Planks
Walnuts
Wheat
Whiskey
White Shad
Wines
Wood Products: Billets, Headings, Oak and Pine Planks, Walnut Planks, Barrel Staves, Hogshead Staves, Pipe Staves, Timber
Wool
Yams
Yards

# APPENDIX F

## Origin and Destination of Exports and Imports

The Naval List of "Imports" of Port Rappahannock for 1765 shows the following sources of origin of the commodities:

| | |
|---|---|
| Glasgow | North Carolina |
| Port Hampton | Philadelphia |
| Halifax | Rhode Island |
| Leith | Salem |
| Liverpool | South Carolina |
| London | Upper District of the James |
| Southampton | Antigua |
| Whitehaven | Barbados |
| Boston | Bermuda |
| Maryland | Lisbon |
| New York | Madeira |

The "Exports" of Port Rappahannock for 1765 were destined for the following places:

| | |
|---|---|
| Ayr | Rappahannock |
| Bideford | Rhode Island |
| Glasgow | Salem |
| Leith | Whitehaven |
| Liverpool | Boston |
| London | Hampton |
| Maryland | Barbados |
| New York | Bermuda |
| Philadelphia | Lisbon |

The "Imports" to the South Potomac for the year 1765 originoted in:

| | |
|---|---|
| Glasgow | London |
| Greenock | Boston |
| Liverpool | Hampton |
| Liverpool and Limerick | Maryland |

New West Jersey               Bordeaux
North Potomac                 Citte (Cette, Cetti)
Philadelphia                  First Entry
Rhode Island                  Gambia
Salem                         Quebec
Barbados                      Rotterdam
Barbados and Saltertudas      Rappahannock

The "Exports" from the South Potomac for 1765 were bound for:

Ayr                           Whitehaven
Cork                          East Florida
Glasgow                       Hampton
Leith                         New England
Liverpool                     Philadelphia
London                        Rappahannock
Lisbon                        Antigua
Barbados                      Bermuda
St. Kitts

The "Imports" to the Rappahannock for 1766 came from the following ports and places:

Ayr                           Philadelphia
Greenock                      Port Hampton
Leith                         Rhode Island
Liverpool                     Salem
London                        South Potomac
Port Glasgow                  York
Whitehaven                    Antigua
Ayr and Port Glasgow          Nevis and
Bordeaux and Greenock         St. Eustatius (Eustatia)
Boston                        Guadeloupe
Madeira                       Rotterdam

The ports and regions to which the "Exports" from the Rappahannock for 1766 were destined were:

Bristol                       Southampton
Glasgow                       Whitehaven
Liverpool                     Boston
London                        Maryland
Port Glasgow                  South Carolina

| | |
|---|---|
| Cadiz | Lisbon |
| Philadelphia | Cork |
| Rhode Island | Falmouth (England) |
| Salem | Greenock |
| Antigua | Kinsale |
| Barbados | Grenados |

The "Imports" for the South Potomac for 1766 represented the following places:

| | |
|---|---|
| Ayr | Maryland |
| Dublin | Philadelphia |
| Greenock | Rappahannock |
| Hull | Salem |
| Limerick | Lisbon |
| Liverpool | Barbados |
| London | St. Kitts (St. Christopher) |
| Port Glasgow | Bermuda |
| Whitehaven | Coasting |
| East Florida | First Entry |
| Hampton | Hamburg |
| Madeira | |

The "Exports" from the South Potomac were sent to:

| | |
|---|---|
| Ayr | St. Kitts |
| Cork | Antigua |
| Leith | Bermuda |
| London | Barbados |
| Glasgow | New England |
| Liverpool | East Florida |
| Whitehaven | Hampton |
| Lisbon | Rappahannock |
| Philadelphia | |

The "Imports" to the Rappahannock for 1767 came from the following ports and places:

| | |
|---|---|
| Bristol | Boston |
| Hull | Piscataqua |
| London | Basseterre |
| Port Glasgow | Rhode Island |
| Whitehaven and | Salem |
| Bordeaux | Antigua |

Barbados                          Quebec
St. Kitts                         North Potomac
St. Eustatius  (St. Eustatia)

The "Exports" from the Rappahannock for 1767 were destined for:

Bristol                           Philadelphia
Glasgow                           Salem
London                            Antigua
Whitehaven                        Barbados
Boston                            Leghorn

The "Imports" for the Rappahannock for 1768 came from the following places:

Bristol                           St. Eustatius
Greenock                          Boston
Falmouth  (England)               Maryland
Liverpool                         Philadelphia
London                            Port Hampton
Port Glasgow                      Rhode Island
Whitehaven                        Salem
South Potomac                     Antigua and
Antigua                           Madeira
Bermuda                           St. Thomas
Jamaica                           Bordeaux
St. Kitts                         Cette (Cetti)
Barbados                          Gibraltar

The "Exports" from the Rappahannock for 1768 were bound for:

Ayr                               Maryland
Glasgow                           North Potomac
Liverpool                         Rappahannock
London                            Salem
Whitehaven                        Antigua
Ayr and                           Barbados
Belfast                           Cadiz
Boston                            Madeira

The "Imports" to the South Potomac for 1768 came from:
Ayr                               London
Dublin                            Port Glasgow

Whitehaven and Dublin
Glasgow
North Potomac
Liverpool and N. Potomac
Hampton and London
London and N. Potomac
Glasgow, Hampton and Bremen
Boston
Philadelphia
Rappahannock
Salem

Hampton
Martinique
Hampton and Rotterdam
Isle of May
Cadiz
London, Hampton
York River
Antigua
Barbados
Bremen
Unknown Port

The "Imports" to the Rappahannock for 1769 hailed from the ports and areas named below:

Boness (Borrowstoness)
Bristol
Greenock
Isle of May
Liverpool
London
Port Glasgow
Whitehaven
Boston
Havre de Grace
Maryland

North Carolina
Philadelphia
Port Hampton
Rhode Island
Salem
Antigua
Barbados
Caracao (Curriso)
St. Croix
Bordeaux
Cette (Cetti)

The "Exports" from the Rappahannock for 1769 were destined for the following ports and places:

Bristol
Cork
Glasgow
Greenock
Liverpool
London
Whitehaven
Philadelphia
Rhode Island
Salem
Antigua

Barbados
St. Kitts
Cadiz
Boston
Maryland
New York
Vigo
Leghorn
Lisbon
Oporto

# APPENDIX G

## MISCELLANEOUS[6]

The following list of items of trade of the Allason Company is interesting for two reasons. It shows the value of slaves who were being bought and sold by a merchant of Falmouth, and the fact that horses and slaves are listed together, both chattel alike.

| | | |
|---|---|---|
| Horses . . . . . . . . . . . . . . . . . . | 30 | pounds |
| Negro boy Moses . . . . . . . . . . . | 57 | " |
| Negroe . . . . . . . . . . . . . . . . . | 80 | " |
| Horse & Mare . . . . . . . . . . . . . | — | — |
| Negroe Evans had of Reuben Pates . . . . | 33 | " |
| Horse . . . . . . . . . . . . . . . | 8 | " |
| Cows with calves . . . . . . . . . . . | — | — |
| Negroe John . . . . . . . . . . . . . | 80 | " |
| Colts . . . . . . . . . . . . . . . | — | — |
| Negro man Jack bought of Dr. Greenwood . . | 45 | " |
| Molattoe boy George bought of Jno. Snelling . | 40 | " |
| Molattoe boy bought of Dr. Greenwood . . . | 15 | " |
| Jack, about 50 years old . . . . . . . . | 45 | " |
| George, 15 . . . . . . . . . . . . . . | 75 | " |
| Lydia . . . . . . . . . . . . . . . | 60 | " |
| Lydia's daughter Nany . . . . . . . . | 60 | " |
| Harry, about 30 years . . . . . . . . . | 60 | " |
| Alice a girl 12 years old . . . . . . . | 50 | " |
| Jean . . . . . . . . . . . . . . . . | 30 | " |
| Jack . . . . . . . . . . . . . . . . | 45 | " |
| George . . . . . . . . . . . . . . . | 60 | " |
| Tom . . . . . . . . . . . . . . . . | 25 | " |
| George . . . . . . . . . . . . . . . | 70 | " |

6. Allason Inventory Book, 1761-2, p. 41; Oct. 1, 1764, p. 13; Oct. 1, 1765, p. 25; Oct. 1, 1766, p. 63; Allason Invoice Book, Oct. 1, 1768, p. 23; 1769, p. 5; 1772, p. 60.

# APPENDIX H

## Schools and Tutors[7]

Academy, Fredericksburg, James Mercer, President
Academy, Medical, Fredericksburg
Alexander School, Rev. Archibald, "Greenwood," Posey Home
Allan School, John, Fredericksburg
Arnaud's French School, Fredericksburg
Barrett School, Bartholomew, Fredericksburg
Berry and Custis School, Fredericksburg
Boucher School, Rev. Jonathan, Port Royal
Brooks School, Dr. Ebenezer, "Oak Hill," John Marshall Home
Callender Singing School, Fredericksburg
Catholic Parish School, "Woodstock," Aquia
Catholic Parish School, "Richland," Aquia
Curley's French and Dancing School, Fredericksburg
Dame School, The, Fredericksburg
Douglas School, Rev. William, "The Ducking Hole," Thomas Jefferson's tutor
English School, Fredericksburg
Fithian School, "Nomini Hall," Robert Carter Home
French Language School, Fredericksburg
Fuller Mathematical and English School, Bartholomew, Fredericksburg
Goolrick School, John, Fredericksburg
Grammar School, Fredericksburg
Grove's School, William or "Master Hobbie," Falmouth

7. George Washington Bicen. Com., *Youth and Manhood; Dic. of Am. Biog.;* *W. & M. Quart., III, VI;* John Harrower, *Diary, 1773-1776* (New York, 1900, reprinted from Am. Hist. Rev., VI, No. 1); Moncure D. Conway, *Geo. Washington's Rules of Civility* (New York: U. S. Book Co., 1890); *Va. Gazette,* 1781; Kate Mason Rowland, *The Life of Geo. Mason, 1725-1792* (New York and London: Putnam, 1892), I; W. G. Stanard, *Va. Mag. of Hist.,* XXI; Samuel Shepherd, The Statutes of Va., II, III (Richmond: Shepherd, 1835-36); Madison Papers, in MS Division, Lib. of Cong.; Mecupian's Washington Letter, Jul. 5, 1778.

Harrower School, "Belvidere," Dangerfield Home
Heely School, "Nottingham," Alexander Spotswood Home
Hudson's Boarding School, Fredericksburg
Jones School, Joseph, Fredericksburg
Jones School, Maria, Fredericksburg
Latin and Greek School, Fredericksburg
Lewis School, Fielding, Fredericksburg
Lewis School or Rappahannock Academy, Charles
Lennegan School, "Smithfield," the Brooke Home
Llangollen University, "Prospect Hill," the Lewis Home
Low's Grammar School, Fredericksburg
Lowe's School, John, "Wakefield," the Washington Home
McPherson Charity School, Fredericksburg
Martin's School, Thomas, James Madison's tutor
Marye School, Rev. James, Fredericksburg
Master Hobby's School
Maury School, Rev. Matthew, Orange County
Maury School, Walker, Thomas Jefferson's tutor
Moore's School, Col. Bernard, "Nottingham," Spotswood Home
"Old Log College," "Nottingham," the Spotswood Home
Price School, William, "Willis Hill," Fredericksburg
Robinson School, Donald, James Madison's tutor
Thompson School, Rev. James, "Oak Hill," the John Marshall
    Home
Victor's Music School, Fredericksburg
Williams School, William, Oak Grove
Williams School, Mason Home, George Mason's tutor
Wylie School, the Mason Home, George Mason's tutor
Yates School, Rev. William, Gloucester County

# APPENDIX I

## American and Foreign Colleges Attended by Colonials from The Rappahannock Valley

Some insight into the cultural life of the people of the Rappahannock Valley, particularly those of the upper class, may be had by noting the colleges to which the leaders of the area went for advanced study. The relatively large number of colonials from the Rappahannock Valley who attended colleges of the North and foreign universities is impressive, and indicates something of the cultural outlook of these men, of their families, and, to an extent, of the people of the region whom they represented.

Thomas Jefferson, James Monroe, John Marshall, John Mercer, *et al*, attended William and Mary College.

Of Southern graduates of Philadelphia College, Dr. Ewing Jordon states that "the first Southern student matriculated in the College, May 25, 1754 . . . . . Previous to 1775, thirty-five Southern students were graduated from our College Department, and about half that number were graduated from our Medical School. Maybe the number of Southern matriculates in our University, previous to the Revolution, numbered at least twice, if not four times, as many as the total number of graduates I have first given."[8]

Michael Kraus in his "Intercolonial Aspects of American Culture," states that "Over thirty southern students . . . . were graduated from the College of Philadelphia before 1775, Princeton had ten and Harvard listed a few."[9]

The following is a list of the names of the students from Virginia given by Dr. Jordon's article as having received their education in Northern colleges. It should be noted that almost the entire number were from the Rappahannock Valley or from the counties immediately contiguous to it. All Southern students who attended Northern Colleges are mentioned in the list, together with their

---

8.  Article in the *W. & M. Quart.*, VI, 217-19.

9.  Michael Kraus, *Intercolonial Aspects of American Culture on the Eve of the Revolution* (New York, 1928), p. 12.

date of graduation, arranged chronologically and with the name of the college each attended. The students whose names are preceded by an asterisk were from the Rappahannock Valley:

*JOHN TODD, Louisa County, Princeton, 1747;

JOHN BROWN, Princeton, 1749;

*DAVID JAMESON, Lt. Gov. of Virginia, Princeton, 1753;

*WILLIAM GRAYSON, Pennsylvania College (University of Pennsylvania) 1760;

JACQUELINE AMBLER, Pennsylvania College, 1761;

*RICHARD LEE, of "Stratford," Pennsylvania College, 1766;

NATHAN RUMSEY, Pennsylvania College, 1771;

*DONALD CAMPBELL, Princeton, 1771;

*JAMES MADISON, Princeton, 1771;

*JOHN TAYLOR, of "Hazelwood," Caroline, Princeton, 1771;

WILLIAM GRAHAM, President of Liberty Hall (Washington and Lee), Princeton, 1773;

*HENRY LEE, General in the Revolution and Governor of Virginia, Princeton, 1773;

*BEVERLEY ROBINSON, Lt. Col., in His Britannica's Majesty's Army, King's College (Columbia University), 1773;

*CHARLES LEE, Attorney General of the United States, Princeton, 1775;

*JOHN CLOPTON, Pennsylvania College, 1776;

THOMAS MAYO, Pennsylvania College, 1780;

ABRAHAM VENABLE, Member of Congress and United States Senator, Princeton, 1780;

*JOHN DAWSON, of Fredericksburg, Harvard, 1780;

*SPENCER BALL, Lancaster, Princeton, 1782;

RICHARD N. VENABLE, Princeton, 1782.

It will be observed that twelve of the twenty persons listed attended Princeton; six attended Pennsylvania College; one was a student at Harvard, and one studied at King's College.

*Rappahannock Valley Virginians Educated in England*

An article appearing in the *William and Mary Quarterly* under the title of "Virginians Educated in Great Britain"[10] gives the following names:

ALEXANDER, PHILIP, Stafford County,

ARMISTEAD, HENRY, Gloucester County,

BEVERLEY, WILLIAM, Essex County,

---

10.  *W. & M. Quart.*, XXI, 196-99.

BEVERLEY, JOHN, ROBERT, HARRY, Middlesex County,
BAYLOR, JOHN, King and Queen,
BAYLOR, JOHN, JR., Caroline,
BROOKE, LAWRENCE, and ROBERT, Spotsylvania County,
CARTER, JOHN, and LANDON, "Cleve," King George,
CORBIN, FRANCIS, and GAWEN, King and Queen,
CAMPBELL, ARCHIBALD, Westmoreland,
FAUNTLEROY, WILLIAM, Richmond County,
FITZHUGH, HENRY, Stafford County,
LEE, ARTHUR, HENRY, JOHN, GEORGE FAIRFAX, RICHARD HENRY,
PHILIP LUDWELL, THOMAS, LANCELOT, and WILLIAM, Westmore-
land County,
PEYTON, VALENTINE, Stafford County,
SPOTSWOOD, ALEXANDER, and JOHN, Spotsylvania County, edu-
cated at Eton, England,
SKINKER, JOHN, King George,
TAYLOE, JOHN, "Mt. Airy," Richmond County,
WARNER, AUGUSTINE, Gloucester,
WASHINGTON, AUGUSTINE, SR. and JR., LAWRENCE, Westmore-
land, educated at Appleby School in England,
WORMLEY, RALPH, URBANNA, Middlesex County.

During the Eighteenth Century Westmoreland and Middlesex
Counties led in sending the largest number of colonials to be educated in England, furnishing nineteen and seventeen respectively,
as shown by the article. There are ten residents of Rappahannock
County represented in the foregoing list, Westmoreland County
having fourteen; Middlesex and Spotsylvania four each; King and
Queen, and Stafford three each; Gloucester and Richmond two
each; and Essex and Caroline one each, making a total of thirty-
seven.

No other region of Virginia can compare with the Rappahannock Valley in the number of colonial Virginians it sent to be
educated abroad.

Edward Alfred Jones has made an extensive study of *American
Members of the Inns of Court*[11] of London. The number of Virginians who were members of this famous Court exceeds that of
any other colony except South Carolina. Allowing for all uncer-

---

11.  Edward Alfred Jones, *American Members of the Inns of Court* (London,
1842), Introduction, pp. ix-xxx, 11-13, 20-21, 28, 34, 40-42, 50, 53, 76-77, 91,
107-08, 122-27, 186.

tainties as to geographical identification, and counting the uncertain ones with other parts of Virginia, we find that there were ten persons who resided outside the Rappahannock Valley admitted to the Court; twenty-four students from the Rappahannock area were granted admission. These twenty-four were:

*Henry Lee Ball,* of "Millenback," Lancaster County, (his wife was Lettice Lee of "Stratford"), admitted to Middle Temple, 1769.

*Joseph Ball,* of "Marattico," Lancaster, half-brother of Mary Ball, mother of George Washington, admitted to Gray's Inn, 1720. It was on his advice, in a letter, dated May 19, 1747, to his half-sister, Mary Washington, that her son, George, then aged 15, was not sent to sea as a mariner.

*Robert Beverley,* son of Harry Beverley of Urbanna (brother of Robert Beverley, the historian), admitted to Middle Temple, 1719. He married the daughter of William Stanard, died at his home, of "Newlands," Spotsylvania County, 1733.

*Robert Beverley,* only son of William Beverley of "Blandfield" (member of Colonial Council of Virginia and patentee of great Beverley Manor tract in Augusta County), educated at Wakefield Grammar School in England, afterwards at Trinity College, Cambridge; entered Middle Temple, 1757. His sympathies were with England during the Revolutionary War.

*William Beverley,* eldest son of Robert Beverley of "Blandfield," went to Trinity College, 1781—where his father had also gone—having been previously at school at Fredericksburg, under the tutorship of Mr. Denholm; admitted to Lincoln's Inn, 1788. He was a Loyalist in the Revolution, and remained in England.

*Carter Braxton,* of King William County, third son of Carter Braxton (signer of the Declaration of Independence), admitted to Inner Temple, 1783. He was later member of the Assembly of Virginia.

*Lewis Burwell,* of "Carter Creek," Gloucester County, admitted to Cambridge, 1729, and entered Inner Temple, 1733. He was a member of the Masonic Lodge of Fredericksburg, Governor of the Council of Virginia, 1744, and of the Colony, 1750-52.

*Lewis Burwell,* eldest son of Lewis Burwell of "Carter Creek," Gloucester, matriculated at Balliol College, Oxford, 1765, admitted to Inner Temple, 1765. Member of the House of Burgesses from Gloucester during several sessions, 1769-1775; member of the Revolutionary Conventions of 1775, 1776; died, 1779.

*George Carter,* youngest son of "King" Carter of Corotoman, admitted to Middle Temple, 1733, called to the English Bar, 1738.

*Robert* ("Councillor") *Carter,* of "Nomini Hall," admitted to Inner Temple, 1749. Later he served as member of the Colonial Council of Virginia, 1758, and as a member of the Committee of Correspondence, 1765.

*John Clayton,* son of Sir John Clayton of Middlesex, England, born 1665, admitted to Inner Temple, 1682; sailed for Virginia, 1705; died, 1737; father of John Clayton, the botanist of Gloucester County, Virginia.

*Francis Corbin,* fifth son of Col. Richard Corbin and youngest brother of Gawen Corbin, of "Laneville," King and Queen; born, 1760; admitted to Inner Temple, 1777. He was a Loyalist in the American Revolution, as were his father and brother, Richard and Thomas.

*Gawen Corbin,* eldest son of Col. Richard Corbin of "Laneville" (member and President of His Majesty's Council and Receiver-General); born, 1738; educated first at Grinstead in Essex County, under a Mr. Harris, and afterwards at Christ's College, Cambridge; entered Middle Temple, 1756. His home was at "Buckingham," Middlesex County. He became a member of the House of Burgesses; appointed to the Council, 1775, the last to receive that appointment under the Crown; died, 1779.

*William Fauntleroy,* eldest son of William Fauntleroy of Essex County; born, 1742; entered Marischal College, Aberdeen, Scotland, 1759; admitted to Middle Temple, 1760; died, 1775.

*Moore Fauntleroy,* 1743-1802, youngest brother of William Fauntleroy, was educated at Marischal College, Aberdeen, Scotland, from which he received the degree of M. D.[12] Being a physician, he never applied for admission to the Court.

*Henry Fitzhugh,* only son of William Fitzhugh of "Eagle's Nest," Stafford; admitted to Middle Temple, 1722, at the age of 15; matriculated at Christ College, Oxford, 1722. He married the daughter of "King" Carter, and served as member of the Colonial Council.

*John Grymes,* son and heir of Hon. John Grymes (1693-1748), of "Brandon," Middlesex, born 1718; entered Inner Temple, 1736.

---

12. New England History and Genealogy Register (Boston, 1842), XLI, 391-92; XLII, 159-61, American Graduates in Medicine at the University of Edinburgh to 1809.

Benjamin Grymes of Spotsylvania County was a descendant of this family.

*Joseph Jones,* son and heir of James Jones; born, 1727; admitted to Middle Temple, 1751. He was one of the most able and influential citizens of Virginia. He served as member of the House of Burgesses from King George County; member of the Committee of Safety, 1775, Convention, 1776; Delegate to the Continental Congress, 1778, 1779. He was a close friend of George Washington and corresponded with him on the limitation of the powers of Congress by the several states, 1780. In 1783, there was a Proposition in the Virginia Assembly to revoke the release to the United States of the territory northwest of the Ohio River, but by the determined opposition of Joseph Jones it was rejected and the Assembly induced to conform to the wishes of Congress concerning the matter. He was a member of the Convention of 1788; died, 1805.

*Arthur Lee,* the sixth and youngest son of Thomas Lee of "Stratford"; born, 1740; studied medicine at Edinburgh University where he took the degree of M. D. in 1764; settled as doctor in Williamsburg; member of the Mississippi Company in 1763, with George Washington, Thomas Ludwell Lee, *et al;* admitted to Lincoln's Inn, 1770; to the Middle Temple, 1773; agent to France as member of the Commission with Franklin and Silas Deane; later sent to the Courts of Spain and Prussia.

*Henry Lee,* affectionately known as "Light Horse Harry Lee," eldest son of Henry Lee, member of the House of Burgesses and of the State Legislature, of "Leesylvania," Prince William County; born, 1756; was graduated from Princeton, 1773; admitted to Middle Temple, 1773. He was a favorite general of George Washington, and was chosen to deliver the funeral oration, 1799, when he uttered the famous words: "First in war, first in peace, and first in the hearts of his countrymen." He was a delegate to the Continental Congress, 1786; member of the Virginia Convention of 1788, where he supported Madison and Washington in favoring the adoption of the Constitution. He served as Governor of Virginia, 1792-1795.

*Philip Ludwell Lee,* eldest son of Hon. Thomas Lee (1690-1750); born, 1726-7; admitted to Inner Temple, 1749; member of the House of Burgesses from Westmoreland; President of the Council of Virginia; successor of his father, Hon. Thomas Lee, as proprietor of "Stratford," birthplace of his brothers, Richard Henry and Francis Lightfoot Lee, signers of the Declaration of Independence. He was a brother of Thomas Ludwell Lee.

*Thomas Ludwell Lee,* son of Hon. Thomas Lee; born, 1730; admitted to Inner Temple, 1748; President of the Virginia Council; member of the Mississippi Company, 1763, with Washington, Arthur Lee, *et al;* member of the House of Burgesses; delegate to the Convention of 1775; member of the Committee of Safety; member of the Convention of 1776; member of the Committee appointed to draft a declaration of rights and of a plan of government. His brothers were Richard Henry Lee, Francis Lightfoot, and Philip Ludwell Lee.

*Thomas Mason,* brother of George Mason of "Gunston Hall," admitted to Middle Temple after previously attending an academy in Stafford County and one in Fredericksburg.

*Christopher Robinson,* son and heir of Christopher Robinson (1681-1727); naval officer of the Rappahannock River; member of the Council of Virginia; matriculated at Oriel College, Oxford, May 16, 1724; from Oxford he was admitted to Middle Temple, 1727; married Judith Wormeley, daughter of Ralph Wormeley of Urbanna; member of the House of Burgesses from Middlesex 1752-1758; died 1768.

The author states that "In these pages may be found as Middle Templars representatives of such conspicuous Virginian families as Ball, Bolling, Churchill, Dowman, Fauntleroy, Fitzhugh, Robinson, Whiting and Wilcox."[13]

To all the aforementioned names of colonials from the Rappahannock Valley, several others should be added:

Lawrence Brooke of "Smithfield," Spotsylvania County, famous surgeon on the *Bon Homme Richard,* received his M. D. degree from Edinburgh University. His brother, Robert Brooke, Jr., was also graduated from Edinburgh University, where he took a degree in law. Robert served in the Revolution, and afterwards became Governor of Virginia, and Attorney-General. Their grandfather, Richard Brooke, accompanied Alexander Spotswood across the Blue Ridge Mountains in 1716.[14]

The Rev. Rodman Kenner, second Rector of St. George's Church, was a scholar at Bee's Grammar School, England, and later went to Glasgow University.[15]

---

13.  *Ibid.,* p. xiv, of the Introduction.
14.  Brooke, *op. cit.,* pp. 6-8.
15.  Virginia Magazine of History, XX, 213-14.

Mann Page was educated at Oxford; Augustine Washington and his sons, Lawrence and Augustine were educated at Appleby School; Col. Theodore Bland was sent to Leeds School in Yorkshire, England.[16]

John Carter, son of Robert Carter of Corotoman, was educated at the private academy of Mile End, London, and later matriculated at Trinity College, Cambridge, 1714;[17] Hugh Mercer was a graduate in medicine from Marshall College, Scotland.[18] Robert Beverley, the historian, was educated in England.

Many of the scholarly tutors mentioned in the discussion of private schools in the preceding chapter, were educated in the universities of Europe. Dozens of others from the Rappahannock Valley went abroad for their education.

Besides those persons whose distinctions have been described above, there were numbers of others from the Rappahannock Valley who were either natives, or who lived in the Valley as tutors and later achieved distinction. Among them was the Rev. William Yates, headmaster of the school in Gloucester, who became President of William and Mary College. Rev. Archibald Alexander, tutor in the home of General Thomas Posey, became President of Hampden-Sydney and founder of the Divinity School of Princeton. The names of Thomas Jefferson, James Madison, James Monroe, John Marshall, are too familiar to require more than mention of the fact that they were identified with the Rappahannock section of Virginia as to birthplace (or schooling) and in the practice of their arts or professions. Henry Lee, already mentioned as the author of the famous expression, "First in war, first in peace, and first in the hearts of his countrymen," and Richard Henry Lee, who introduced the resolution: "Resolved, That these colonies are, and of a right ought to be, free and independent states," are names well-known to every school child in America.

European schools, colleges, and universities represented by Rappahannock Valley men are Appleby, Bee's Grammar School, Cambridge University, Leeds Academy, Mile End Academy, Inner Court-Gray's, Lincoln's, Inner and Middle Temple, Oxford University, Paris University, Eton, Edinburgh University, Glasgow Uni-

16. *W. & M. Quart.*, II, 149-53.
17. Virginia Magazine of History, XXI, 82.
18. John T. Goolrick, Hugh Mercer (New York & Washington: The Neale. 1906), p. 13.

versity, Wakefield Grammar School. Most of the well-known universities of France, the Netherlands, Italy, and Germany were attended
by one or more of the tutors in private homes or schools of the
Rappahannock Valley, or by colonial students from the section.

INDIANS OF THE RAPPAHANNOCK VALLEY, TRIBES ON THE
PERIPHERY, AND BEYOND WITH WHOM COLONIAL
FREDERICKSBURG CAME INTO CONTACT*

*In the Immediate Vicinity of the Falls* (8 Tribes)

I. *Powhatan Indians (Algonquians)*: Between the Potomac and
the James Rivers and the Bay, to the falls of
these rivers.
    1. Cuttatawomen (north side of Rappahannock River
near Lamb's Creek).
    2. Mattaponi (on the Mattaponi River in Spotsylvania
and Caroline).
    3. Nantaughtacund (in Caroline and Essex Counties).
    4. Potomac (in Stafford and King George—seat at the
mouth of Potomac Creek—gave the Potomac River its
name).

II  *Siouan Indians (Manahoacs)*: Both sides of the Rappahannock River around and above falls.
    1. Hassininga (at the falls—HASSININGA VILLAGE at
top of the falls).
    2. Manahoac (in Stafford near the falls—MAHASKAHOD
VILLAGE on the heights above present Falmouth).
    3. Shackaconia (on south bank of Rappahannock River
in Spotsylvania County).
    4. Tanxnitania (on the north side of the Rappahannock
River in Fauquier County).

---

* There were 16 Powhatan villages on both banks of the Rappahannock between the falls and Leedstown site, and 13 Manahoac villages on the Rappahannock and Rapidan Rivers between the falls and the mountains.

## On the Periphery (9 Tribes)

III *Powhatan Indians* (Cont.):
1. Pissasec (in King George and Westmoreland).
2. Rappahannock (in Richmond County—gave the Rappahannock River its name).

IV *Siouan Indians* (Cont.):
1. Ontponea (Manahoac stock—in Orange County).
2. Saponi (in Culpeper County—Pony Top—near Culpeper, named after them).
3. Monacan (between North Anna and the James Rivers west of the falls of these rivers).

V *Conoy Indians* (in Md.—closest relatives the Delaware, Nanticoke, Powhatan. Once lived in Virginia on Kanawha River, whence the name.)
1. Doeg (north side of the Rappahannock River near present Dogue Creek. May have preceded any other Indians in the falls territory of Rappahannock.)
2. Seneca (from Md.—crossed Potomac to Virginia c.1660, South side Potomac).
3. Piscataway (from Md.—South side Potomac River).
4. Secawocomoco (from Md. to South side Potomac).

## Beyond the Periphery (8 Tribes)

VI. *Iroquois Indians* (Mohawk Valley and central New York main body).
1. Nottaway (on Nottaway River in southeastern Virginia. Kin to Meherrin and Susquehanna.)
2. Meherrin (on Meherrin River in Virginia and North Carolina—closest relatives the Nottaway).
3. Iroquois (constantly invaded the area from the North).
4. Susquehanna (neighbors of the Manahoacs on the northwest).
5. Catawba (in North Carolina below the Virginia line).
6. Tuscarora (on the lower Roanoke River, neighbors of the Nottaways).
7. Cherokee (in southwestern part of Virginia at the end of the Appalachia, in Tennessee, North Carolina, etc.).
8. Shawnee (one of their earliest seats was on the Cumberland River).

LIST OF PORTS, ISLANDS, REGIONS, AND OTHER PLACES
INCLUDED IN THE TRADE OF THE MERCHANTS OF
COLONIAL FREDERICKSBURG, 1727-1775

*Atlantic Seaboard* (43)
Annapolis
Accomac
Baltimore
Bath Town
Beauford
Boston
Brunswick
Burlington
Charles Town
Chester
Cohensy
Currituck
Edenton
Falmouth (Mass.)
Halifax
Island of St. Johns
James River Towns
Marblehead
Mobile
Nantucket
New Bern
Newfoundland
New Castle (Pa.)
New Haven
New London
New York
Norfolk
Patuxent
Pensacola
Perth Amboy
Philadelphia
Piscataqua
Pocomoke
Port Royal (S.C.)

Potomac River Towns
Quebec
Rappahannock River Towns
Rhode Island (Province
    Town)
Roanoke River Towns
Salem
St. Augustine
Sansbury
Savannah
York River Towns
Yorktown
Wilmington (N.C.)
Wynyaw

*The Back Country* (c. 100)
(The larger volume of Colonial Fredericksburg's trade came from the back country which included):

*The Piedmont* (which extended northwest to the Potomac River Country and southwest to the James River regions).

*The Shenandoah Valley* (to the west).

*The Ohio Country* (The Monongahela, The Konaway, or New River, Clinch and Holston Rivers, and the Cherokee and Shawnee countries).

WEST INDIES (14)
  Antigua
  Barbados
  Bermuda
  Curacao
  Guadeloupe
  Jamaica
  Martinique
  Nevis
  St. Croix
  St. Eustatius (Eustatia)
  St. Kitts (St. Christopher)
  St. Thomas
  Sal Tortuga
  Turk's Island

*Extra-Continental* (58)
  AFRICA (7)
    Bonny (Idzo)
    Calabar (Callabar)
    Dunbar
    Gambodia
    Gold Coast
    Guinea Coast
    Ivory Coast

ATLANTIC PORTS AND
    ISLANDS (5)
  Azores
  Canaries
  Cayenne
  Madeira
  Cape Verde

ENGLAND (15)
  Barnstaple
  Beaumaris
  Bristol
  Exeter
  Falmouth
  Leith
  Liverpool

London
Milford
Plymouth
Scarborough
Southampton
Topsham
Weymouth
Whitehaven

FRANCE (2)
  Bordeaux
  Cette (Citti or Cettes)

GERMANY (2)
  Bremen
  Hamburg

HOLLAND (3)
  Amsterdam
  Rotterdam
  Utrecht

IRELAND (9)
  Ayr
  Belfast
  Bideford
  Cork
  Greenock
  Irvine
  Kinsale
  Hull
  Limerick

ITALY (3)
  Florence
  Leghorn
  Venice

SCOTLAND (3)
  Edinburgh
  Glasgow
  Kirkcudbright

SPAIN  (7)                          Oporto
    Cadiz                           Madrid
    Granada                         Valencia
    Gibraltar                       Cartagena


## MINING IN THE FREDERICKSBURG AREA DURING THE COLONIAL PERIOD

### *Iron Ore*

*Spotsylvania County*
  1. Eight mines on Mine Run and above, located 3 miles west of Chancellorville.
  2. Two mines on Massaponax River, lower and upper.
*Stafford County*
  1. Accokeek (Washington) Mines on Accokeek Creek near Mountain View.

### *Copper*

*Orange County*, near Orange; Taylor's Copper Mine operated only short time.

*Culpeper County*, near Stevensburg; slight development in colonial times.

*Fauquier County*, southeast of Warrenton on Elk Run; five mines in this area.

### *Lead*

Somewhere in the Fredericksburg area. Mined extensively during the Revolution and before.

### *Slate*

*Fauquier County*, Quarries in area of White Sulphur Springs, worked before 1839.

*Culpeper*, *Stafford*, and *Spotsylvania Counties*, slate outcroppings.

### *Granite*

*Along Rappahannock River banks,* in front of Fredericksburg and above the town and on *Hazel Run;* forms the 3rd most important source of granite in Virginia; used by the early builders of Fredericksburg, as early as 1732; stone obtained from Quarries on Hazel Run for the Presbyterian Memorial Chapel. *Stafford County,* quarries on Aquia Creek; stone for the early government buildings in Washington City obtained from the Aquia quarries.

### Salt

*Subterranean deposits* found by drilling, in Fredericksburg vicinity, location undetermined; *Salt Works* at Fredericksburg referred to in Executive Journals during the Revolutionary War; mentioned by Dr. Schoepf in 1782.

### Ocher

*Fall Hill* banks, above Fredericksburg; used by the Indians and by the early white settlers in the Fredericksburg area for making paints.

### Mica

*Rappahannock* and *Hazel Run banks,* near Fredericksburg; slight use made of mica during the colonial period.

### Pyrite

*Louisa County,* near Mineral City, south of North Anna River, across southwest county line of Spotsylvania; sulphur works started in early colonial times, Waller papers describe Wm. Waller's Sulphur Mines here; large scale mining operations begun here in 1834, one of the most important sulphur mines in America up to 1900.

### Gold

(See special chart on Gold, pages 294, 295)

## COLONIAL IRON WORKS IN
## THE FREDERICKSBURG VICINITY*

*Accokeek* or *Washington Iron Works,* c.1725-1780—Abandoned in 1753, revived during the Revolution, ceased operation c.1780. (On the upper waters of the Accokeek Creek in Stafford County, north side of the Rappahannock River short distance from Fredericksburg.)

*Bloomery Iron Works,* c.1750-1772 (on south bank of Rappahannock River in the lower part of town).

---

* Six of these iron mines were in Spotsylvania County close to Fredericksburg; two were in Stafford County, one on the north bank of the Rappahannock just above Fredericksburg, and the other in the same county; the last named being a subsidiary of the Principio Co. of Md., the largest exporter of iron in the colonies, managed by Augustine Washington, the father of George Washington.

*Catherine Furnace,* c.1730? (on upper waters of the Po River, 3 miles
West of Chancellorville, old Mine Road).

*Fredericksville Iron Works,* c.1730? (between Douglas and Pigeon
Runs, on the old Catharpin Road, in southwest corner of Spotsylvania).

*Gunnery Iron Works,* 1775-1785 (on Hazel Run, lower side of Fredericksburg).

*Hunter's Iron Works,* c.1750-1790 (on north bank of Rappahannock
River just above Falmouth, opposite Dixon Island).

*Massaponax Blast Furnace,* c.1730-1785 (at the mouth of Massaponax River, south bank of the Rappahannock a few miles
below Fredericksburg).

*Rappahannock* or *Tubal Iron Works,* 1714-c.1785 (on Mine Run,
south side of the Rappahannock, a few miles up the river from
Fredericksburg).

## GOLD MINING IN THE FREDERICKSBURG AREA[*]

*Spotsylvania County:*
1. *Whitehall Gold Mines;* gold discovered here in 1806; yield,
   1806-1881, $1,800,000.
2. *United States Mines;* opened prior to 1836; these mines were
   producing $30,000 per year at that date.
3. *Marshall Mines;* opened prior to 1854; yield up to that date
   was $300,000.

*Orange County:*
1. *Grasty Gold Mines;* first gold mining company in Virginia
   operated these mines, the Virginia Mining Company; operations began in 1829; very profitable yield.
2. *Vaucluse Mines;* began operations in 1832; large producing
   mines.
3. *Melville Mines;* began operations around 1835; rich and
   valuable ore.

*Culpeper County:*
1. *Culpeper Gold Mines;* opened in 1832; large yield.

---

[*] Gold was first discovered in Va. by Thomas Jefferson near Fredericksburg
in 1782; it was first discovered in Spotsylvania Co. at Whitehall in 1806. Mining
operations for gold did not commence in the Fredericksburg area until 1806.
A total of 72 gold mines are listed above; yield nearly $3,000,000. All these mines
were within 24 miles or less of Fredericksburg.

2. *Love Gold Mines;* operated before and after the Civil War; rich vein.

3. *Greenwood Mines;* one of the old mines; yield perhaps $250,000.

*Stafford County:*

1. *Eagle Gold Mines;* first worked as early as 1834; large yield.

*List of Gold Mines Operated in the Fredericksburg Area*

### SPOTSYLVANIA COUNTY
(South Side of Rappahannock)
*Mine Run—Hunting Run*

| | |
|---|---|
| United States Mines | 5 |
| Total | 5 |

*Upper Po River*

| | |
|---|---|
| Whitehall Mines | 6 |
| Pulliam Mines | 2 |
| Huggin's Mines | 2 |
| Grindstone Hill Mines | 3 |
| Johnston's Mines | 3 |
| Total | 16 |

Tributaries of North Anna

| | |
|---|---|
| Mitchell Mines | 2 |
| Goodwin's Mines | 2 |
| Total | 4 |

### CULPEPER COUNTY
(South Side of Rapidan)

| | |
|---|---|
| Culpeper Mines | 2 |
| Love Mine | 1 |
| Embry Mine | 1 |
| Rossin's Mt. Mine | 2 |
| Cromarty Mine | 2 |
| Total | 8 |

### ORANGE COUNTY
(South Side of Rapidan)
*Upper Mine Run*

| | |
|---|---|
| Virginia Mines (Including Grasty & Dickey Mines (N.W. of Wilderness Run) | 3 |
| Vaucluse Mines | 2 |
| Coalter's Mines | 2 |
| Greenwood Mines | 2 |
| Melville Mines | 2 |
| Orange Grove Mfg. Co. Mines | 3 |
| H. Gordon's Mine | 1 |
| Wilderness Run Mine | 1 |
| Total | 16 |

### North Side of the Rappahannock River

### STAFFORD COUNTY
(Opposite U. S. Mines)

| | |
|---|---|
| Eagle Mines | 2 |
| Horsepen Mines | 2 |
| Stafford Mines | 2 |
| Newhope Mines | 2 |
| Rattlesnake Mines | 2 |
| Rappahannock Mines | 2 |
| Total | 12 |

### FAUQUIER COUNTY
*Rock Run—Summerduck Run —Deep Run*

| | |
|---|---|
| Liberty Mines | 3 |
| Union Mines | 3 |
| Bancroft Mine | 1 |
| Kelly Mine | 1 |
| Franklin Mine | 1 |
| Total | 9 |

A Partial List of the Businesses, Occupations, Trades, and Professions in Colonial Fredericksburg\*

Apothecary Shops (Drug Stores)
Bakery Shops
Blacksmith Shops
Boat Building
Book-Binders
Breweries
Brick Layers
Brick-making Kilns
Builders
Butcher Shops
Cabinet-making Shops
Candle-making Shops
Carpenters
Carpenter Shops
Cider Mills (Presses)
Clearing Houses (Counting or Customs)
Clock and Watch Making
Coach and Wagon Making Shops
Cobbler Shops (Boots and Shoes)
Cooper Shops (Barrels, Casks, etc.)
Coppersmith Shops
Enameling Workers
Engraving (Stone, Plate, etc.)
Entertainers (Players, Theaters, Market Hall)
Extractive Industries (Sumac, Malt, Linseed Oil)
Ferrymen (4 Ferries across river)
Flour and Grist Mills
Forges (Foundries)
Furrier Shops
Goldsmith Shops
Hatter Shops
Horse-Racing
Inns (Taverns, Ordinaries)

---

\* There were at least 179 separate business concerns in colonial Fredericksburg. A conservative estimate of the total number of such concerns, trades, and professions found in the city would exceed 350. This compares with 583 today, 1956.

Iron Works  (8 in and near the City)
Jockey Clubs
Jewelry Shops
Kilns  (Lime, Brick, Pottery, Malt, etc.)
Livery Stables
Lock-smiths
Lumber Mills and Yards  (Staves, Hoops, etc.)
Manufactures  (Carts and Wagons, Carriages, Coaches, Extractive,
     Hemp, Tobacco, Snuff, etc.)
Merchant Stores  (Native and Foreign Establishments)
Mines and Quarries  (Iron, Granite, etc.)
Milliners
Milling  (Flour and Grist Mills—17 along river banks, between
     Hazel Run and the Falls)
Painters and Painter Shops
Peddlers
Pewter Making Shops
Plasterers
Planters and Farmers
Postal Employees
Pottery Shops
Powder Making
Pot-Ash Yards
Printers
Printer Establishments
Public Officials  (Town, Parish, Public Warehouses)
Rope-Making
Saddler Shops
Salt Works
Saw Mills
Ship-Building
Shipping Business
Silver-Smiths
Slave Trafficking
Spinning
Stage-Coach Making
Stave Mills
Stone Cutters  (Stone Masonry)
Surveying
Tailor Shops

Tallow and Candle-Making
Tanneries
Tin-Plate Shops
Tinners
Teachers and Tutors
Traders
Tobacco Factories
Ware-Houses (Tobacco, Hemp, Wheat)
Weavers Shops
Wheelwright Shops
Wig-Maker Shops
Wineries

## FREDERICKSBURG (NEWPOST) SEAT OF POSTAL SYSTEM OF "THE BRITISH DOMINIONS OF NORTH AMERICA AND THE WEST INDIES," 1730-1753*

*British Dominions in North America*
Hudson Bay Region (Rupert's Land—Canadian Northwest)
Labrador
New Brunswick
Newfoundland (St. John's Island)
Nova Scotia (Acadia)
Prince Edward Island
The American Colonies:
1. Connecticut (her territorial claims extended to the Mississippi River)
2. Delaware
3. Georgia (her territorial claims extended to the Mississippi River)
4. Maryland
5. Massachusetts (her territorial claims extended to the Mississippi)
6. New Hampshire
7. New Jersey

* Mail from and to all parts of the world cleared through this Post Office. Fredericksburg, therefore, was a world communications center during this period.

8. New York (extensive territorial claims)
9. North Carolina (her territorial claims extended to the Mississippi, including what is now the State of Tennessee)
10. Pennsylvania (extensive territorial claims)
11. Rhode Island
12. South Carolina (her territorial claims extended to the Mississippi)
13. Virginia (her territorial claims extended to the Mississippi and to the Great Lakes region)

*English West Indies (Caribbean Region)*

Antigua
Bahama Islands (Grand Bahama, Andros Island, New Providence, San Salvador—there are 3,000 islands in the group)
Barbados
Bermuda (in the Atlantic Ocean)
Jamaica
Leeward Islands
Nevis
St. Kitts (St. Christopher)
St. Vincent
Trinidad
Windward Islands

## Membership of The Fredericksburg Masonic Lodge, Distribution of Membership, 1769*

Albemarle County—2 Members (Charlottesville)
Amherst County—1 Member (southwest of Charlottesville)
Caroline County—1 Member (Port Royal)
Charles City County—1 Member (on the James River above Williamsburg)
Culpeper (town and County)—4 Members (in forks of Rappahannock and Rapidan above Fredericksburg)
Essex County—1 Member (Hobes or Tappahannock)

---

* There are 4 widely separated towns or cities represented in the membership, 18 counties, including 2 counties south of the James River, 4 counties south of the York River, 3 Middle Peninsula counties, 2 Lower Northern Neck counties, 4 Upper Northern Neck counties (including Spotsylvania and Orange), and 1 county in the Shenandoah Valley.

Falmouth—9 Members (across river above Fredericksburg)
Fauquier County—1 Member (north side of Rappahannock River above Stafford County)
Frederick County—1 Member (Winchester)
Fredericksburg—68 Members
Gloucester County—5 Members (Gloucester and Gloucester C. H.)
King George County—3 Members (north side of the Rappahannock little below Fredericksburg)
Louisa County—1 Member (Louisa Courthouse)
Mecklenberg County—1 Member (on Roanoke River near North Carolina line)
Norfolk—1 Member (at Mouth of the James River below Williamsburg)
Philadelphia—1 Member (Pennsylvania)
Prince William County—2 Members (north side of Rappahannock near mountains)
Spotsylvania County—13 Members
Stafford County—3 Members (opposite Fredericksburg)
Westmoreland County—1 Member (Leedstown—Wakefield)


## MEMBERSHIP IN THE AMERICAN PHILOSOPHICAL SOCIETY, 1769-1785*

Alsace (1 Member—Strasburg U.)
Am. Colonies (11 Held Membership):
    Connecticut (4 Members—YALE)
    Delaware (3 Members)
    Georgia (1 Member)
    Maryland (5 Members)
    Massachusetts (10 Members—HARVARD)
    New Jersey (11 Members—PRINCETON and RUTGERS)
    New York (11 Members—KING'S COLLEGE)
    Pennsylvania (157 Members—PHIL. ACADEMY and PA. U.)
    Rhode Island (2 Members—BROWN UNIVERSITY)

* 35 Countries, 17 States, and 51 Universities, Colleges, and Learned Societies Throughout the World Held Membership: A Revealing Index to World Outlook of Fredericksburgers and to Their Trade, Travel, Correspondence, and Cultural Contacts and Relationships.

South Carolina (5 Members)
Virginia [11 Members (10 of them from Rappa. Valley)]
Antigua (1 Member)
Austria (1 Member—UNIV. of VIENNA)
Barbados (4 Members)
Belgium (1 Member—UNIV. of BRUSSELS)
Bohemia (1 Member—UNIV. of PRAGUE)
Denmark (3 Members—UNIV. of COPENHAGEN)
England (10 Members—CAMBRIDGE, INNS of COURT, OX-
    FORD)
France (14 Members—UNIV. of PARIS and SORBONNE)
German States:
    Hamburg (1 Member—UNIV. of HAMBURG)
    Palatinate (1 Member—UNIV. of HEIDELBERG)
    Prussia (1 Member—UNIV. of BERLIN)
Iceland (1 Member —UNIV. of REYKJAVIK)
India (1 Member—UNIV. of MADRAS)
Ireland (3 Members—UNIV. of DUBLIN)
Italy (3 Members—UNIV. of MILAN)
Jamaica (4 Members)
Kgd. of the Sicilies (2 Members—UNIV. of NAPLES)
Latvia (1 Member—UNIV. of RIGA)
Lithuania (2 Members—Nogorod and Vilna)
Majorca (1 Member)
Netherlands (4 Members—UNIV. of AMSTERDAM, LEYDEN,
    UTRECHT)
Netherlands Indies (1 Member—Batavia)
Nova Scotia (1 Member)
Papal States (4 Members—UNIV. of ROME, BOLOGNA, FLOR-
    ENCE)
Poland (2 Members—UNIV. of CRACOW and WARSAW)
Portugal (2 Members—ROYAL ACADEMY OF SCIENCES)
Prussian States:
    Hanover (1 Member—Osnabruck)
    Rhine (1 Member—UNIV. of COLOGNE)
    Saxony (1 Member—ROYAL ACADEMY OF ARTS)
Russia (2 Members—UNIV. of ST. PETERSBURG—ACADEMY
    OF SCIENCES)
St. Croix (1 Member)
Santo Domingo (2 Members—Santo Domingo City)

Scotland (10 Members—UNIV. of ABERDEEN, EDINBURGH, GLASGOW)
Spain (7 Members—UNIV. of BARCELONA, MADRID, VALENCIA)
Sweden (1 Member—UNIV. of STOCKHOLM)
Venetian Republic (1 Member—ACADEMY OF FINE ARTS)
West Florida (1 Member—New Orleans)

# BIBLIOGRAPHY

## SOURCE ACCOUNTS

### Manuscripts

BEVERLEY, ROBERT, Letters, 1761-1791, MSS., Library of Congress.

BEVERLEY, WILLIAM, Letter Book, 1737-44, I, MSS., Force Collections, New York Public Library.

BROOKE, FRANCIS T., Narrative of My Life, Richmond, Va.; Macfarlane & Ferguson, 1849.

CARTER, ROBERT, The Councillor, Letter Books, MSS., Virginia Historical Society, Richmond.

CHALMERS, GEORGE, MSS., Virginia, III. New York Public Library.

CLAYTON, JOHN, Letters, Peter Force Collection, Tracts and other papers, III, No. 12. Washington: Government Printing Office, 1836-46.

COUNCIL MINUTES OF THE CITY OF FREDERICKSBURG, 1782-1800, MSS., City Hall, Fredericksburg, Va.

COURTHOUSE RECORDS, MSS., Clerk's Office, Courthouse, Fredericksburg.

DINWIDDIE PAPERS, 2 vols. MSS., Virginia Historical Society, Richmond.

DIXON, CAPT. EDWARD, MSS., Library of Congress.

DOCUMENTS RELATING TO THE BOUNDARIES OF THE NORTHERN NECK, Contributed by Charles E. Kemper. MSS., Library of Congress.

EXECUTIVE COMMUNICATIONS, MSS., Archives Division, Virginia, State Library, Richmond.

FAIRFAX, LORD THOMAS, Letters, 1739-1751, Relating to the Dispute over the Boundary of the Northern Neck. Fairfax v. Hite . . . . Papers Relating to the Report of the Board of Trade, Documents relating to the Boundaries of the Northern Neck, contributed by Charles E. Kemper, MSS., Library of Congress.

FORCE, PETER, MSS., Library of Congress.

FREDERICKSBURG COURTHOUSE RECORDS, MSS., Clerk's Office, Courthouse, Fredericksburg.

HUGUENOT EMIGRATION, n. s. 5., MSS., Virginia Historical Society Collections, Richmond.

JEFFERSON, THOMAS, Papers, MSS., Library of Congress.

JONES, CADWALLADER, An Essay about the Indian Trade with a MS Map or Plot of Louisiana, MSS., Library of Congress.

LAND OFFICE, Patent Books, MSS., Land Office, Richmond.

LIST OF CONTRIBUTORS TO THE BOSTONIANS, MS., Virginia State Library, Richmond.

MADISON, JAMES, Papers, MSS., Library of Congress.

MASON, GEORGE, Declaration of Rights, MS., Virginia State Library, Richmond.

MASONIC LODGE MINUTE BOOKS, Fredericksburg Lodge No. 4., Fredericksburg, Virginia.

MERCER, HUGH, Account Book, MSS. belonging to George H. S. King, Fredericksburg, Virginia.

MERCER, HUGH, MSS., Virginia Historical Society, Richmond.

MINUTES AND OTHER PAPERS, MSS., Friends Meeting House, Baltimore, Maryland.

MSS. 712, Spotsylvania County, Virginia, Committee of Safety Resolutions, 1774, MSS., Library of Congress.

MORGAN, GEORGE, Papers, 4 vols. MSS., Library of Congress.

NAVAL OFFICE LISTS OF IMPORTS AND EXPORTS OF THE RAPPAHANNOCK AND SOUTH POTOMAC, MSS., Public Records Office, London: Transcripts, University of California Library.

NAVAL OFFICERS BOOK OF ENTRIES AND CLEARANCES, 1785-1787, MSS., Accomac County Courthouse, Accomac, Virginia; photostatic copy, Virginia State Library, Richmond.

NAVAL RETURNS, Rappahannock, to 1789, MSS., Virginia State Library, Richmond.

PUBLIC STORES, Fredericksburg Station, Books 6, 9, 10, 11, and 12, MSS., Virginia State Library, Richmond.

PETITIONS, Baptists, to the House of Burgesses, Governor, and Council, MSS., University of Richmond Library.

PETITIONS to the House of Burgesses, Governors and Council, MSS., Virginia State Library, Richmond.

REPORT OF THE COMMITTEE OF REVISORS Appointed by the General Assembly of Virginia, MSS., Virginia State Library, Richmond.

RITCHIE, JAMES AND COMPANY, Papers, MSS., George H. S. King, Fredericksburg.

ST. GEORGE'S VESTRY BOOKS, I and II, MSS., University of Virginia Library; photostatic copy, Rector's study, Fredericksburg.

Spotsylvania County Records, MSS., Spotsylvania County Courthouse.

Stephens, Adams, Papers, 1763-1776, MSS., Library of Congress.

U. S. Post Office, Correspondence File, 1914, 14707-C-AC, MS.,
U. S. Post Office, Washington, D. C.

Winder Abstracts, MSS., Archives Division, Virginia State Library,
Richmond.

## Public Documents

*Biographical Dictionary of the American Congress,* 1774-1927.
Washington: Government Printing Office, 1928.

*Calendar of State Papers, Colonial Series, American West Indies,*
I-XX. London: British Record Office, 1860-1925.

*Calendar of Treasury Papers.* 11 vols. London: Public Record
Office, 1868-1903.

*Calendar of Virginia State Papers and other Manuscripts.* 11 vols.
Richmond: State Printing, 1875-1893.

*Executive Journals of the Council of Colonial Virginia.* Richmond:
Superintendent of public printing, 1925.

Hening, William Waller, *The Statutes of Virginia at Large.*
New York: R. & W. & G. Bartow, I-II; Philadelphia: Thomas
Desilver, III and XIII; Richmond: Franklin Press, IV-XII;
Series I-XII, 1823.

*Journal of the Commissioners for Trade and Plantations, 1704-1722.*
4 vols. London: H. M. Stationery Office, 1920-25.

*Journals of the Continental Congress.* 24 vols. Washington: Government Printing Office, 1904-1937.

*Journals of the Council of Colonial Virginia,* ed. by H. R. Mc-
Illwaine. 3 vols. Richmond: The Colonial Press, 1918-19.

*Journals of the House of Burgesses, 1727-1776,* ed. by H. R. Mc-
Illwaine. 27 vols. Richmond: The Colonial Press, 1905-1910.

*Journals of the United States Congress,* I. Washington: Way &
Gideon, publishers, 1823.

*Minutes of the Council and General Court of Colonial Virginia.*
Richmond: The Colonial Press, 1924.

*Official Letters of the Governors of Virginia,* ed. by H. R. Mc-
Illwaine, I, II, III. Richmond: Virginia State Library, 1926-
29.

Shepherd, Samuel, *The Statutes of Virginia at Large.* 3 vols. Richmond: S. Shepherd, 1835-36.

*U. S. House Documents,* Vol. I, No. 19, 24th Congress, 2nd. Session,

1836-37, *"Memorial of Jannette Taylor, et al.,"* pp.1-8. Washington: Government Printing Office, 1837.

*Virginia: Convention of Dec. 1, 1775: A Collection of Laws, Statutes, etc.* Richmond: Nicolson & Prentis, 1785.

### Published Books and Articles

ALVORD, CLARENCE W., and BIDGOOD, LEE, editors, *The First Explorations of the Trans-Allegheny Region by Virginians.* Cleveland: Arthur H. Clark & Co., 1912.

ANBUREY, THOMAS, *Travels through the Interior Parts of America.* 2 vols. London: printed for W. Lane, 1789.

ANDERSON, ADAM, *An History and Chronological Deduction of the Origin of Commerce,* II. London: printed by J. Watters, 1788.

ASPLUND, JOHN, *The Annual Register of the Baptists Denomination in North America to 1790.* Richmond: n.p., 1791.

BEVERLEY, ROBERT, *The History of the Present State of Virginia.* London: R. Parker, 1705.

BIRKET, JAMES, *Some Cursory Remarks Made by James Birket on his Voyage to North America, 1750-1751.* New Haven: Yale University Press, 1916.

BRISSOT de WARVILLE, JACQUES PIERRE, *New Travels in the United States of America, 1788.* London: T. & J. Swords, 1792.

BULLITT, THOMAS, Travels of Colo. Thomas Bullitt, *Calendar of Virginia State Papers,* I, p. 308.

BURNABY, REV. ANDREW, *Travels through the Middle Settlements of North America in the Years 1759 and 1760.* London: T. Payne, 1775.

BYRD, WILLIAM, *Writings of Colonel William Byrd,* ed. by J. S. Bassett. New York: Doubleday, Page & Co., 1901.

CASTIGLIONI, LUIGI, *Travels in the United States.* 2 vols. Milan: G. Merilli, 1790.

CHASTELIUX, FRANCIS JEAN, MARQUIS de, *Travels Through North America, 1780-1783.* London: G. G. J. & J. Robinson, 1787.

CLAYTON, JOHN, *Letters,* Peter Force Collection. *Tracts and Other Papers,* III, No. 15. Washington: Government Printing Office, 1836-46.

COKE, THOMAS, *Extracts of the Journals of Rev. Dr. Coke's Five Visits to America.* London: G. Paramore, printer, 1793.

COLLES, CHRISTOPHER, *A Survey of Roads of the United States, 1789.* New York: n.p., 1789.

COMMONS, JOHN R., *et al.,* eds., *A Documentary History of American Industrial Society.* Cleveland: A. H. Clark Co., 1910-11.

COXE, TENCH, *A View of the United States of America, 1787-1794.* Philadelphia: Printed for William Hall, et al., 1794.

CRESWELL, NICHOLAS, *The Journal of Nicholas Creswell, 1774-1777.* New York: The Dial Press, 1924.

DARLING, WILLIAM, *Memorials of John Bartram and Humphrey Marshall.* Philadelphia: Lindsay & Blackister, 1849.

FITHIAN, PHILIP VICKERS, *Journal and Letters, 1767-1774.* Princeton: Princeton University Library, 1900-1934.

FONTAINE, JACQUES, *Memoirs of a Huguenot Family,* trans. by Ann Maury: Journal of Travels in Virginia, 1715-1716. New York: G. P. Putnam & Co., 1853.

FRY, JOSHUA, *Memoirs of Col. Joshua Fry, Sometime Professor in William and Mary College, Virginia,* ed. by Philip Slaughter. Richmond: Randolph & English, 1880.

GORDON, LORD ADAM, *Journal of an Officer's Travels in America and the West Indies, 1764-1765,* ed. by N. D. Mereness. New York: Macmillan Co., 1916.

GRATZ, B. & M., *Merchants of Philadelphia, 1754-1798,* ed. by Wm. Vincent Byars. Jefferson City, Missouri: The Hugh Stephens Printing Co., 1916.

GWATHMEY, JOHN H., *Historical Register of Virginians in the Revolution, 1775-1783.* Richmond: The Dietz Press, 1938.

HADFIELD, JOSEPH, *An Englishman in America, 1785,* ed. by D. S. Robertson. Toronto: 1933.

HARROWER, JOHN, *The Diary of John Harrower, 1773-1776.* New York: n.p., 1900.

HUTCHINS, THOMAS, *A Topographical Description of Virginia.* London: The Author, 1778.

*The Jefferson Encyclopedia,* ed. by John P. Foley. New York and London: Funk & Wagnalls, 1900.

JEFFERSON, THOMAS, *Notes on the State of Virginia.* Paris: J. Stockdale, 1784-85.

JEFFERSON, THOMAS, *The Writings of Thomas Jefferson,* ed. by Paul Leicester Ford, vols. 12. New York and London: G. P. Putnam's Sons, 1892-99.

JONES, JOSEPH, *Letters of Joseph Jones,* ed. by Worthington C. Ford. Washington: Department of State, 1889.

KAUFMAN, C. H., *The Dictionary of Merchandise and Nomenclature in All Languages.* Philadelphia: James Humphreys, Printer, 1805.

LA ROCHEFOUCAULD-LIANCOURT, F. A. F., *Travels Through the United States of North America, 1795-1797.* London: R. Phillips, 1799.

*Letter* of George Washington to William Fitzhugh, Mann Page, *et al.*, July 5, 1778. This letter is in the possession of Miss Eliza Roy, Fredericksburg, Virginia.

LEWIS, THOMAS, *The Fairfax Line: Journal of 1746,* ed. by John W. Wayland, New Market, Virginia: Henkel Press, 1925.

LINDSAY, HUGH, *Journal, 1773 and 1774.* Brooklyn: Norton Co., 1867.

MERENES, N. D., *Travels in the American Colonies.* New York: The Macmillan Co., 1916.

MESICK, JANE LOUISE, *The English Traveler in America, 1785-1835.* New York: Columbia University Press, 1922.

MIRANDA, FRANCISCO, *Diary . . . . Tour of the United States, 1783-1784,* ed. by W. S. Robertson. 2 vols. New York: Hispanic Society, 1928.

MONAGHAN, FRANK, comp., *French Travellers in the United States, 1765-1932.* New York: New York Public Library, 1933.

MITCHELL, JOHN, *American Husbandry.* 2 vols. London: J. Bew, 1775.

MORRISON, ALFRED J., *Travels in Virginia in Revolutionary Times.* 2 vols. Philadelphia: Campbell Co., 1911.

NORTON, JOHN, AND SONS, *Merchants of London and Virginia, Being the Papers from their Counting House for the Years 1750 to 1795,* ed. by Frances Norton Mason. Richmond: The Dietz Press, 1937.

PERRY, WILLIAM S., *Historical Collections Relating to the American Colonial Church in Virginia, 1650-1774,* I. Hartford: Church Press Co., 1879.

PEYTON, JOHN HOWE, *Memoirs of John Howe Peyton, in Sketches of His Contemporaries,* comp. by John Lewis Peyton. Staunton, Virginia: A. B. Blackburn & Co., 1894.

PRINCE, THOMAS, *The vade mecum for America: or a Companion for traders and travellers.* Boston: S. Kneeland and T. Green. 1782.

SCHAW, JANET, *Journal of a Lady of Quality, 1774 to 1776,* ed. by Evangeline W. and C. M. Andrews. New Haven: The Yale University Press, 1939.

SHEFFIELD, LORD, *Observations on the Commerce of the American States.* London: J. Debrett, 1784.

SMITH, CAPT. JOHN, *The Generall Historie of Virginia, 1642*, ed. by
Edward Arber. Birmingham, England: The Author, 1884.

SMITH, CAPT. JOHN, *True Travels, Adventures, and Observations*.
Richmond: Republished at the Franklin Press, 1819.

SMITH, WILLIAM L., *Journal, 1790-91*. Cambridge: The Harvard
University Press, 1917.

SMYTH, JOHN F. D., *A Tour of the United States of America*. 2 vols.
London: Printed for G. Robinson . . . ., J. Robson . . . .,
and J. Sewell, 1784.

SPARKS, JARED, *The Writings of George Washington*. 12 vols. New
York: Harper & Son, 1847.

SPOTSWOOD, ALEXANDER, *The Official Letters of Alexander Spotswood*, ed. by R. A. Brock. 2 vols. Richmond: Virginia Historical Society, 1882-85.

STRACHEY, WILLIAM, *The Historie of Travaile in Virginia Britannia*,
ed. by R. H. Major. London: Hakluyt Society, 1849.

VIRGINIA BROADSIDE PORTFOLIO 180, no. 4, *A Topographical Analysis
of the Commonwealth, 1790-1*. Philadelphia: Charles Cist,
1791. Library of Congress.

VIRGINIA BROADSIDE PORTFOLIO 181, no. 24, 1805, *A Plan for Establishing Iron Works in Spotsylvania County*. Plan proposed by
John Strode, included with a letter of Col. Richard Bland Lee,
dated, April 29, 1805, and addressed to James Madison, which
concerns the Plan of John Strode. No place or publisher of the
publication of the Broadside is given.

WANSEY, HENRY, *An Excursion to the United States of America, in
the Summer of 1794*. Salisbury, England: J. Easton, printer,
1798.

WASHINGTON, GEORGE, *Writings of George Washington*, ed. by
W. C. Ford. 4 vols. New York: G. P. Putnam & Co., 1889-93.

WELD, ISAAC, *Travels Through the States of North America, and
the Provinces of Upper and Lower Canada, during the years
1795, 1796 and 1797*. London: John Stockdale, Printer, 1800.

*Periodicals and Newspapers*

AMERICAN PHILOSOPHICAL SOCIETY, *"List of Members, 1769 to 1838."*
Philadelphia: J. & W. Kite, printers, 1838.

AMERICAN PHILOSOPHICAL SOCIETY, *Register of papers published in
the Transactions and Proceedings* of the American Philosophical Society. Philadelphia: McCalla & Stavely, printers, 1881.

LETTER OF GEORGE WASHINGTON TO WILLIAM FITZHUGH, MANN PAGE,

JR., *et al.*, July 5, 1778. This letter is in the possession of Miss
Eliza Roy, Fredericksburg, Virginia.

*Maryland Gazette* (Annapolis).

*Virginia Gazette,* (Williamsburg), 1736-1775.

*Virginia Herald,* (Fredericksburg), 1787-1800.

## Maps

BOWEN, EMMANUEL, A Map of the British American Plantations,
extending from Boston in New England to Georgia; including
all the back Settlements in the respective Provinces as far as
Mississippi, from the *London Magazine and Monthly Chroni-
cler,* July 1749. Library of Congress.

EVANS, LEWIS, Map of the Middle British Colonies in America,
1755. Library of Congress.

HENRY, JOHN, A New and Accurate Map of Virginia, 1770. Library
of Congress.

HERMAN, AUGUSTINE, Map of Virginia and Maryland, 1673. Library
of Congress.

HUTCHINS, THOMAS, A New Map of the Western Parts of Virginia,
Pennsylvania, Maryland, and North Carolina, 1778. Library
of Congress.

JEFFERSON, PETER, and BROOKE, ROBERT, Map of the Northern Neck
of Virginia, 1749. Library of Congress.

JEFFERSON, PETER, and FRY, JOSHUA, Map of the Most Inhabited
Parts of Virginia, 1751. Library of Congress.

MADISON, JAMES, *Map of Virginia,* 1807. Library of Congress and
Virginia State Library.

A MAP OF THE WESTERN PARTS OF THE COLONY OF VIRGINIA, 1754.
Printed for the *London Magazine,* 1754. Library of Congress.

MAPS OF FREDERICKSBURG AND SPOTSYLVANIA COUNTY. Virginia State
Library.

MARTIN, COL. LAWRENCE, The Debt of the United States of America
to Spain. Library of Congress.

MAYO, WM., A Map of the Northern Neck of Virginia. The Territory of the Right Honourable Lord Thomas Fairfax, 1737.
Library of Congress.

MERCER, JAMES, Plot of Charles Dick's Lots, Deed Book A, p. 268.
Courthouse, Fredericksburg.

MITCHELL, JOHN, Map of the British and French Dominions in
North America, 1755. Library of Congress.

Moll, Herman, Map of Virginia and Maryland, 1729. Library of Congress.

Smith, C., Map of Fredericksburg. Clerk's Office, Courthouse, Fredericksburg, "Land Causes and Appeals, 1808-1821," p. 51.

Spotsylvania County, 1820, Virginia State Library, Map No. 441.

Warner, John, Map of the Northern Neck, 1737. Library of Congress.

*Miscellaneous*

Masonic Cemetery, data from tombstones. Fredericksburg, Virginia.

St. George's Church Cemetery, data from tombstones. Fredericksburg.

## Secondary Works

Abernethy, Thomas, *Western Lands and the American Revolution.* Cleveland: Arthur H. Clark & Co., 1912.

Adams, H. B., "Washington's Interest in Western Lands," Johns Hopkins University *Studies in Historical and Political Science,* III, 55ff.

Adams, J. T., *Provincial Society, 1690-1763.* New York: Macmillan Co., 1936.

Alvord, Clarence W., *The Mississippi in British Politics.* Cleveland: A. H. Clark Co., 1917.

American Philosophical Society, *List of Members, 1769 to 1838.* Philadelphia: J. & W. Kite, printers, 1838.

Andrews, C. M., "Colonial Commerce," *The American Historical Review,* XX (1914-15), 43-63.

Andrews, C. M., *The Colonial Period of American History,* II. New Haven: Yale University Press; London: Oxford University Press, 1934-38.

Andrews, C. M., *Colonial Self-Government, 1652-1689,* Vol. 5 of *American Nation Series,* ed. by A. B. Hart, 27 Vols. New York and London: Harper & Bros., 1906-08.

Bean, Robert B., *The Peopling of Virginia.* Boston: Chapman & Grimes, 1938.

BASSETT, J. S., *A Short History of the United States*. New York: Macmillan Co., 1913.

BECKER, CARL L., *Beginning of American People*. Boston and New York: Houghton Mifflin Co., 1915.

BLANTON, W. B., *Medicine of Virginia in the Eighteenth Century*. Richmond: Garrett & Massie Co., 1931.

BOLTON, H. E., *History of the Americas; Western Land Schemes Before the Revolution*. New York: Ginn & Co., 1935.

BOLTON, W. B., *The Colonization of North America, 1492-1783*. New York: Macmillan Co., 1920.

BROCK, R. A., *Early Iron Manufacture in Virginia, 1619-1776, Proceedings* of the U. S. National Museum, VII (1885), 77-80.

BROOKES, RICHARD, *General Gazetteer; or a New and Compendious Geographical Dictionary*. London: J. Johnson, 1809.

BUCKINGHAM, J. S., *The Slave States of America*. 2 vols. London and Paris: Fisher, Son & Co., 1842.

BRUCE, KATHLEEN, *Virginia Iron Manufacture in the Slave Era*. New York and London: The Century Co., 1930.

BURKE, JOHN DALY, *The History of Virginia From its First Settlement to the Revolution*. 3 vols. Petersburg: Dickin & Pescud, printers, 1822.

BUSHNELL, DAVID I., *The Manahoac Tribes in Virginia, 1608*. Washington: The Smithsonian Institution, 1935.

BUSHNELL, DAVID I., *Indian Sites Below the Falls of the Rappahannock, Virginia*. Washington: The Smithsonian Institution, 1937.

CAMPBELL, CHARLES, *The History of Virginia*. Philadelphia: J. B. Lippincott & Co., 1860.

CAMPBELL, JOHN WILSON, *The History of Virginia From its Discovery Till the Year 1781*. Petersburg: J. W. Campbell, 1813.

CARMAN, H. J., and McKEE, SAMUEL, *A History of the United States*. Boston and New York: D. C. Heath & Co., 1931.

CARTER, C. E., "British Policies Toward the Indians in the South, 1763-8," *English Historical Review* (January, 1918), pp. 37-56.

*Catalogue of the College of William and Mary in Virginia, from its foundations to the present time, 1859*. Williamsburg, 1859. Rare Book Collection, Library of Congress.

CHITWOOD, OLIVER P., *A History of Colonial America*. New York and London: Harper Brothers, 1931.

COLLINS, V. L., *President Witherspoon, II*. Princeton: Princeton University Press, 1925.

CONWAY, MONCURE C., *George Washington's Rules of Civility*. New York: The United States Book Co., 1890.

COOKE, JOHN E., "Virginia in the Revolution," *Harper's New Monthly Magazine*, No. 313 (June, 1876), Vol. 53, pp. 1-5.

COTTERILL, ROBERT S., *The Old South, the geographic, economic, social, political, and cultural expansion, institutions, etc*. Glendale, Cal.: A. H. Clark & Co., 1936.

CRAVEN, AVERY O., *The United States, experiment in democracy*.

*Dictionary of American Biography*, ed. by Allen Johnson and Dumas Malone. 20 vols. New York: Charles Scribner's Co., 1928-36.

DRIVER, CARL S., *John Sevier, Pioneer of the Old Southwest*. Chapel Hill: The University of North Carolina Press, 1932.

EMBREY, ALVIN T., *History of Fredericksburg, Virginia*. Richmond: Old Dominion Press, 1937.

FAULKNER, HAROLD U., *American Political and Social History*. New York: F. S. Crofts & Co., 1937.

FEUERLICHT, MORRIS M., "Influence of Judaism on the Founders of the Republic," *Yearbook* of the Central Conference of American Rabbis, XXVI, (1926) pp. 213-46.

FISH, CARL R., *The Development of American Nationality*. New York and Cincinnati: American Book Co., 1913.

FISKE, JOHN, *The American Revolution*. Boston and New York: Houghton Mifflin Co., 1891.

FITZHUGH, WILLIAM, "Letter," *Virginia Magazine of History and Biography*, I (July, 1893), pp. 17-53.

FORMAN, S. E., *Our Republic; a brief history of the American people*. New York: G. P. Putnam & Co., 1922.

FURCRON, A. S., *Geology and Mineral Resources of the Warrenton Quadrangle*, Virginia Geological Survey Bulletin 54. Charlottesville: University of Virginia Press, 1939.

GILPIN, THOMAS, *Exiles in Virginia*. Philadelphia: Sherman, printer, 1848.

GOODWIN, EDWARD L., *The colonial church in Virginia, with biographical sketches of the first six bishops of the diocese of Virginia, and other historical papers together with biographical sketches of the colonial clergy of Virginia*. London: A. R. Mowbray, & Co., 1927.

GOOLRICK, JOHN, *Hugh Mercer*. New York and Washington: The Neale Brothers, 1906.

GRANT, DOROTHY F., *Margaret Brent*. New York and Toronto: Longmans Co., 1944.

GREENE, EVARTS B., *American Population before the Federal Census of 1790*. New York: Columbia University Press, 1932.

GREENE, EVARTS B., *The Foundations of American Nationality*. New York and Cincinnati: American Book Co., 1922.

GWATHMEY, JOHN H., *Twelve Virginia Counties Where Western Migration Began*. Richmond: The Dietz Press, 1937.

HARLOW, RALPH V., *The Growth of the United States*. New York: Henry Holt & Co., 1943.

HARREL, ISAAC, *Loyalism in Virginia*. Durham, N. C.: Duke University Press, 1926.

HARRISON, FAIRFAX, *Landmarks of Old Prince William*. Richmond: The Old Dominion Press, 1924.

HART, FREEMAN H., *The Valley of Virginia in the American Revolution*. Chapel Hill: The University of North Carolina Press, 1942.

HASKELL, DANIEL C., *American Historical Prints, Early Views of American Cities*, from the Phillip Stokes and other collections by I. N. Phelps and Daniel C. Haskell. New York: The New York Public Library, 1932.

HICKS, JOHN D., *The Federal Union; a History of the United States to 1865*. Boston, New York: Houghton Mifflin Co., 1937.

HOCKETT, HOMER C., *Political and Social Growth of the United States*. New York: Macmillan Co., 1933.

HUHNER, LEON, *The Jews in Virginia from the Earliest Times to the Close of the Eighteenth Century*. Baltimore: Leon Huhner, 1911.

HULBERT, A. B., *Historic Highways*. 16 vols. Cleveland: A. H. Clark Co., 1902-5.

HULBERT, A. B., *Boone's Wilderness Road*. Cleveland: A. H. Clark Co., 1903.

HULBERT, A. B., *Braddock's Road*. Cleveland: A. H. Clark Co., 1903.

HULBERT, A. B., *The Cumberland Road*. Cleveland: A. H. Clark Co., 1904.

JOHNSON, J. STODDARD, *First Explorations of Kentucky*, Filson Club Publications, No. 13, pp. 4-166. Louisville, Ky.: J. P. Morgan & Co., 1898.

JONES, EDWARD, *American Members of the Inns Court*. London: St. Catherine Press, 1924.

JORDAN, DAVID STARR, *Your Family Tree*. New York and London: D. Appleton Co., 1929.

KEMPER, R. A., *The History of Germantown*. Fauquier Historical Society Bulletin 2, 1922.

KEMPER, WILLIS M., *Genealogy of the Kemper Family in the United States*. Chicago: G. K. Hazlitt & Co., 1899.

KIRKLAND, EDWARD C., *A History of American Economic Life*. New York: C. F. Crofts & Co., 1933.

KONWISER, HARRY M., *Colonial and Revolutionary Posts*. Richmond: The Dietz Press, 1931.

KRAUSE, MICHAEL, *Intercolonial Aspects of American Culture on the Eve of the Revolution*. New York: Columbia University, 1928.

LEDNUM, JOHN, *A History of the Rise of Methodism in America Containing Sketches of Methodist Itinerant Preachers From 1736 to 1785*. Philadelphia: The Author, 1859.

LINDLEY, HARLOW, "The Quakers in the Ohio Northwest," reprinted from the *Proceedings* of the Mississippi Valley Historical Association, V (1911-12), pp. 60-72.

LIVERMORE, SHAW, *Early American Land Companies*. New York: The Commonwealth Fund; London: Oxford University Press, 1939.

LOVETT, HOWARD MERIWETHER, *Llangollen*.

MCDONALD, JOHN, *Biographical Sketches . . . . General Simon Kenton*. Cincinnati: E. Morgan & Son, 1838.

MCGILL, WILLIAM, *Outline of Mineral Resources of Virginia*. Virginia Geological Survey, Bulletin 47, Series 3. Charlottesville: University of Virginia Press, 1936.

MCILLWAINE, H. R., *The Struggle of Protestant Dissenters for Real Religious Toleration in Virginia*. Baltimore: John Hopkins Press, 1894.

MARTIN, JOSEPH, A New and Comprehensive Gazetteer of Virginia, Charlottesville, J. M. Martin, 1836.

MEADE, BISHOP WILLIAM, *Old Churches, Ministers and Families of Virginia*. Philadelphia: J. B. Lippincott & Co., 1857.

MORTON, LOUIS, *Robert Carter of Nomini Hall*. Williamsburg: Colonial Williamsburg, Inc., 1941.

MORRISON, ALFRED J., "The Virginia Indian Trade to 1673," William and Mary College Quarterly Historical Magazine, Vol. I. Series 2, (October, 1921), pp. 217-236.

MORRISON, SAMUEL S., and COMMAGER, HENRY S., *The Growth of the American Republic.* London, Toronto, etc.: Oxford University Press, 1942.

MUZZEY, DAVID S., and KROUT, JOHN A., *American History for Colleges.* Boston, New York, etc.: Ginn & Co., 1933.

MUZZEY, DAVID S., *The United States,* I. Boston, New York, etc.: Ginn & Co., 1922.

NICHOLS, JEANNETTE P., and ROY F., *The Republic of the United States.* New York and London: D. Appleton-Century Co., 1942.

OPPENHEIM, SAMUEL, *The Jews and Masonry in the United States Before 1810.* New York: The Author, 1910.

PASCOE, C. F., *Two Hundred Years of the Society for the Propagation of the Gospel.* London: The Society, 1901.

PEASE, T. C., *The United States.* New York: Harcourt, Brace & Co., 1927.

PHILLIPS, U. S., Plantation and Frontier Documents, 1642-1863. *A Documentary History of American Historical Society.* 2 vols. Cleveland: A. H. Clark Co., 1910-11.

QUINN, S. J., *History of Fredericksburg.* Richmond: Hermitage Press, 1908.

RAMSEY, JAMES G. M., *The Annals of Tennessee to the End of the Eighteenth Century.* Kingsport, Tenn.: The Kingsport Press, 1926.

ROWLAND, KATE MASON, *The Life of George Mason 1725-1792.* New York and London: G. P. Putnam Co., 1892.

ROYALL, MRS. ANNE, *Sketches of the History, Life, and Manners in the United States.* New Haven: The Author, 1826.

SABINE, LORENZO, *The American Loyalists.* Boston: Little Brown & Co., 1847.

SCHLESINGER, ARTHUR M., *The Colonial Merchant and the American Revolution, 1763-1776.* New York: Columbia University Press, 1917.

SEMPLE, ROBERT B., *History of Baptists in Richmond, Virginia.* John O'Lynch, printer, 1810. Rare Book Collection, Library of Congress.

SHANNON, FRED A., *Economic History of the People of the United States.* New York: Macmillan Co., 1934.

SLAUGHTER, PHILLIP, *A Brief Sketch of William Green, LL.D., Jurist and Scholar.* Richmond: W. E. Jones, Printer, 1883.

SMART, GEORGE K., "Private Libraries in Colonial Virginia," *American Literature*, X (March, 1938), pp. 24-52.

SONNECK, OSCAR G., *Early Concert Life in America, 1731-1800*. Leipzig: Breithopf & Hartel, 1907.

STANARD, MARY MANN PAGE, *Colonial Virginia, Its People and Customs*. Philadelphia and London: J. B. Lippincott & Co., 1917.

SUTHERLAND, STELLA H., *The Distribution of Population in the American Colonies*. Urbanna, Ill.: University of Illinois Press, 1931.

SWANK, JAMES M., *History of the Manufacture of Iron in All Ages*. Philadelphia: The Author, 1884.

TAYLOR, JAMES B., *Lives of Virginia Baptist Ministers*. Richmond: Yale & Wyatt Co., Baltimore: Armstrong & Berry Co., 1838.

THOM, WILLIAM, *The Struggle for Religious Freedom in Virginia, The Baptists*. Baltimore: Johns Hopkins Press, 1900.

THOMAS ISAIAH, *The History of Printing in America*. American Antiquarian Society *Collections*, Vol. II. Worcester, Mass.: The Society, 1874.

TUGWELL, REXFORD G., *American Economic Life*. New York: Harcourt, Brace & Co., 1925.

TURNER, FREDERICK J., *The Frontier in American History*. New York: Henry Holt & Co., 1920.

TYLER, LYON G., *Encyclopedia of Virginia Biography*. 5 vols. New York: Lewis Historical Publishing Co., 1915.

TYLER, LYON G., *Tyler's Quarterly Historical and Genealogical Magazine*, I. Richmond: Whittett & Shepperson, printers, 1920.

*Virginia Magazine of History and Biography*. 30 vols. Richmond: Virginia Historical Society.

*Virginia Register*, 8 vols. Richmond: n.p., 1860.

WADDELL, J. A., *Annals of Augusta County, Virginia, 1726-1871*. Richmond: W. E. Jones, 1866.

WASHINGTON BICENTENNIAL COMMISSION, *Youth and Manhood of George Washington*, Program Three. Washington: Government Printing Office, 1931.

WATSON, T. L., *Economic Products of the Virginia Coastal Plain*: *Virginia*, Geological Survey Bulletin, no. 4. Charlottesville: University of Virginia Press.

WATSON, T. L., *Mineral Resources of Virginia*. Lynchburg: J. A. Bell Co., 1907.

WERTENBAKER, T. J., *The First Americans, 1607-1690*, Vol. II of the American Life Series. Arthur M. Schlesinger and Dixon Ryan Fox, eds. 12 vols. New York: Macmillan Co., 1927-44.

WERTENBAKER, T. J., *The Planters of Colonial Virginia*. Princeton: Princeton University Press, 1922.

WHITNEY, J. D., *The Metallic Wealth of the United States*. Philadelphia: J. B. Lippincott Co.; London: Trubner & Co., 1854.

WIRT, WILLIAM, *Sketches of the Life and Character of Patrick Henry*. Philadelphia: Webster Co., 1818.

WITHERS, ALEXANDER S., *Chronicles of Border Warfare*, ed. by Reuben G. Thwaites. Cincinnati: The R. Clarke Co., 1895.

WRIGHT, LOUIS, *The First Gentlemen of Virginia*. San Marino, Cal.: The Huntington Library, 1940.

*William and Mary College Quarterly Historical Papers*, Series 1, IV, VI-VII, XXI, XXVII. Williamsburg: College of William and Mary.

# Errata

page 49, line 23: *other* should read *otter*.

page 112, line 24: *ambassador to the Court of St. James* should read *consul to Liverpool*.

page 115, line 10: *intricate* should read *integral*.

page 161, line 24: *1681/2* should read *1698*.

page 206, line 1: *human* should be omitted.

page 241, line 17: *German* should read *Germany*.

page 242, line 1: *1643* should read *1642*.

DATE DUE